Shakespeare & Money

Shakespeare &

Series Editors:
Graham Holderness, *University of Hertfordshire*
Bryan Loughrey

Volume 7
Shakespeare & Money
Edited by Graham Holderness

Volume 6
Shakespeare & His Biographical Afterlives
Edited by Paul Franssen and Paul Edmondson

Volume 5
Shakespeare & the Ethics of War
Edited by Patrick Gray

Volume 4
Shakespeare & Creative Criticism
Edited by Rob Conkie and Scott Maisano

Volume 3
Shakespeare & the Arab World
Edited by Katherine Hennessey and Margaret Litvin

Volume 2
Shakespeare & Commemoration
Edited by Clara Calvo and Ton Hoenselaars

Volume 1
Shakespeare & Stratford
Edited by Katherine Scheil

Shakespeare & Money

Edited by
Graham Holderness

berghahn
NEW YORK · OXFORD
www.berghahnbooks.com

Published in 2020 by
Berghahn Books
www.berghahnbooks.com

© 2020 Berghahn Books

Originally published as a special issue
of *Critical Survey*, volume 30, number 3,
unless otherwise noted.

All rights reserved. Except for the quotation of short passages
for the purposes of criticism and review, no part of this book
may be reproduced in any form or by any means, electronic or
mechanical, including photocopying, recording, or any information
storage and retrieval system now known or to be invented,
without written permission of the publisher.

Library of Congress Cataloging-in-Publication Data
Names: Holderness, Graham, editor.
Title: Shakespeare & money / edited by Graham Holderness.
Other titles: Shakespeare and money
Description: New York : Berghahn, 2020. | Series: Shakespeare & ; volume 7
| Includes bibliographical references and index.
Identifiers: LCCN 2020006099 (print) | LCCN 2020006100 (ebook) | ISBN
9781789206715 (hardback) | ISBN 9781789206722 (paperback) | ISBN
9781789206739 (ebook)
Subjects: LCSH: Shakespeare, William, 1564-1616--Criticism and
interpretation. | Shakespeare, William, 1564-1616--Knowledge--Economics.
| Money in literature. | Economics and
literature--England--History--16th century. | Economics and
literature--England--History--17th century.
Classification: LCC PR3021 .S524 2020 (print) | LCC PR3021 (ebook) | DDC
822.3/3--dc23
LC record available at https://lccn.loc.gov/2020006099
LC ebook record available at https://lccn.loc.gov/2020006100

British Library Cataloguing in Publication Data

A catalogue record for this book is available from the British Library

ISBN 978-1-78920-671-5 hardback
ISBN 978-1-78920-672-2 paperback
ISBN 978-1-78920-673-9 ebook

Contents

Introduction
    Shakespeare, Minted   1
    Graham Holderness

Chapter 1   15
    Shakespeare and Derivatives
    David Hawkes

Chapter 2   29
    Shakespeare, Reciprocity and Exchange
    John Drakakis

Chapter 3   48
    Offshore Desires
    Mobility, Liquidity and History in Shakespeare's Mediterranean
    Rui Carvalho Homem

Chapter 4   70
    Pity Silenced
    Economies of Mercy in The Merchant of Venice
    Alessandra Marzola

Chapter 5   87
    'Love Merchandized'
    Money in Shakespeare's Sonnets
    Manfred Pfister

Chapter 6   97
    Timon of Athens **in the Downturn**
    James Tink

Chapter 7
'Fill Thy Purse With Money'
Financing Performance in Shakespearean England
Tiffany Stern
    109

Chapter 8
Biography and Shakespeare's Money
Portraits of an Economic Persona
Paola Pugliatti
    125

Chapter 9
Shakespeare and the Hybrid Economy
Sujata Iyengar
    142

Afterthought
'Best for Winter'
Graham Holderness
    160

Index
    167

Introduction
Shakespeare, Minted

Graham Holderness

Shakespeare made money, enabled many others to make money and wrote extensively about money. In 1970, Shakespeare *became* money. The cover design of this book features a detail from the British £20 note, first issued by the Bank of England in 1970 and withdrawn from circulation in 1991. Shakespeare was the first non-royal historical personality to appear on a banknote. From this privileged position on the national currency, his image presided over a two-decade period of enormous economic turbulence, which saw deindustrialization of Britain's heavy industries (coal, steel and motor production), declines in manufacturing and infrastructure, the failure of a Labour government to resolve the crisis, and the triumph of Margaret Thatcher. By the end of those two decades, the £20 note Shakespeare stood on was worth, as a consequence of inflation, eight times less than it had been.

The image of Shakespeare on the note, designed by Bank of England employee Harry Ecclestone, was derivative, being that of the best-known sculpted representation of Shakespeare, the marble

Notes for this section begin on page 13.

statue commissioned by public subscription, designed by William Kent, executed by Peter Scheemakers and erected in Westminster Abbey as a memorial to the national poet in 1741. Sculpture from this period tended to commemorate rather than imitate the person, overtly using the person's physical attributes as a source for the direct communication of cultural meaning. It functioned therefore both as a collective tribute, drawing on what was already a substantial fund of reverence and admiration; as a memorialization of a pre-eminent genius of English culture; and as an official emblematization of Shakespeare's reception into the structures of national authority and power, constituted by church, state and monarchy. Housed in Westminster Abbey, the image of a writer becomes expressive of the spirit of a nation. Here representation is at its most impersonal, a lapidary codification of the signs of cultural power. The features of Shakespeare scarcely resemble any of the extant portraits, but are constituted by those conventions of idealized depiction that transformed the eighteenth-century English aristocracy into a pantheon of classical characters.

The semiotics of the statue also enact in microcosm a relation between the figure and its institutional space. The form of Shakespeare is shown leaning on a pedestal, embossed with the faces of a pantheon of English monarchs. The supportive pedestal expresses monumental authority and links the image to its surrounding context of royal and state power. The figure by contrast expresses relaxed contemplation and nonchalant mastery: the pose is derived from the conventional Elizabethan image of the melancholy young man leaning against a tree (as in Nicholas Hilliard's famous miniature of 'Young Man among Roses'). Thus, the artefact juxtaposes the weight and stability of the monumental context against an aristocratic insouciance, a relaxed grace and elegant languor appropriate to the eighteenth-century image of the man of letters. The pile of books surmounting the pedestal partakes of both dimensions: the solid, weighty, heavily bound records of monumental achievement – they are merely props for the casual elbow of the leaning poet, rapt in an impassioned stillness of meditation.

The history of its reproduction actually began very early, and in a context that neatly illustrates the relationship between bardolatrous reverence for the symbol of cultural hegemony, and its reduction to tourist curiosity in the acquisition of commodified bardic mementos. In the form of a leaden copy executed in a mass-production factory at Hyde Park Corner, Scheemakers's statue appeared as a centrepiece in David Garrick's Great Shakespeare Jubilee, held in Stratford in 1769. Garrick's Jubilee can be regarded as the great formal inauguration of 'bardolatry' as a national religion: the moment, in the words of one scholar, that 'marks the point at which Shakespeare stopped being regarded as an increasingly popular and admirable dramatist, and became a god'. At the same time, it employed as a central symbolic icon an image of Shakespeare which became, in a later age of mechanical reproduction, an instantly recognizable souvenir. In terms of cultural commerce, the Scheemakers statue offered the perfect form for reproduction and circulation and, as a miniature souvenir, became a standard item in the old curiosity shops of Stratford-upon-Avon. The movement from fetishized object of worship to fetishized token of commodity production is a graphic curve typical of the cultural distribution of the Shakespeare industry.

The contradictory apotheosis of this statuesque image was its incorporation into the design of the British £20 note, where the mystical aura of monumental magnificence and the millionfold multiplicity of mechanical reproduction occupied a single dimension. The device on the banknote transacted a complex exchange of values: the currency of Shakespeare as a cultural token, a symbol both of high art and national pride, enhanced the material worth of the promissory note, while the high value of the note itself conferred a corresponding richness on the symbol of national culture. A banknote is both a sign of value and a legal contract, a 'bond' between citizen and state: the exchange of such symbolic tokens represents both a constitutive material activity and a process of bonding and socialization. The fortunate holder of a Shakespeareanized banknote possessed both monetary wealth and aesthetic richness, and by virtue of that possession was integrated, both materially and culturally, into the dominant cultural-financial system. Here, the solid bulk of another major apparatus of British society, the Bank of England, was articulated with the marble gravity of Shakespeare and the immense solidity of Westminster Abbey, in an institutional configuration grouped to link the strength of a currency with the power of traditional authority.

The paper portrait of Shakespeare probably represents the culmination of eighteenth-century bardolatry: but it represents also its terminal point. Here, all the contradictions of the bardic ideology are held in a paradoxical unity. That which is specific, unique and supremely individual, here appears in its most generalized, impersonal form. The incomparable, irreplaceable, unrepeatable genius of Shakespeare is fragmented by the process of mechanical reproduction into millions of identical simulacra. Those specialized public domains which are in reality the private spaces of our society's prominent individuals are here offered for imaginative occupation by anyone possessed of that minimal financial qualification, as Buckingham Palace used to be occupied every morning by a million breakfast plates slapped onto a million cheap table mats. But the overriding premise of this ideological structure is that authority and power are vested in the material presence of a concrete substance, embodied in the solidity and weight of a positivistic 'reality'. The banknote may be merely fragile paper, but it bears the signature of authority, the images of reliability, the stamp of power. The mysterious potency symbolized by the financial token is by definition absent (even a banknote is really abstract 'credit', declares itself explicitly to be a 'promise'): but it is a god with a countenance of marble, with feet of lead and with printing presses of solid steel. What happens however when, as we see today, the identity of money as abstract value supersedes and obliterates the character of money as material substance?

In the contemporary, social economy money is, as David Hawkes explains in this volume, 'derivative': money is plastic or virtual, debt and credit, profit and investment, figures scrolling across a computer screen, even an invisible 'digital currency', as much for the private citizen as for the industrialist or commercial entrepreneur. Wealth is no longer piled up in greasy banknotes or accumulated amid the clashing cacophony of industrial production, but instead amassed through technological media, realized in the vacuous non-existence of the futures market. Commercial exchange at even the simplest level is more likely to proceed via the plastic or digital authorization of credit as through an exchange of physical tokens like coins or notes.

The traditional iconography of Shakespeare reproduction traded in effects of mass and solidity, gravity and substance. But in the late 1980s, banks began to issue 'cheque guarantee cards' that incorporated an image of Shakespeare into a new postmodern iconography of credit authorization. Whereas the bardic image on the banknote only symbolically authorized value, on the 'Bardcard' it did so literally, since the image was depicted in the form of a high-technology visual 'hologram', designed to inhibit fraudulent use and reproduction. Most of the holograms used the Droeshout portrait of Shakespeare, but one was developed from a photograph, which was not a copy of a standard Shakespeare portrait but rather a photo of a costumed actor pretending to look like Shakespeare.

The authenticity of the card was thus demonstrated not by a display of cultural power, but by a technological coup d'œil. In terms of content, the image approached grotesque self-parody, since the proof of individual ownership, by the cardholder, of certain resources of credit held by a bank was attested by the most fraudulent and artificial means imaginable: a hologram of a photograph of an actor pretending to be ... Shakespeare. Where the traditional imagery of the Scheemakers statue invoked cultural and economic solidity, the image of the Bardcard was pure postmodernist surface, yielding to the efforts of interpretation only a ludicrous self-reflexive playfulness. Where the £20 note pointed to the legitimate state ownership and control of both economic and cultural power, the Bardcard proved your title to credit by displaying the image of a major author whose responsibility for the cultural productions attributed to him has been consistently and systematically questioned. This quality was compounded by the reverse of the card, where the holder's signature authorized individual ownership of its power, irresistibly recalling the hugely contested scrawl of the six signatures attributed to Shakespeare. One wonders how the bank would react to a cardholder who signed their name with the flexible and cavalier approach to spelling also visible in those 'Shakespearean' autographs. The police asked a thief arrested in possession of a stolen Bardcard why he hadn't used it. 'It didn't', he confessed, 'look a bit like me'.

Shakespeare and money: boom or bust? Whether we agree with John Maynard Keynes that 'we were just in a financial position to afford Shakespeare when he presented himself', or with Douglas Bruster that in fact, since Shakespeare entered the theatre business in a time of economic slump, poor harvests and theatre closures, he arrived just as we were least able to afford him, Shakespeare's art has been inextricably involved with the market economy, and with emergent and eventually dominant capitalism.[1] Capitalizing on the emergence of a professional theatrical market in late sixteenth-century London, Shakespeare, in the course of becoming one of the greatest writers in history, made money for himself, and created the basis for incalculable sums subsequently made by those who have profited from reproducing, selling and trading in his work.

Notwithstanding the obviousness of this relationship between art and commerce, as Siobhan Keenan and Dominic Shellard have pointed out, 'the world of Shakespeare studies has been slower to acknowledge the economic importance of Shakespeare's works and name, despite the fact that the scholarly Shakespeare industry has itself been partly based on the ongoing marketability of England's most famous playwright and his art'.[2]

As well as being a successful entrepreneur in the metropolitan theatre industry, Shakespeare himself was also, as Paola Pugliatti reminds us in her chapter in this volume, a moneylender and a speculator in property (both in Stratford and London), in land, in agricultural produce and supplies, and in ecclesiastical tithes. In fact his biographical record displays an overwhelming abundance of evidence about money, property dealings, and commercial transactions, compared with a relative deficiency of evidence pertaining to writing, acting and theatrical entrepreneurship. This discrepancy has long troubled admirers of his work, and even prompted some to speculate that Shakespeare the businessman and Shakespeare the poet may even have been two different people. Since the eighteenth century there has been a sense of incongruity about the sort of financial activity Shakespeare clearly was involved in (e.g. usury and the legal pursuit of small debtors, the proposed enclosure of common lands, and dubious property speculations), which do not sit well with the lofty moral character expected of a national poet and universal bard. The Shakespeare who may have lied in court about a financial bond, bought a house through trustees so his wife couldn't inherit it and participated in a planned enclosure of common land in Stratford seems in some way unqualified to be the author of *Timon of Athens, The Merchant of Venice*, and *King Lear*.[3] This incongruity is actually reflected in the design of the £20 note, which features the balcony scene from *Romeo and Juliet*. The choice of play seems at first glance curiously inappropriate: is not this drama the great poetic protest of romantic passion against mercenary morality and commercialized relationship? Utterances of elevated and idealized passion – 'Beauty too rich for use, for earth too dear' – seem to juxtapose incongruously with ironic effect against the symbolism of monetary value. Until, that is, we realize, as Manfred Pfister demonstrates here in his chapter on the sonnets, that the languages of love and finance are in Shakespeare's poetry inextricably involved: 'rich', 'use' and 'dear' all have double meanings, both romantic and commercial.

Shakespeare's biographers have tended to be divided between approval and antipathy towards Shakespeare the businessman. It would on the other hand, be probably true to say that most Shakespeare criticism is anti-capitalist, formed as it was in the heat of Victorian intellectual critiques of industry, finance, commerce and the accumulation of wealth, and dominated into the twentieth century by critical schools resolutely hostile to the culture of capitalism, demonized as 'mass civilization'. When Marx invoked Shakespeare's work in support of his critique of capitalism, as well as subsuming continental philosophy, he was building on a long British tradition of radical rhetoric, albeit often mounted from a reactionary perspective, condemning the system as, in Thomas Carlyle's phrase, reductive of all social relations to the 'cash nexus between man and man'.

But when, from the 1980s onwards, some radical critics began to study Shakespeare as an economic and cultural phenomenon, as the Shakespeare 'industry', the Shakespeare 'trade' or what Terry Hawkes influentially styled 'Bardbiz',[4] their emphasis was far more focused on matters of politics and philosophy, especially around the concept of ideology, than it was with the economic studies that were central to Marx's project. In the 1970s, teachers and students were certainly reading Marx, but in the relatively accessible form of the *Economic and Philosophical Manuscripts of 1844* rather than the forbidding economic theory of *Capital* or the *Grundrisse*. Both John Drakakis and David Hawkes remind us, in their chapters in this volume, of the centrality of the economic in Marxist-influenced critical interpretations of Shakespeare.

It is only in the past decade that this deficiency in Shakespeare studies has been more widely addressed, and Shakespeare as *Homo economicus* once again brought to the fore. Scholars such as Douglas Bruster, S. P. Cerasano, Andrew Gurr, Siobhan Keenan, Melissa Aaaron and Roslyn Lander Knutson have produced new studies of the Elizabethan and Jacobean theatre industries and the economic contexts surrounding the playwrights and the acting companies.[5] Other critics have explored Shakespeare's poetry and plays in relation not only to the economic context of their production, but also to modern economic theories, following the school known as 'New Economic Criticism', which is concerned not only with 'the social, cultural and economic contexts in which individual or related works have been produced' but also with 'understanding texts as systems of exchange' and with more formalist emphases such as 'studying exchanges between characters and economic tropes in language'.[6] As Peter F. Grav, author of *Shakespeare and the Economic Imperative*, has observed in 2012, 'New Economic critical work' is 'rooted in semiotic and historicist practices' but also, 'often employs formalist methods to discuss the interplay between literature and the economic'.[7] The contributors to this volume make full use of these new, or newly current, critical paradigms. For example, in her chapter on *The Merchant of Venice,* Alessandra Marzola deploys the methods of the new economic criticism, situating the familiar moral dilemmas of the play within historic debates about the role of morality within economics and religion.

We are now in a much better position, as the international contributors to this volume abundantly demonstrate, to evaluate Shakespeare's importance within the global economy. Shakespeare's works can be read to prompt awareness of the growing importance of collapsing and reforming trade barriers between nations in the present, as well the close and complex relationship between economic and political power and culture in a historical perspective. Rui Carvalho Homem, in his chapter, situates some of Shakespeare's less familiar plays within a modern global context of contemporary financial and geopolitical crises. Shakespeare's characters and stories certainly played an important role in his own time in a historical and cultural context in which a new system of mercantile economy was developing out of geographical discoveries, and common law was trying to keep pace with current debates and regulations aimed at facilitating commerce. It should therefore come as no surprise that economic themes and motifs rank high among the pressing cultural concerns to which Shakespeare gave shape in his works. This rapid, dramatic rise to prominence of economic questions is typically reflected in the pervasive monetary subtext of Shakespeare's language, and the sometimes surprising ubiquitousness, as Manfred Pfister ingeniously demonstrates in his chapter on the sonnets of economic language and metaphor in his plays and poems.

Collectively, the authors in this volume have made substantial contributions to financial, economic and commercial studies of Shakespeare, to work on early modern cultural, political and economic power, and to detailed analyses of Shakespeare's most economically-focused plays, including *The Merchant of Venice* and *Timon of Athens*.

David Hawkes is author of *The Culture of Usury in Renaissance England* (London: Palgrave Macmillan, 2010), and *Shakespeare and*

Economic Theory (London: Bloomsbury, 2015). His chapter 'Shakespeare and Derivatives' argues that the twenty-first century has witnessed the rise to power of images in every aspect of human endeavour, including those of commerce, finance and economics. Speculative financial derivatives have achieved a predominant place in the economy, spin and perception rule the political sphere, and technological media ensure that we spend our lives surrounded by images of all kinds. Reading the works of Shakespeare reveals the roots of this process in the early modern period, when the iconoclasm of the Reformation, popular protests against usury, and the campaign against ritual magic combined to provide an ethically based popular resistance to the power of signs.

John Drakakis, well known as the editor of *Alternative Shakespeares*, also edited the Arden 3 edition of *The Merchant of Venice*.[8] In 'Shakespeare, Reciprocity and Exchange', Drakakis invokes Kojin Karatani's *The Structure of World History* (2014), which argues that too little attention has been paid in Marxist historiography to the issue of 'exchange'.[9] In several Shakespearean texts, 'exchange' and 'reciprocity' are of vital importance in sustaining social cohesion; in *Romeo and Juliet*, for example, radical disruptions of patterns of reciprocity and exchange expose an ambivalence that, in certain critical circumstances, inheres in language itself. The disruption that results from the perversion of these values is felt at every level of the social order, but particularly in the sphere of the 'economic', where money and trade become metaphors for the disturbance of the relation between language and action, word and object. This disruption is represented as a product of 'nature' but it also becomes a feature of a historically over-determined human psychology, and leads to a critical examination of different forms of government and social organization.

Rui Carvalho Homem is co-editor of *Gloriana's Rule: Literature, Religion and Power in the age of Elizabeth*.[10] In 'Offshore Desires: Mobility, Liquidity and History in Shakespeare's Mediterranean', Homem probes the ability of Shakespearean drama to provide expressive resources for coming to terms (conceptually, discursively) with current crises. These include both the power games of global finance and those disasters that ostensibly concern other strands of geopolitics. This chapter focuses on two plays, *The Comedy of Errors* and *Pericles*, the actions of which unfold in the eastern Mediterranean – an area of the world associated, in the late modern imagination, with either mobility as pleasure (mass tourism and its apparatus) or mobility as crisis (disputed territories, the plight of displaced populations). It highlights the close bonds between prevalent modes – satire and farce in *The Comedy of Errors*, romance in *Pericles* – and the plays' distinct strategies for representing human mobility: the sense of agency proper to acquisitive urges the victimhood of forced displacement.

Alessandra Marzola is co-author of *Shakespeare and the Power of Difference*.[11] In 'Pity Silenced: Economies of Mercy in *The Merchant of Venice*', Marzola argues that while the mercantile value of mercy in *The Merchant* has been often highlighted, the diminished role of pity has received scant attention. She demonstrates that the ways mercy is shown to subsume and eventually incorporate pity throw light on the play's negotiation of contentious religious and political approaches to the spectres of poverty and/or impoverishment that threaten the emerging mercantile economy. A rereading of relevant scenes retraces the Catholic implications of the safety-net potential of pity, which, unlike the Protestant worldly pity of the sonnets, here seems bound for repression. In Portia's final donation to the merchants of Venice, even the lingering allusions to Catholicism are neutralizsed and put to the service of vested interests: a conflation of Christian and Jewish usury that cuts across all religious divides. Such allusions, she contends, are possibly reminiscent of the Monti di Pietà (Mounts of Piety) existent in Italy since 1462 to counter Jewish usury.

Manfred Pfister is co-editor of *Venetian Views, Venetian Blinds: English Fantasies of Venice*.[12] In '"Love Merchandized": Money in Shakespeare's Sonnets', Pfister re-examines the famous love poems that are, as he observes, not the obvious first choice for discussing matters of finance, money and economic transaction. He argues that in fact the ideas outlined by Karl Marx on 'The Power of Money' in his *Economic and Philosophic Manuscripts* are as relevant to the sonnets as they are to plays such as *Timon of Athens*. Pfister's reading foregrounds their dialogue with terms and developments in early modern banking and focuses on metaphors of economic transaction that run through the whole cycle; indeed, a third of them figure love, its wealth and truth, use and abuse, in terms of investment in order to project an alternative economy beyond the self-alienating world of banking/financial gain. This imbrication of the erotic with the economic comprises also the writing of love sonnets, a competitive gamelike economic transaction. Soneteering is a way of 'merchandizing love' that inevitably casts a capitalist shadow across the supposedly most sincere expression of love.

James Tink, editor of *Seeing Animals after Derrida*,[13] examines the challenges of localizing Shakespeare though theatrical adaptation and considers some of the problems of 'presentist' approaches to the early-modern text. His chapter 'Staging *Timon of Athens* in the Downturn' analyses the production of *Timon* at the Royal National Theatre, London in 2012, directed by Nicholas Hytner and starring Simon Russell Beale. This was a defiantly topical and localized interpretation of the play that made reference to the current economic downturn in the U.K. and Europe, and the recent protests in the City of London by the Occupy movement. The chapter discusses how significantly the text was revised and adapted to fit these topical British concerns about London, politics and the finance sector and assesses how successfully these changes were developed in performance. The chapter also considers in what other ways Shakespeare and Middleton's text has been received in recent literary criticism of the play in order to better understand how the drama has been interpreted as a commentary on the present economic situation. In particular, the theme of linguistic and symbolic breakdown in the drama can be related to contemporary arguments in political philosophy, such as by Slavoj Žižek, regarding language, authority and the social order. The chapter also speculates on how the drama lends itself to ideas of politics, and in what ways the London production illustrated some limitations of the presentist approach. The chapter finally speculates on the ramifications of contemporary Shakespeare reception in local and global contexts.

Although Shakespeare is known to have enjoyed considerable financial success, actors and playwrights of the early modern period were known to be poor. In her chapter '"Fill Thy Purse With Money": Financing Performance in Shakespearean England', Tiffany Stern, author of *Making Shakespeare: from Page to Stage*[14] and *Documents of Performance in Early Modern England*,[15] explores the question of what it meant for Shakespeare to be a 'sharer' in his theatre company, and to what extent the theatres were focused on economic gain as much as the production of successful plays. She takes into consideration the infrastructural and contextual economic practices of the theatres, including transport and the consumption of goods such as food, tobacco, drinks, books and jewellery, and connects these patterns of commercial exchange to monetary and financial allusions in the plays.

Paola Pugliatti is author of *Beggary and Theatre in Early Modern England*.[16] In 'Biography and Shakespeare's Money: Portraits of an Economic Persona', Pugliatti cites Robert Bearman's *Shakespeare's Money* as 'the first economic biography of William Shakespeare', but also as the latest specimen of an innovative trend in Shakespeare biography which has come to the fore over the last decade.[17] While the vein of cradle-to-grave biographies seems to be exhausted, new attention is being devoted to parts of Shakespeare's life, with an attitude that has been seen as 'microhistorical' or 'disintegrationist'. The chapter discusses this new kind of sensitivity to biography in general, and Shakespeare biography in particular. It starts out by addressing certain developments in the theory and practice of life writing during the second half of the twentieth century, which are today becoming ever more substantial; it then examines the progress of Shakespeare biographies and, in particular, how the issue of money has been tackled since Nicolas Rowe first dealt with it.

Sujata Iyengar, author of *Shakespeare's Medical Language*,[18] argues in her chapter 'Shakespeare and the Hybrid Economy' that the established critical terms 'adaptation' and 'appropriation' should be considered under a new rubric as 'transformation'. To evoke either 'adaptation' or 'appropriation' is to evoke copyright law. She suggests that Shakespearean appropriations potentially metamorphose or mutate culture, literary form, creativity, pedagogy and, most provocatively, the market economy, in part because Shakespearean texts antedate current copyright law, and thus any use we make of them is already 'transformative'. In particular, Shakespearean appropriations transform creative production and intervene in contemporary commodity culture or the hypermediatized, monetized creative self. Shakespearean transformations in both legacy and emerging media also offer models for the new hybrid creative economies predicted ten years ago by Lawrence Lessig, in part because of Shakespeare's 'spreadability' (Jenkins, Ford, and Green's term for content that can be remixed, shared, grabbed and so on) and its 'stickiness' (a marketing term popularized by Grant Leboff that connotes the power to draw repeat users who forge a lasting connection with the source material).

The afterthought appended to this volume, a short story entitled 'Best for Winter', is a creative attempt to imagine what might have gone on in Shakespeare's mind as he was writing *The Winter's Tale*, thinking about his financial and property dealings and reacting to his immediate physical surroundings. The stream-of-consciousness method imitates James Joyce and Anthony Burgess. Quotations from *The Winter's Tale* and other plays are mingled with imagined memories of Shakespeare's rural childhood, extracts from the documents recording his commercial transactions and everyday details from his London biography. The story attempts to connect the Shakespeare biography, the working of the creative imagination and the historical economic context into a single complex discourse. The 'hybridity' explicitly discussed in the play, here identified as an inextricable interweaving of the imaginative, the social and the economic, is shown to be the very essence of both writing and of life.

Graham Holderness is the author or editor of some 60 books. His work can be divided into three strands: literary criticism, theory and scholarship, especially in Shakespeare studies; the pioneering of an innovative new method of 'creative criticism'; and creative writing in fiction, poetry and drama. Key critical works include *The Shakespeare Myth* (Manchester UP, 1988), *The Politics of Theatre and Drama* (Routledge, 1992), *Shakespeare: The Histories* (Bloomsbury, 2000), and *The Faith of William Shakespeare* (Lion Books, 2016). Works of creative criticism, which are half criticism and half fiction, include *Nine Lives of William Shakespeare* (Bloomsbury-Arden Shakespeare, 2011); *Tales from Shakespeare: Creative Collisions* (Cambridge University Press, 2014) and *Re-writing Jesus: Christ in 20th Century Fiction and Film* (Bloomsbury, November 2014). He has also published two novels: *The Prince of Denmark* (University of Hertfordshire Press, 2001), and the historical fantasy novel *Black and Deep Desires: William Shakespeare Vampire Hunter* (Top Hat Books, 2015).

Notes

1. John Maynard Keynes, *A Treatise on Money*, 2 volumes (New York: Harcourt Brace and Co., 1930), vol. 2, 124, and Douglas Bruster, *Drama and the Market in the age of Shakespeare* (Cambridge: Cambridge University Press, 1992) 18.
2. Siobhan Keenan and Dominic Shellard, 'Introduction' to their edition *Shakespeare's Cultural Capital: his economic impact from the sixteenth to the twenty-first century* (London: Palgrave Macmillan, 2016), 1.
3. See Graham Holderness, *Nine Lives of William Shakespeare* (London: Bloomsbury, 2011), 76–89.

4. See Graham Holderness (ed.), *The Shakespeare Myth* (Manchester: Manchester University Press, 1988); Barbara Hodgdon, *The Shakespeare Trade* (University of Pennsylvania Press, 1998), and Terence Hawkes, 'Bardbiz', in *Meaning by Shakespeare* (London: Routledge, 1992).
5. S. P. Ceresano, 'Theatrical Entepreneurs and Theatrical Economics', in Richard Dutton (ed.), *The Oxford Handbook of Early Modern Thehatre* (Oxford: Oxford University Press) 380–95; Andrew Gurr, *The Shakespeare Company, 1594–1642* (Cambridge: Cambridge University Press, 2010); Siobhan Keenan, *Acting Companies and their Plays in Shakespeare's London* (London: Bloomsbury, 2014); Melissa Aaron, 'Theatre as Business', in Arthur F. Kinney (ed.), The *Oxford Handbook of Shakespeare* (Oxford: Oxford University Press, 2012), 421–32; Roslyn Lander Knutson, *Playing Companies and Commerce in Shakespeare's Time* (Oxford: Oxford University Press, 2001).
6. Mark Osteen and Martha Woodmansee, 'Taking Account of the New Economic Criticism: an Historical Introduction', in their edition *The New Economic Criticism: Studies at the Intersection of Literature and Economics* (London: Routledge, 1999), 35, 36, 37.
7. Peter F. Grav, 'Taking Stock of Shakespeare and the New Economic Criticism', *Shakespeare* 8.1 (2012), 111–136. And see his book *Shakespeare and the Economic Imperative, "What's aught but as 'tis valued?"* (New York and Abingdon: Routledge, 2008).
8. John Drakakis (ed.) *Alternative Shakespeares* (London: Methuen, 1985) and (ed.) *The Merchant of Venice*, Arden 3rd series (London: Bloomsbury, 2010).
9. Kojin Karatani, *The Structure of World History* (Durham, NC: Duke University Press, 2014).
10. Rui Carvalho Homem and Fátima Vieira, eds, *Gloriana's Rule: Literature, Religion and Power in the Age of Elizabeth* (Porto: University of Porto, 2006).
11. Davide Del Bello and Alessandra Marzola, *Shakespeare and the Power of Difference* (Rome: Aracne, 2011)
12. Manfred Pfister and Barbara Schaff, eds, *Venetian Views, Venetian Blinds: English Fantasies of Venice* (Amsterdam: Brill Rodopi, 1999).
13. James Tink, *Seeing Animals After Derrida* (Lanham: Rowman and Littlefield, 2017).
14. Tiffany Stern, *Making Shakespeare: from Page to Stage* (London: Routledge, 2004).
15. Tiffany Stern, *Documents of Performance in Early Modern England* (Cambridge: Cambridge University Press, 2009).
16. Paola Pugliatti, *Beggary and Theatre in Early Modern England* (Aldershot: Ashgate, 2003).
17. Robert Bearman, *Shakespeare's Money* (Oxford: Oxford University Press, 2016).
18. Sujata Iyengar, *Shakespeare's Medical Language* (London: Arden Shakespeare, 2011).

Chapter 1
Shakespeare and Derivatives

David Hawkes

This chapter explores Shakespeare's role in describing the progressive autonomy of representation that has characterized the last four hundred years of financial history. That process began in Shakespeare's lifetime, when London's goldsmiths began issuing bank-notes for values in excess of the gold bullion in their possession, thus establishing the practical efficacy of independent financial symbols. The signs that stand for exchange-value grew progressively more abstract, and less referential, over the next three centuries until, in the twentieth century, all pretence that money referred to a physical signified was finally abandoned along with the gold standard. Over the last twenty or thirty years, this progressive abstraction of financial symbols has entered a new stage, as the economy dominates society, the financial sector rules the economy, and finance itself takes on new symbolic forms that are collectively known as 'derivatives'.

Shakespeare has continued to comment on such matters long after his death, through the readings to which his texts have been subjected by generations of critics. He lived in the last historical era before what T. S. Eliot called the 'dissociation of sensibility', when 'economic' forms of representation were isolated and distinguished from other kinds of signifying practice, such as literature and aesthetics. Shakespeare was therefore able clearly to perceive the connections between the 'economy' and what we consider discrete areas of life such as art, religion or sexuality. This enabled him to attain an ethical perspective on finance that eludes most modern economists, but which we would do well to recapture today.

According to most estimates, the notional value of the market in financial derivatives currently accounts for over twenty times the collective GDP of the entire world – a combined value of 1.2 quadrillion dollars. This staggering power has largely been achieved over the past three decades, and it has profound implications for the relation of the economy to society, and indeed on the relation of representation to reality in general. Some of these implications are already becoming manifest: the Barings Bank scandal, the bankruptcy of Orange County, the sub-prime mortgage crisis and sundry other financial disasters show the damage that can be caused by reckless trading in derivatives. As early as 2002, the well-known investor Warren Buffet called them 'financial weapons of mass destruction'.[1]

The general term 'speculative derivatives' refers to various kinds of transaction – forwards, futures, options or swaps – by means of which traders exchange the value of various underlying assets, rather than trade in the assets themselves. They are financial instruments that represent signs of other financial instruments. They do not point to any referent in the real world, nor even to a sign of such a referent, but to the signs of such signs – derivatives are symbols of symbols of symbols. As Niall Ferguson observes, regarding an especially intricate form of derivative: 'a synthetic Credit Default Option is a yet higher, almost parodic, level of abstraction – a metaphor of a metaphor of a metaphor'.[2] Derivatives are thus the economic expression of the cultural phenomenon that postmodernists like Jean Baudrillard call 'hyper-reality'.

When President Nixon abandoned the gold standard in 1973, exchange-value finally floated free of its last physical incarnation, and massive price volatility in exchange and interest rates ensued. This volatility made speculation in financial instruments immensely profitable. Meanwhile, the rapid growth of computing capacity made it possible to design and market hugely complicated packages of swaps and options in order to hedge and speculate with superhuman speed and efficiency. During the 1990s the sudden relaxation of government oversight known as 'deregulation' removed most practical obstacles to derivatives' domination of the financial sector.[3] The logic of derivation provided an extra gear, an additional source of symbolic exchange-value, through which the financial sector consolidated its pre-eminence within the economy.

Financial value, like linguistic meaning, is represented through a system of symbols. In such systems, money and words possess analogous signifying properties, which form what Jean-Joseph Goux calls 'the structural homology between money and language'.[4] The symbolic nature of financial value is perceptible in the most basic form of exchange. It originates in the ability to perceive the symbolic value of one object in the physical body of another. In order for a pig to be exchanged for a cow, both participants in the bargain must perceive the animals as representing each other: the pig must be worth the same as the cow; their values must be the same. They must be regarded as equivalent – although they are of course essentially distinct. The most elementary form of commodification thus obtrudes image onto essence, and Shakespeare regularly uses the term 'commodity' in this sense. In *King John,* Phillip the Bastard describes '[t]hat smooth-faced gentleman, tickling Commodity', as 'that same purpose-changer, that sly devil ... This bawd, this broker, this all-changing word ...' (2.1.592–93).

In societies that have developed beyond elementary barter, economic exchange demands the mediation of a universal equivalent, a common denominator, in terms of which the value of any commodity can be expressed. This common denominator is 'exchange-value', and it is represented in the objective form of money. The growth in the power of money thus imposes a false equivalence on the world of essentially different things. It replaces essence with appearance, and it grafts representation onto reality. As Karl Marx pointed out, Shakespeare often remarks on this property of money. On four separate occasions Marx quoted Timon of Athens's well-known description of money's destructive effect on essential identity: 'Thus much of this [gold] will make black white, foul fair, / Wrong right, base noble, old young, coward valiant ...' and so on (4.3.28–9). According to Marx and Engels: 'Shakespeare notes ... [money's] transformation of all human and natural properties into their contraries, the universal confounding and distorting of things'.[5]

Marx often invoked Shakespearean characters like Falstaff, Dogberry and Mistress Quickly, in support of his economic theories. Above all, he repeatedly cited Shylock as the incarnation of capitalist psychology. In *The Merchant of Venice*'s courtroom scene, Shylock's moral claim to equality before the law is based on a false equivalence, the grafting of an apparent similarity onto what, from the perspective of the play's Christians, is an essential difference. He asserts that, as a Jew, he is: 'fed with the same food, hurt with the same weapons, subject to the same diseases, healed by the same means, warmed and cooled by the same winter and summer, as a Christian is ... and if you wrong us, will we not revenge? If we are like you in the rest, we will resemble you in that'.

As Linda Woodbridge has recently pointed out, the vogue for revenge drama in early modern England reveals the period's interest in getting even, in the imposition of equality on essentially different phenomena. Woodbridge describes, for example, the process by which the word 'fair' came to mean 'beautiful' as well as 'equal'. When in George Chapman's *Bussy D'Ambois*, Charlotte is asked, 'Shall we revenge a villainy with a villainy?' she replies with the typical voice of the age: 'It's not equal?' It is this desire for false equivalence that turns *Coriolanus*'s plebians against the hero for, as Brutus comments, Coriolanus 'hath no equal' (1.1.276). In *Titus Andronicus*, Tamora Queen of the Goths appeals to a similar equality when she asks the Romans for clemency: 'if thy sons were ever dear to thee, / O, think my son to be as dear to me' (1.1.124–25). But Demetrius regards any claim of equality between Romans and barbarians as the archetype of false equivalence: 'Oppose [compare] not Scythia to ambitious Rome' (1.1.132).

Thus Shakespeare records the earliest stirrings of autonomous representation, and notes its destructive impact on essential identity. This tendency culminates in the postmodern condition, in which signs generate meaning from their relations to other signs, in the absence of external referents. Within the economy, it is exemplified by the development of financial derivatives. Even when the referent, or 'underlier', of a derivative is a material commodity, as for example in wheat futures, derivatives make it possible to own the price, the value – the meaning – of the wheat without owning the wheat itself. Instead of purchasing a bushel of wheat, an investor can buy the right to dispose of a pattern of variations in the price of wheat over a specific period of time. Derivatives thus separate value from its referent, give it a price, and allow it to reproduce autonomously. They lay bare the semiotic nature of all financial value, for the recognition of exchange-value is already a successful imposition of image on reality, and a bestowal of efficacious power on an image. Derivatives simply apply the logic of exchange-value to exchange-value itself. In doing so, they provide a new kind of universal equivalent, a medium in which the value of any part of production, distribution, exchange or consumption can be expressed – an 'objective correlative' of financial value.

Derivatives extend the logic of money to money itself, and this has led some commentators to describe them as 'the money of money'. As Matthew Bishop remarks: 'people often forget that one of the earliest derivatives was money, which for many centuries derived its value from the gold into which it could be converted'.[6] In this respect derivatives play the same role today as gold bullion did in the Middle Ages, and as the gold standard did until the early twentieth century.

The semiotic role of the gold standard was subjected to a remarkably perspicuous, but hitherto little-known analysis by T. S. Eliot, during his employment by Lloyds Bank. Like Marx, Eliot often had recourse to Shakespeare in his reflections on economic representation, and in his work literary and financial signifying systems converge in striking fashion.

Eliot's friends had initially been worried when poverty forced him to take the job at Lloyds. As his wife told his mother: 'I shed *tears* over the thought of Tom going into a Bank! I thought it was the most terrible catastrophe'.[7] Yet Eliot soon became intrigued by the strange, symbolic power of money. He told his sister that: 'Anything to do with money – especially foreign money – is fascinating, and I hope to learn a little about finance while I am [at Lloyds]'.[8] Two days later he wrote to a friend: 'I should like to think that I shall come to learn something of that extraordinary science of banking, if I can grasp any of it'.[9]

The First World War had left the currencies of Europe a heap of broken images – empty signifiers, with no real value. Banks on the victorious side, like Lloyds, were charged with restoring some semblance of order, and Eliot described his role as 'trying to elucidate knotty points in that appalling document, the Peace Treaty'. The most pressing practical task facing him was the collection of war reparations from Germany. Germany had attempted to meet its obligations by simply printing paper money and paying government workers in marks of arbitrary value, which increased inflation to levels that made money meaningless. As a solution, the victorious allies proposed the Dawes Plan, for which Eliot argued tirelessly in the monthly column he wrote for *Lloyds Bank Monthly*. The restoration of the gold standard in Germany was the plan's major requirement, and Eliot saw it as the only feasible way out of Europe's crisis.

His inaugural column, published in October 1923, scoffs at the fictional, non-representative paper notes being printed by the German government: 'inflation figures at the Reichsbank have become utterly fantastic, the bank officials there have been working twenty hours a day – mostly writing noughts, one would imagine'.[10] Two months later he reminded British investors that the mark was 'nominally a token currency, though it appears to retain a vitality to which it is not entitled'. For Eliot such non-referential value was practically fraudulent. He frowned upon the new currencies issued by regional banks in Hamburg and Bavaria: 'Most of these new issues are denominated "gold" issues, with one qualification or another, but it is to be noted that a "goldmark" of any kind is not necessarily backed by gold, and is never, of course, convertible into gold'. He even described a reversion to barter: 'a leather manufacturer in Saxony paid part of his wages in soles, stamped with the date and the value at that date. It is not stated whether these symbols were accepted by the local tradesmen'. To Eliot's consternation, the Saxons were literally selling their soles.

Eliot warned his readers of the danger in taking such financial signs for wonders. He insisted that mere 'symbols' such as 'printing press' paper or the soles of shoes, are not real money, because they do not refer to the ultimate source and guarantor of financial value, which is gold bullion. His 'Foreign Exchanges' columns are dominated by a fear of chaos, of dissolution and disintegration – of the dissociation of sensibility, and the loss of universally acknowledged standards of value.

During his years at Lloyds, Eliot was expressing similar concerns in his literary criticism, and he found Shakespeare a source of especially apt examples. In the essay 'Hamlet and His Problems', he contrasted *Hamlet* with *Macbeth,* praising the latter for its 'complete adequacy of the external to the emotion'. In the most successful art, Eliot claimed, the objective representation corresponds precisely with the subjective experience:

> The only way of expressing emotion in the form of art is by finding an 'objective correlative;' in other words, a set of objects, a situation, a chain of events which shall be the formula of that *particular* emotion; such that when the external facts, which must terminate in sensory experience, are given, the emotion is immediately evoked.[11]

What Eliot demanded was a stable medium through which subjective feelings can be consistently and reliably represented in external form. Faced with the political and cultural disintegration of Europe, he urged recourse to an absolute source and ultimate referent of symbolic value.

Without such an objective correlative, he believed the nations of Europe would remain in the condition of Hamlet, a state of hyper-reality in which symbol and referent are indistinguishable. As Eliot saw it:

> Hamlet is up against the difficulty that his disgust is occasioned by his mother, but that his mother is not an adequate equivalent for it; his disgust envelops and exceeds her. It is thus a feeling which he cannot understand; he cannot objectify it, and it therefore remains to poison life and obstruct action.

Gertrude is not an adequate objective correlative for Hamlet's subjective feelings of disgust, and in fact this inadequacy of representation is itself the ultimate reason for his disgust. The triumph of the irrational within Hamlet's psyche springs from this failure of representation: 'it is just *because* her character is so negative and insignificant that she arouses in Hamlet the feeling which she is incapable of representing'. In precisely analogous fashion, Eliot the financier pointed out that, in the absence of an adequate objective correlative in the form of physical gold, the value of the paper money issued by the printing presses of Europe would fluctuate in an irrational fashion:

> In connection with the return of so many European nations to the gold standard ... It is, perhaps, not too much to say that the well-being of the whole world depends, in a great measure, upon a speedy return by all countries to sound monetary conditions ....

In the absence of such 'sound' conditions, Eliot believed, an economic Babel would ensue, as 'merchants of different nationalities' chaotically compete in their 'respective currencies' – a prospect that Eliot found culturally as well as economically disconcerting.

The most prominent of Eliot's literary acquaintances who had been horrified by his accepting the position at Lloyds was Ezra Pound. Pound knew that Eliot was engaged in usury, which he regarded as an immoral form of representation, since it projected an illusory efficacy onto an arbitrary system of signs. Usury, according to Pound, works by 'destroying the symbols'. That is to say, by ceasing to treat money as referential, usury robs it of its symbolic nature. A symbol, by definition, refers to something, but usury assumes that money is inherently valuable. By fetishizing the symbol, usury turns it into an idol.

In Pound's view, 'Money is not interesting until it CAN represent something fecund, such, namely AS rams and ewes.'[12] Pound's allusion here is to *The Merchant of Venice,* where Antonio scoffs at

Shylock's attempt to rationalize interest by analogy with the breeding of sheep: 'Was this inserted to make interest good? / Or is your gold and silver ewes and rams?' (1.3.92–93) Shylock's gloating response epitomizes the usurer's confounding of nature and custom: 'I cannot tell, I make them breed as fast' (1.3.94).

Shakespeare employs the association of usury with barren, concupiscent sexuality to ironic effect in *The Sonnets*. In the opening procreation sequence the male speaker describes his homosexual lover as a 'profitless usurer' who has 'traffic' with 'thyself alone'. He urges the youth to loan his love to women, and to reap interest in the form of offspring. Shakespeare alludes to the contemporary legal exemption whereby usury was permissible if both parties benefitted: 'That use is not forbidden usury / Which happies them that pay the willing loan'.[13] The speaker's plan misfires, however, and he comes to realize that it is the youth's female lover who truly possesses him, while he himself is merely a borrower: 'Thou usurer, that put'st forth all to use …. Him have I lost through my unkind abuse'.[14]

While the gold standard provided an apparently invariant, ultimately material referent for financial value, the system of derivatives is made up entirely of representation. The self-referential nature of derivatives links them conceptually, as well as historically, to the self-generating verbal signs of post-structuralist linguistics, and several critics of the postmodern economy describe themselves, in the words of Christopher Schinkus, as 'inspired by post-structuralism'.[15] The founder of structural linguistics, Ferdinand de Saussure, divided the linguistic sign into two parts: the 'signifier' (for example the word 'cow') and the 'signified' (for example the concept of a cow). In this model, the sign no longer derives its meaning from its referent (which is the actual animal that says 'moo'), but from the signified – which is a factor internal to the sign.

That is a decisive moment in the history of linguistics, and of representation in general, for it locates reference within the sign, rather than in any pre-linguistic 'real world'. But meaning remains referential in Saussure's model, in the sense that the signifier refers to the signified. By the 1960s, however, post-structuralists like Jacques Derrida were deconstructing the polarity between signifier and signified, arguing that concepts were themselves semiotic in nature, and that they could not be separated from their expression as signifiers. Derrida criticized the notion that signifiers refer to signifieds, or that signs derive their meaning from a reality that lies beyond or beneath them. Instead, he viewed linguistic meaning as the product of *differance*: an endless chain of signifiers, each one differing from the next, but none of them referring to any extra-linguistic sphere. In analogous fashion, and at the same historical moment, financial value was peeling off from reference to the external world, adhering instead to the self-generating power of financial symbols.

Derrida was inspired by the work of J. L. Austin, whose *How To Do Things With Words* distinguished between 'constative' statements, which refer to an extra-linguistic reality and can therefore be evaluated as either true or false (for example 'the fox is brown'), and 'performative' statements, which refer to nothing beyond themselves, but rather perform the action they describe (for example 'I name this ship the Queen Elizabeth' or 'Open Sesame!'). Performative statements are neither true nor false; they can only be evaluated as successful or unsuccessful. Austin eventually concluded that, while all constative utterances are also performative, not all performatives are constative. A statement like 'the fox is brown' can be evaluated as either true or false, and also as either successful or not. However, a statement like 'this country is at war with Germany' is neither true nor false; it can only be judged as either successful or unsuccessful, depending on who says it in which circumstances. The performative turns out to be logically prior to the constative. This contention cast doubt on some of the most fundamental assumptions of Western metaphysics. It challenged the idea that meaning is the product of a conscious subjectivity, the belief that verbal signs derive their meaning from their reference to a pre-linguistic reality and, in the interpretations of Austin's most radical readers, even the existence of truth itself.

Although Austin chose not to emphasize, and may not have fully appreciated, the radical implications of his theory, these were fully exposed by Derrida. According to him, subjectivity itself was inescapably mediated through various representational discourses, of which the financial and the linguistic were homologous examples, and on which Derrida bestowed the general term 'writing'. On this basis, the post-structuralist followers of Derrida constructed an ethics of performativity, whose radical implications were announced by Judith Butler:

> If gender attributes ... are not expressive but performative, then these attributes effectively constitute the identity they are said to express or reveal ... gender cannot be understood as a role which either expresses or disguises an interior 'self'.... As performance which is performative, gender is an 'act'... which constructs the social fiction of its own psychological interiority.[16]

For Derrida and Butler, significance is produced by the autonomous force of 'writing', whose central characteristic is 'iterability', the capacity to retain its meaning when repeated in the author's absence. The financial theorist Elie Ayache stresses that this quality of 'iterability' is shared by the financial signs of the derivatives market, which he therefore classifies as a type of 'writing'. According to Ayache, the value of derivatives is produced by their 'writing' alone: 'It is the pure, material writing of contingency. It is pure difference. Writing is difference, as Derrida would say'.[17]

A future contract, forward, option or swap relies on the same instrument having a different value in an altered context. It depends, as Ayache notes, on iterability, and for this reason he takes Jorge-Luis Borges' story 'Pierre Menard, Author of the *Quixote*' as his illustrative model. In Borges' fable, a twentieth-century French author reproduces sections of Cervantes's text word-for-word, thus revealing a wholly new, and vastly richer, set of meanings within the unchanged text. Ayache argues that profit from derivatives emerges out of a similar elevation of value above reference. The derivatives market is dependent on techniques for measuring value – for measuring measurement itself – because value, rather than substantive commodities, is what it trades in. This is a dramatic departure from conventional economics. In the realist or traditional view, as summarized by Arjun Appadurai:

> ... the derivative is above all a linguistic phenomenon, since it is primarily a referent to something more tangible than itself: it is a proposition or a belief about another object that might itself be similarly derived from yet another similar object. Since the references and associations that compose a derivative chain have no status other than the credibility of their reference to something more tangible than themselves, the derivatives' claim to value is essentially linguistic.[18]

Ayache agrees that the value of a derivative is 'essentially linguistic', but he disputes the referential model of value described by Appadurai. Derrida argued that identity and meaning emerge out of the difference between signs, so that *differance* itself becomes the fundamental, constitutive category in the construction of meaning and identity. In similar fashion, Ayache conceives of derivatives as the primary financial instrument, not as secondary or supplemental. They are not, in other words, derivative. Ayache declares that 'derivative' is a misnomer since, like *differance*, derivatives are a primary and not a secondary phenomenon. He criticizes the view that that they derive their value from their underlying referent:

... we should no longer think of derivatives as derivatives ... we have something called the underlying upon which the derivatives are written, and the underlying according to the metaphysics of possibility and probability is going to find itself in several possible states of the world ... the derivative is a function of those states, hence 'deriving' from those states.... So, in the end, the derivatives are not absolute because they depend on the underlying.[19]

In his criticism of this traditional conception of derivatives, Ayache takes up the postmodern hostility to 'metaphors of depth': for him even financial value is an essentialist fantasy. Only price, the surface expression of value, its symbol, is real. The notion that the price of something might not express its true value is impossible for Ayache. In a world ruled by performative signs, every price is the *justum pretium*, and appearance is the only reality.

Today, many philosophers hail the autonomous power of representation as politically and personally liberating. Western universities are packed with ardent advocates of performativity, which they portray as enabling a revolt against the oppressive constrictions of essentialist identity. But the connection between the rise of performativity in identity politics and the rise of financial derivatives is not often expressed by today's radical philosophers. In my opinion, however, this connection is the proverbial elephant in the philosophical drawing room. Once we understand that performative theories of personal identity are conceptually implicated in, as well as historically simultaneous with, the logic of derivative-based finance capitalism, the entire field of identity politics, and its relations to the politics of the 'economy', will have to be substantially re-conceived.

The independence of signs from their referents is not an ontological but an historical fact. It is salutary to remember just how egregious a violation of traditional ethics it involves. The attribution of subjective agency to symbols has traditionally been the definition of idolatry and ritual magic as well as of usury. In England the dawn of the capitalist era was marked by widespread popular and intellectual revolts against the practical power of symbols. The great 'witchhunt', which killed around one hundred thousand people over the sixteenth and seventeenth centuries, was an hysterical reaction to the unprecedented power of autonomous images. At the same time, the iconoclasm of the Reformation instructed the population in the dangers of worshipping images, or idolatry.

This was also the period when theoretical and practical restrictions on usury were lifted, and Shakespeare often noted the homologies between the magical, idolatrous and financial forms of 'derivation'. In *The Comedy of Errors,* Antipholus identifies the performative power of commodities with the efficacious symbols of magic:

> Some offer me commodities to buy.
> Even now a tailor called me in his shop
> And showed me silks that he had bought for me,
> And therewithal took measure of my body.
> Sure, these are but imaginary wiles,
> And lapland sorcerers inhabit here. (4.3.6–11)

At the same time, popular tracts like the anonymous *The Ruinate Fall of Pope Usurie, Deriv'd From Pope Idolatrie* (published in 1580) drove home the connections in between usury and idolatry. This dialogue claims that usury occurs when a man 'useth the gain of his stock, turned from wares into money, supposing such dealing to be as lawful as to have the increase of his money, as of wares, considering not the difference that is between wares and money'. The tract objects to usury's confusion of 'wares' and 'money', because money is value itself – the 'equall value' that 'governeth all unequall values'. If the value of value itself fluctuates, there can be no objective value, and so the author declares that: 'Money must not be used as wares, nor wares as money'.

In such complaints, the people of early modern England expressed their indignation at the prospect of being ruled by signs. If we are to develop an ethical critique of derivative finance, the postmodern world needs to re-learn what the pre-modern world understood: magical totems, liturgical idols and self-generating money are different species of performative representation. Each of them can be, and often has been, subjected to ethical criticism, on the grounds that they encourage and express the human tendency to fetishism. The moral problem with fetishism, or idolatry, is that it involves worshipping 'graven images', signs that are the products of human labour. In the words of Psalm 115: 'Their idols are silver and gold, the works of men's hands'.[20] The Psalm goes on to prognosticate that the consequence of fetishism is psychological objectification: 'Those who make them are like unto them, so is every one that trusteth in them'.[21] The postmodern displacement of *logos* by *eidola*, and the consequent impact on human thought and behaviour, can be read as the ultimate fulfilment of that prophecy.

After all, performative speech-acts abolish human intention as a factor in the formation of significance. The couple is objectively married once the priest declares them so, even if he subjectively intends them to remain single. The witch-hunters of the seventeenth century said the same about the tokens and talismans of ritual magic: they operate efficaciously without regard to the intention of the magician. In the metaphysical discourse of the age, the source of representation's magical efficacy was personified as Satan, the declared enemy of the human soul. We do not need to resort to such anachronistic terminology to see that the power of financial derivatives is fundamentally destructive and antihuman. That seems clear on practical grounds alone. Is there also an ethical case to be made against the autonomous power of linguistic representation? Is there a logical or even a causal link between the self-referential signifiers of postmodernist philosophy and the self-referential signs of twenty-first century finance? And if we find the rule of autonomous finance to be morally reprehensible, should we not extend that criticism to performative representation as a whole? Shakespeare's Henry V suggested so when he asks:

> ... what art thou, thou idol ceremony?
> What kind of god art thou, that suffer'st more
> Of mortal griefs than do thy worshippers?
> What are thy rents? What are thy comings in?
> O ceremony, show me but thy worth!
> What is thy soul of adoration? (4.1.219–24)

As Marx noted on the first page of *Capital*: 'In English writers of the seventeenth century, we still sometimes find "worth" employed to mean use-value, and "value" to refer to exchange-value'. Here, the King indicates that idolatry consists in the occlusion of 'worth' or 'soul'– of essence, in short – beneath the empty form of appearance. It is here that Shakespeare provides his most damning verdict on the effect of derivatives, broadly conceived. The 'logic of the derivative' may have liberated humanity from the constrictions of essentialism, but such revolutionary liberations always carry a price. If the effect of autonomous representation is the destruction of essence, and if the soul is the essence of a human being, then we are surely justified in asking whether that price is worth paying.

David Hawkes is Professor of English Literature at Arizona State University. His seventh scholarly monograph, *The Reign of Anti-Logos: Performativity in Postmodernity*, is forthcoming with Palgrave Macmillan in 2020.

Notes

1. Berkshire Hathaway Annual Report, 2002, http://www.fintools.com/docs/Warren%20Buffet%20on%20Derivatives.pdf (accessed 31 July 2016).
2. Niall Ferguson, *The Ascent of Money: A Financial History of the World* (London: Allen Lane, 2008), 98.
3. As LiPuma and Lee remind us: 'the secretary of the Treasury in the late 1990s, Robert Rubin, his successor Paul O'Neill, and the present vice-president Dick Cheney, all commanded companies that are architects of, and principals in, derivatives trading'. Edward LiPuma and Benjamin Lee, *Financial Derivatives and the Globalization of Risk* (Durham, NC: Duke University Press), 199n2.
4. Jean-Joseph Goux, *The Coiners of Language* trans. Jennifer Curtiss Gage (Norman: University of Oklahoma Press, 1984), 4. The term 'homology' was first used in this context by Marc Shell, in *The Economy of Literature* (Baltimore, MD: Johns Hopkins University Press, 1978). Fascinating though it is, the debate about the distinction between 'homology' and 'analogy' is best conducted elsewhere.
5. 'The Economic and Philosophical Manuscripts of 1844', trans. and ed. Robert C. Tucker, *The Marx-Engels Reader* (Second Edition) (New York, 1978), 167–68. See also Marshall Berman, 'All That is Solid Melts into Air', *The Experience of Modernity* (New York, 1982).
6. Matthew Bishop, 'A Brief History of Derivatives', *The Economist*, 338, no. 7952 (1996), 6–9, here 1.
7. Valerie Eliot, *The Letters of T. S. Eliot*, volume one, revised edition, eds. Valerie Eliot and Hugh Haughton (Yale, 2011), 197.
8. *Ibid.*, 182.
9. *Ibid.*, 446.
10. Quoted from the 'Foreign Exchanges' column of *Lloyds Bank Monthly*, consulted courtesy of the Lloyds Bank archive, Victoria, London. The columns are unsigned, although composing them was Eliot's job.
11. T. S. Eliot, 'Hamlet and His Problems', in *Selected Essays, 1917–1932* (London: 1932), 96.
12. Leonard William Doob (ed.), *Ezra Pound Speaking: Speeches of World War Two* (London), 176.
13. Sonnet 6, 5–6 in Harold Bloom (ed.), *Shakespeare's Poems and Sonnets* (New York: 2009).
14. Sonnet 134, lines 10, 12.
15. Christophe Schinkus, 'Semiotics of Financial Marketplace', *The Interdisciplinary Journal of Economics* 22 (2010), 317–33.
16. Judith Butler, 'Performative Acts and Gender Constitution: An Essay in Phenomenology and Feminist Theory', *Theatre Journal*, 40, no. 4 (1988), 519–31, here 528.
17. Elie Ayache, *The Blank Swan: The End of Probability* (Chichester: Wiley, 2010), xix.
18. Arjun Appadurai, *Banking on Words; The Failure of Language in the Age of Derivative Finance* (Chicago, IL: University of Chicago Press, 2016), 4.
19. 'The Blank Swan: Dan Tudball talks to Elie Ayache', *Wilmott* April 2007, 43.
12. Psalms 115: 4.
13. Psalms 115: 8.

Chapter 2
Shakespeare, Reciprocity and Exchange

John Drakakis

Exchange

In 1859 Marx began his *Contribution to the Critique of Political Economy* with a reference to Aristotle's *The Politics*. His concern was with 'the wealth of bourgeois society' and its capacity for accumulating 'commodities' where the commodity 'has a two-fold aspect – *use-value* and *exchange-value*'.[1] Aristotle, who was concerned with the political organization of the Republic also made this distinction, although his concern was not primarily with what we might term the 'capital' to be derived from the exchange value of a commodity. He thought that the process and 'technique of exchange' had its origin 'in a state of affairs often to be found in nature' whereby 'men having too much of this and not enough of that' sought 'to re-establish nature's own equilibrium of self-sufficiency'.[2] For Aristotle, productive labour is stimulated by need, and the form of acquisition of which he approves is

> in accordance with nature, a part of household-management, in that either the goods must be there to start with, or this technique of

Notes for this section begin on page 46.

property-getting must see that they are provided; goods, that is, which may be stored up, as being necessary for providing a livelihood, or useful to household or state as associations. And it looks as if wealth in the true sense consists of property such as this.[3]

Indeed, he goes on to argue that 'wealth is a collection of tools for use in the administration of a household or a state'[4] while at the same time recognizing that the process of acquisition through 'trade' raises certain problems: firstly, 'one, which is necessary and approved of, *is to do with household management*', (my italics) but the other 'which is to do with trade and depends on exchange, is justly regarded with disapproval, since it arises not from nature but from men's gaining from each other'.[5] This is followed by an often quoted passage that vilifies usury:

> Very much disliked also is the practice of charging interest; and the dislike is fully justified, for the gain arises out of currency itself, not as a product of that for which currency was provided. Currency was intended to be a means of exchange, whereas interest represents an increase in the currency itself. Hence its name [*Tokos*], for each animal produces its like, and interest is currency born of currency. And so of all types of business this is the most contrary to nature.[6]

Of course, before *The Politics* Aristotle had discussed 'the household' in his *Oeconomica*, a text some of whose major concerns were later echoed in Sir Thomas Smith's *De Republica Anglorum* (1583). The point to emphasize is that the processes of exchange were regarded as instrumental in maintaining the order of the household, and that the acquisition of goods (*chrēmatistikē*) as part of household management is to be distinguished from the unrestrained amassing of wealth. Exchange, and the ethics governing exchange, therefore, were regarded by Aristotle as instrumental and crucial to the organization, sustenance and political stability of the household, and, by implication, the 'state'.

Marxism has traditionally placed its emphasis on 'modes of production', the forms of social organization that are designed to sustain, distribute and reproduce particular kinds of material existence. But recently Kojin Karatani has sought to revisit the connections between production, consumption and exchange in an attempt to establish the dynamic, and often adversarial, mechanisms of exchange as crucial to the process of social evolution.[7] Indeed, Karatani launches out from what Marx identified as 'the commodity' (the object of exchange); this is, as Marx defines it, 'the direct *unity* of use-value and exchange-value, [while] emphasizing, at the same time, that it is a commodity only in relation to other commodities'. Marx continued,

> The *exchange process* of commodities is the *real* relation that exists between them. This is a social process which is carried on by individuals independently of one another, but they take part in it only as commodity-owners; they exist for one another only in so far as their commodities exist, they thus appear to be in fact the conscious representatives of the exchange process.[8]

Karatani regards this exchange process as both constitutive and contingent, and not confined to a capitalist economy, and he seeks to explore its evolution over time through an anthropological investigation of 'the reciprocity of the gift'.[9]

He begins by identifying three types of exchange: firstly, a 'generalized reciprocity' that is rooted in the institution of the family (mode A); secondly, the positive or 'balanced reciprocity' to be found within larger settlements, and underpinned by law – the balance that law produces is impeded by 'negative reciprocity' that can exist between communities who move from consensual agreement to the kind of violence that Karatani refers to as 'the vendetta' (mode B);[10] and thirdly, 'commodity exchange' (mode C) '[t]hat arises when exchange is neither constrained by the obligations inherent in gift-giving, as in mode of exchange A, nor imposed through violence, as in the pillaging of mode of exchange B'.[11] Of initial interest to him, and for this chapter, are the first and second types of 'reciprocity', or the reciprocity that exists within communities on the scale of a single household and the reciprocity that exists in relations between communities'.[12]

In the historic shift from nomadism to a sedentary community, what Karatani calls 'reciprocal exogamy' leads to 'the establishment of a higher-order community' that replaces 'kin-based societies' determined by 'relations of blood' with 'social bonds created through the power of the gift'. Karatani argues that the whole process becomes 'a problem of reciprocal exchange in general',[13] in which exchange both within and between communities is perceived as an expression of the desire to trade,[14] but 'commodity exchange' itself is made possible between communities by 'the existence of the state, which punishes as legal infringements any acts of theft or failures to uphold contracts'. What accelerates the acquisition of commodities and trade in general is the emergence of money as a means for establishing equivalence in value; although, as Marx observed, it is the process of commodification that guarantees exchangeability and an equalization of 'unequal values' through the medium of money, and that systematizes the 'accidental' nature of the relationship through the mediator – 'the merchant, who compares money prices and pockets the difference. It is through this movement that the equivalence is established'.[15] To this Karatani adds the suggestion that the process of exchange is responsible for establishing rule and purchasing services 'without having to rely on either fear or the constraints of reciprocity'.[16] But, contrary to Marx, Karatani does not see this process in historically progressive terms. Indeed, he argues that:

> a single social formation arises as a combination of three different modes of exchange – or the three different forms of power that derive from these, forms that are mutually in conflict yet also mutually interdependent.[17]

His claim is that all three modes of exchange coexisted, and that '[e]ven in pre-capitalist social formations mode of exchange C (commodity exchange that is associated directly with capitalism) was an important factor' although, despite its indispensability, it 'was always placed in a position of inferiority'.[18] In other words, before the accumulation of wealth (*Chrēmatistikē*) became 'capital' it was subjected to forms of moral and ethical control whose long history can be traced back to Aristotle.

Karatani's revision of Marx opens up an important avenue of enquiry that may help to unlock a number of interpretative issues in relation to a range of Shakespearean texts. For example, the question of 'reciprocity' and its difficulties is central to *Romeo and Juliet*; the nature of exchange and the concept of 'value' become the focus of attention in *Troilus and Cressida*; and in *Timon of Athens* the 'economy' of the Athenian republic as seen through early seventeenth-century English eyes, and its relation to questions of 'friendship', is a key idea.

Romeo and Juliet: 'reciprocity and 'exchange'

> Two households both alike in dignity
> In fair Verona, where we lay our scene,
> From ancient grudge break to new mutiny,
> Where civil blood makes civil hands unclean.
> —The Prologue: ll.1–4[19]

The form of the Prologue is an Italian sonnet, and this introduces an additional, disturbingly adversarial layer of intertextuality into a drama that will embed the play's love interest and the potentially comic form, its 'aesthetic', in a distinctly hostile environment. The Verona that the play depicts is one of warring households in thrall to the structure of a 'vendetta' whose origin is so 'ancient' that it is irrecoverable. The love interest might lead us to expect a structure in which reciprocity and the exchange of the lovers will ameliorate, if not eliminate, the hostility between the two houses. What we are offered instead is a return to the hostility between two communities, nominally mediated by an ineffectual representative of the 'state', the Prince Escalus, whose authority is persistently undermined by 'Rebellious subjects, enemies to peace, / Profaners of this neighbour-stained steel' who will not 'hear'. (I. i. 79–81) In short, Verona is a dangerously unbalanced 'economy' in the Aristotelian sense of the term, both at the wider communal level and at the level of the household. Indeed, everything that would maintain a balance in the community is undermined by the ancient grudge and the cumulative violence that it produces. It is in this dangerous environment that the playful sexual hostility of 'star-crossed lovers', is embedded, and it is this context that is responsible for perverting the reciprocity of marriage as an institution that would heal, enrich and enlarge the community. Instead, 'Verona's ancient citizens'

> Cast by their grave-beseeming ornaments,
> To wield old partisans in hands as old,
> Cankered with peace, to part your cankered hate. (I. i. 90–93)

What should be the 'gravity' of the community is transformed into a partisan struggle, a 'canker' that infects the entire play, leading to a constitutive ambivalence that, as the Friar will later indicate in quasi-Aristotelian fashion, is inscribed in the moral economy of nature itself:

> O, mickle is the powerful grace that lies
> In plants, herbs, stones and their true qualities,
> For naught so vile that on the earth doth live
> But to the earth some special good doth give,
> Nor aught so good but, strained from that fair use,
> Revolts from true birth, stumbling on abuse.
> Virtue itself turns vice, being misapplied,
> And vice sometime by action dignified. (II. iii. 11–18)

This becomes a language of paradox that infiltrates the play's love discourse from the very outset, with Romeo lamenting 'O brawling love, O loving hate, / O anything of nothing first create', (I. i. 174–5) defining love as 'O heavy lightness, serious vanity, / Misshapen chaos of well seeming forms' (I. i. 176–7) and 'a smoke made with the fume of sighs' or 'a madness most discreet, / A choking gall and a preserving sweet' (I. i. 188, and 191–93). In this dialogue Romeo and Benvolio discuss the relative and absolute value of the love object that Benvolio takes up again at the end of the following scene.

Left entirely to the emotions, love is a capricious force, hence the need for some kind of institutional containment. Act I scene 2 opens with Paris approaching Capulet for permission to marry Juliet. The judicious father, aware of the pitfalls of marriage, resists because of Juliet's age, but his first consideration is his own future: 'She is the hopeful lady of my earth' (I. ii. 14). However, he confesses that his own authority is but one determining factor in the process, since, initially, at any rate, Juliet will have some say in her own future: 'My will to her consent is but a part, / And, she agreed, within her scope of choice / Lies my consent and fair according voice' (I. ii. 16–18). Juliet is cast initially both as a potentially willing party *and* an object of exchange in what is a larger inter-family negotiation. What follows frustrates this negotiation, and that frustration is a consequence of what the play posits as the 'natural' volatility of human behaviour that imitates the precarious balance of 'nature' itself.

That volatility throws Romeo and Juliet together, while the ancient feud claims the lives of Mercutio and Tybalt. But that is not all. Following the night of the consummation of Romeo and Juliet's relationship, her mother seeks to prepare her daughter for marriage to Paris. Juliet grieves for Romeo's departure, while her mother thinks that she weeps for the death of her cousin at Romeo's hand. Each interprets 'revenge' differently, although the hostility felt by her mother is an indication of a radical inter-familial hostility that the two lovers have already violated. They surmount the conflict between the two families, but not, as we would say, in the conditions of their own making. When Capulet himself enters, the limits of Juliet's resistance are spelled out in no uncertain terms:

> Thank me no thankings nor proud me no prouds,
> But fettle your fine joints 'gainst Thursday next
> To go with Paris to Saint Peter's church,
> Or I will drag thee on a hurdle thither.
> Out, you green-sickness carrion! Out, you baggage,
> You tallow-face! (III. iv. 152–57)

And it gets worse! It is at this point that Capulet exerts his authority over his household, in the face of his wife's and the Nurse's protestations at his ferocity. In this play, the ambivalence of 'nature' is projected into the human world characterized by an almost pathological disharmony, where all exchanges that would seek to cement union and produce social harmony are frustrated.

Juliet's mock death brings this chaos to a head, and the inadvertent failure of the Friar's letter to reach its destination prompts an extreme strategy from Romeo. His visit to the Apothecary represents the one form of exchange whose intentions are not in some way masked. He recalls the Apothecary 'in tattered weeds, with overwhelming brows, / Culling of simples' (V. i. 39–40), but in a context very different from that of the Friar earlier. The Apothecary possesses deadly and, more importantly, illegal drugs, but it is Romeo who glosses his extreme poverty:

> Famine is in thy cheeks,
> Need and oppression starveth in thine eyes,
> Contempt and beggary hangs on thy back,
> The world is not thy friend, nor the world's law;
> The world affords no law to make thee rich,
> Then be not poor, but break it and take this. (V. i. 69–74)

What begins here as 'need' is quickly transformed into a potentially dangerous form of commodity exchange that appears to exist *underneath* 'the law'. The Apothecary's response is simple in its excusing of his recourse to the logic of commodity exchange: 'My poverty but not my will consents' (V. i. 75). Quite out of the blue, there follows a comment from Romeo that addresses directly a fundamental Aristotelian hostility that lurks at the heart of the process of exchange as it emerges in the play:

> There is thy gold, worse poison to men's souls,
> Doing more murder in this loathsome world
> Than these poor compounds that thou mayst not sell.
> I sell thee poison; thou hast sold me none. (V. i. 80–84)

Ironically the events at the end of the play will transform this claim, although this formulation offers a key to an understanding of the consequences of perverting the social mechanisms of exchange. In fact, the play ends in a curious kind of gift exchange, with Capulet asking for Montague's 'hand' in a truncated form of marriage: 'give me thy hand. / This is my daughter's jointure, for no more / Can I demand' (V. iii. 295–7). Montague doesn't reciprocate: rather, in accordance with the logic of gift-giving, he raises the stakes in such a way that transforms a dangerous material substance into an icon of unity:

> But I can give thee more,
> For I will raise her statue in pure gold,
> That whiles Verona by that name is known,

>   There shall no figure at such rate be set
>   As that of true and faithful Juliet. (V. iii. 298–302)

Capulet then raises the stakes even further in order to reinforce some element of equality in the exchange: 'As rich shall Romeo's by his lady lie, / Pure sacrifices of our enmity' (V. iii. 303–4). Montague places a value on the statue of Juliet, and Capulet reciprocates. This is indeed, 'a glooming peace', as the only exchange available is one that fetishizes the figures of Romeo and Juliet in a substance that is the unstable, and radically sterile medium of exchange, 'gold': a substance that has the capacity to impoverish even as it enriches.

Troilus and Cressida and the value of value

In *Troilus and Cressida* normative questions of value, exchange and reciprocity are laid open to radical questioning, which reach an apotheosis in the very aesthetic form of the play itself. At the heart of the action is the abduction of Helen, 'Menelaus' queen' (Prologue i. 9) and the affront it poses to the socially essential ritual act of marriage. Sexual desire and military honour are brought together in a series of encounters that repeat the initial 'ravishing' and its devaluation of representation in the liaison between Troilus and Cressida, and the acts of exchange that produce the dilemma. It is clear that acts of exchange themselves involve tactical manoeuvring that expose, even as they threaten, the integrity of everything that binds society together. The Prologue's recourse to the proverbial 'Now good or bad, 'tis but the chance of war' (i. 31) is initially re-articulated as a 'sex war' that is a perversion of the basic familial unit; indeed, it is the kind of hostility that the scabrous Thersites insists lies at the root of the Trojan war: 'All the argument is a whore and a cuckold; a good quarrel to draw emulous factions and bleed to death upon' (II. iii. 69–71). The fate of Troilus and Cressida, while rooted from the outset in the discourse of romantic chivalry, is circumscribed by a series of contingent events that radically undermine the foundation of their relationship. Not only that, but Troilus characterizes himself as a merchant engaged in the purchase of commodities in his pursuit of Cressida:

>   Her bed is India; there she lies, a pearl:
>   Between our Ilium and where she resides,
>   Let it be called the wild and wand'ring flood,
>   Ourself the merchant, and this sailing Pandar
>   Our doubtful hope, our convoy and our bark. (1. i. 96–100)

Here, the romantic and the venal are brought into alignment with each other so that relationship is perceived as a purchase and an exchange. Two scenes later, in the disorganized Greek camp, the image of the merchant re-appears as part of a military tactic; Nestor is worried how the choice of an opponent to face Hector will reflect on the Greeks' judgement, but Ulysses's strategy reveals the sophistication, and the capacity for deception that inheres in the act of exchange:

> Let us, like merchants, show our foulest wares,
> And think perchance they'll sell; if not,
> The lustre of the better yet to show
> Shall show the better. (I.iii. 360–63)

This strategy is formulated in the wake of a much more detailed definition of order that takes its metaphorical and teleological force both from the organization of bees (I. iii. 81–83), and that of the universe, in which everything exists 'in all lines of order' (I. iii. 88). However, most important of all is how Ulysses describes 'communities':

> How could communities,
> Degrees in schools and brotherhoods in cities,
> Peaceful commerce from dividable shore,
> The primogeneity and due of birth,
> Prerogative of age, crowns, sceptres, laurels,
> But by degree stand in authentic place? (I. iii. 103–8)

Without these checks and balances anarchy is given free rein, and power expresses itself as unrestrained desire: 'will' and 'appetite', which are metamorphosed into a 'universal wolf' that will ultimately consume itself. Each of these categories depends upon balanced rituals of exchange and reciprocation within a symbolic order in which no element is isolated.[20] Also, although each element, as Ulysses's plan suggests, must retain a certain amount of flexibility, the process of differentiation that holds them all together is indispensable if society is not to collapse into anarchy. Moreover, the articulation of military combat as a means of conferring chivalric honour, also permits its further reformulation as a commercial relation in which seller and buyer jockey for position in the act of exchange. The terms of these discourses are integrated, although within the context of the play that integration betrays some strain, and is under threat.

At the heart of the play's complex network of exchanges is Helen, whose abduction is the cause of hostility. Her reclamation involves revenge for Meneleus's cuckoldry, but on both sides questions are raised about 'value': the Greeks assess the methods by which she can be reclaimed while the Trojans question the 'value' of keeping her. Hector's practical observation that Helen 'is not worth what she doth cost / The holding' (II. ii. 51–2), provokes a subjective account of value that appears to be unconditional, a mere product of unrestrained will. We know from Ulysses's analysis where that leads to, and Troilus's question provokes a practical definition that provides a Trojan revision of the Greek account of order. Hector appeals to reason and to the principle of intrinsic value and warns that ''Tis mad idolatry / To make the service greater than the god' (II. ii. 56–7). Troilus, on the other hand, deploys a mercantile metaphor of exchange to explain marriage itself:

> How may I avoid,
> Although my will distaste what it elected,
> The wife I chose? There can be no evasion
> To blench from this, and to stand firm by honour.
> We turn not back the silks upon the merchant
> When we have soiled them; nor the remainder viands
> We do not throw in unrespective sieve
> Because we now are full. (II. ii. 65–72)

Given the circumstances surrounding the 'rape' of Helen as an act of 'vengeance' for the abduction of Paris's 'old aunt' (II. ii. 77), Troilus's example, as David Bevington has suggested, 'could hardly be more inept'.[21]

But Hector invokes Aristotle to counter Troilus's 'reasons' which, he insists 'do more conduce / To the hot passion of distempered blood', and he goes on to link the institution of marriage with 'nature':

> Nature craves
> All dues be rendered to their owners. Now,
> What nearer debt in all humanity
> Than wife is to the husband? If this law
> Of nature be corrupted through affection,
> And that great minds, of partial indulgence
> To their benumbed wills, resist the same,
> There is a law in each well-ordered nation
> To curb those raging appetites that are
> Most disobedient and refractory.
> If Helen then be wife to Sparta's king,
> As it is known she is, these moral laws
> Of nature and of nations speak aloud
> To have her back returned. (II. ii. 173–86)

Karatani's mode of exchange C is present here, but as a threat to the normative balance of mode of exchange B. Spoken 'in way of truth', this does not, in itself, provide Hector with a reason for returning Helen. The 'cause' in which her abduction has now been caught up 'hath no mean dependence / Upon our joint and several dignities' (II. ii. 192–3), where 'dependence' suggests a contingent relation. Despite Hector's quasi-Aristotelian analysis of Troilus's predicament, he affirms the prudence of the merchant who has exchanged one commodity for another that is superior, and then *justifies* his decision in that the Greek challenge threatens Trojan honour. Indeed, both the Greek and Trojan camps embed their analyses of exchange, reciprocity and hostility in the 'administration of a household' and hence in 'Oeconomica', in Aristotle's sense of the term:

> Of such administrations there are four main types, under which all others may be classified. We have the administration of a king; of the governors under him; of a free state; and of a private citizen.[22]

And it is, of course, Thersites who punctures the general self-deceiving rhetoric of chivalry and honour, with his wholly reductive account of the consequences of military incompetence: 'After this, the vengeance on the whole camp! Or rather, the Neapolitan bone-ache! For that, methinks, is the curse dependent on those that war for a placket' (II. iii. 16–19).

The Trojan debate about Helen's value is revised in Diomed's Greek evaluation later in the play, just before Cressida is bargained away for Antenor. And here again the imagery is that of a transaction, an exchange; for example, Diomed's dispraising of Helen is met with Paris's exposure of the pitfalls of exchange:

> Fair Diomed, you do as chapmen do,
> Dispraise the thing that you desire to buy.
> But we in silence hold this virtue well:
> We'll not commend what we intend to sell. (IV. i. 77–80)

In the same way that Helen was seized in exchange for Paris's 'old aunt', so Cressida will now be exchanged for Antenor. In a hostile environment where petty jealousies and dishonourable actions are common, the vows that Troilus and Cressida exchange, observed by Pandarus, will prove to have little substance. Indeed, there is something wrong with the principle of reciprocity as it emerges in the progress of the two lovers. Troilus laments that 'the will is infinite / and the execution confined; that the desire is boundless and the act a slave to limit' (III. ii. 78–80), while Cressida detects a perfidy that she herself will be forced to embrace later in the play:

> They say all lovers swear more performance than they are able, and
> yet reserve an ability that they never perform, vowing more than the
> perfection of ten and discharging less than the tenth part of one.
> They that have the voice of lions and the act of hares, are they not
> monsters? (III. ii. 81–86)

At the point when the lovers realize that they must part, it is Troilus who resorts to a vocabulary of mercantile exchange, as if the proclaimed ethical 'truth' of constancy is always undermined by the venal foundation of exchange:

> We two, that with so many thousand sighs
> Did buy each other, must poorly sell ourselves
> With the rude brevity and discharge of one. (IV. iv. 37–40)

In the Greek camp the captive Cressida has no alternative but to make use of her own sexual attributes, but the consequence of breaking her vow to Troilus is to undermine the very foundation of linguistic exchange. Indeed, as Giorgio Agamben has observed, where there is no correspondence 'between the signifier and the signified, between words and things' then there remains 'a void and a gap' between the semiotic and the semantic'. The result is that 'oath and perjury, bene-diction and male-diction correspond to this double possibility inscribed in the *logos*, in the experience of which the living being has been constituted as speaking being'.[23] To put it another way, trade of a particularly empty kind underwrites the venal exchange in which the prostitute is engaged. As Ulysses points out: 'Set them down / For sluttish spoils of opportunity / And daughters of the game' (IV. v. 62–64).

This fundamental corrupting of the language and the act of exchange, and of the moral and ethical structure that sustains it, drains the cause to which Troilus finally commits himself of all substance. State, household, and private citizen finally have no value, and Pandarus's closing appeal to 'Good traders in the flesh' (V. xi. 45) follows Troilus's final nihilistic resolution to entertain 'Hope of revenge' as a means of masking 'our inward woe' (V. xi. 31). Revenge is the projection of disappointment with the fundamental imbalances of the exchange process that threaten to undermine the social order. The reduction of exchange and community to a venal trading in flesh, reaches its apotheosis in the figure of the pander, the facilitator whose activity both encourages and threatens to undermine the very acts of reciprocity that guarantee the health of community. *Troilus and Cressida* is a dramatic demonstration of what we might call negative economics.

Friendship and society in *Timon of Athens*

The fate of Cressida and the dilemma of Troilus point towards a suspicion of unrestrained commerce, and of language itself. Invoking Fernand Braudel's observation that during the Renaissance there was a 'popular mistrust of money' as a means of mediation, David Hawkes recently observed that 'the commodification of money implies the commodification of mediation *per se*'.[24] *Timon of Athens* provides a demonstration of where that process of increasing commodification, along with the perversion of acts of exchange and reciprocity, leads to. Early Jacobean writers may well have had some knowledge of *The Funeral Declaration of Pericles* from the second book of Thucydides's history of the Peloponnesian War, translated by Thomas Nicolls from the French and published by John Waylande in 1550. Two of the issues that Pericles' speech touches on are friendship and hospitality:

> we use furthermore the offices of vertue, by contrary reasone and manner, that the othere people do. For that, that we attempte and goo aboute to get frends, more by doinge them some plaisir and benefit, than in recyuinge it, of them. Also in kepinge the amytie and benyuolence, he that receyueth the plaisir and benefytt, is in worse condition than he that doth it. For, for him that doth it, yt is ynough to concerue it by benyuolence. But he that hath receyued it, understandeth this that in rendringe the like he gratifieth not but rather dothe render the plaisir whyche he hath receyued. Also we do gratefie nobly and liberally our frends, more for to profit them than for to shewe, that we use our liberality towards them. (sig. Liiii^v)[25]

Thucydides via Nicholls' translation offers some hints as to how we might read Athenian benevolence, liberality and aristocratic modesty, transplanted into early modern political and social discourse. Indeed, it is in *Timon of Athens* (c.1606) that Shakespeare, and a possible collaborator, Thomas Middleton,[26] focused more particularly on representing from a critical standpoint the internal state of Athens on the cusp of an encroaching tide of commodification. Of course, they were looking at the Athenian republic from the perspective of an English absolute monarchy that was still a centralized sovereign state.[27]

Timon of Athens opens with a gathering of four representative figures who are an integral part of the cultural economy of the city. They are all attracted by a shamelessly pecuniary 'Magic of bounty' (I. i. 6) that their efforts will receive from 'Lord Timon'. The poet speaks for his fellow parasites in his representation of the fraud that they collectively perpetrate:

> When we for recompense have praised the vile.
> It stains the glory in that happy verse
> Which aptly sings the good. (I. i. 16–18)

But those who profess friendship to Timon have a utilitarian motive that Aristotle regarded in his *Ethics* as impermanent, and that the duplicitous Poet proleptically ascribes to a changeable Fortune:

> When Fortune in her shift and change of mood
> Spurns down her late beloved, all his dependants,
> Which laboured after him to the mountain's top
> Even on their knees and hands, let him slip down,
> Not one accompanying his declining foot. (I. i. 86–90)

This echoes part of Aristotle's account of friendship, which he regarded as a necessary safeguard against misfortune:

> A gret suretie it is to a man to haue frendes, for so much as a man is in the degree of gretnes, the more egal he is to fal, and his fal most perilous... For a manne that hath no frende, is alone in his dedes: And when he is with his frend, he hathe companye and helpe to brynge his worke to passe.[28]

Timon's friendship is expressed through his lavish 'hospitality' and his generosity that requires no reciprocation. He is the Maussian gift that goes on giving; what Timon gives he gives without expecting recompense: 'there's none / Can truly say he gives, if he receives' (I. ii. 10–11); but in a society driven by venality, his generosity is open to exploitation. The dynamics of what Derrida in his *The Politics of Friendship* (1997) would call 'the invisible theatre of hospitality'[29] are played out to a nihilistic conclusion in which the protagonist completely loses faith in the society that his generosity had done much to sustain. Indeed, Timon's 'unconditional hospitality' is brought into conflict with, to use Derrida's terms, 'a hospitality circumscribed by law and duty', which can always be used to corrupt it, 'and this capacity for perversion remains irreducible'.[30]

Like his hospitality, Timon's unconditional friendship is predicated upon an understanding of society in which 'self' and 'other' are united in a love that Montaigne defined as a kind of intimate mutuality: 'If a man urge me to tell wherefore I loved him, I feele it cannot be expressed, but by answering; Because it was he, because it was my selfe'.[31] However, Montaigne follows Aristotle in distinguishing between 'this sovereigne and mistris Amitie' that implies total commitment, and 'vulgar and customary friendships' within which 'a man must march with the bridle of wisdome and precaution in his hand'. It was this latter category that persuaded Montaigne to recall Aristotle's oft-repeated saying: '*Oh you my friends, there is no perfect friend*'.[32] In *Timon* money is necessary but not sufficient to define the social order. Timon's liberality is a marker of social status, but in a society riven by what Joyce Oldham Appleby has called 'competing descriptions of reality, where money was dealt with simultaneously as an analytical concept, a psychological force, and a practical problem'.[33] For Timon, the gift is an expression of love that requires no immediate material reciprocation. What is exchanged is love for love, whose material foundation, as David Hawkes has reminded us, has, until recently become 'largely invisible'.[34] It is only when Timon is, himself, in need that the non-reciprocal utilitarian foundation of the friendship that he has practised is exposed. In practical terms his failure to reproduce the conditions of his own lifestyle leaves him despondent in a society now built on the impersonal mechanisms of credit and selfish prudence.

As Timon's substance diminishes, he becomes more conscious of the devaluation of language and gesture, the media through which he articulates his friendship and his hospitality. Only the loyal steward Flavius shows a willingness to reciprocate love in the face of adversity, but his appraisal of Timon's dilemma is accurate:

> His promises fly so beyond his state
> That what he speaks is all in debt – he owes
> For every word. He is so kind that he now
> Pays interest for't; his land's put to their books.
> Well, would I were gently put out of office
> Before I were forced out.
> Happier is he that hath no friend to feed,
> Than such that do e'en enemies exceed. (I. ii. 200–8)

In the new democratic world controlled entirely by the relativity of market values, gifts are transformed into perverse examples of exchange, and the 'honourable' and 'honest' Timon's generosity that binds language and society together is made to seem pathological, as the incredulous Senator explains:

>   Still in motion
> Of raging waste? It cannot hold, it will not
> If I want gold, steal but a beggar's dog
> And give it Timon, why, the dog coins gold.
> If I would sell my horse and buy twenty more
> Better than he, why, give my horse to Timon –
> Ask nothing, give it him – it foals me straight
> And able horses. (I. i. 4–10)

'The usuring senate' (III. vi. 109), ostensibly the friends and beneficiaries of Timon's magnanimity, turn out to be the enemies and agents of his destruction; to use Derrida and Dufourmantelle's formulation, they represent the opposing meanings of the 'host': 'foreigner (*hostis*) welcomed as guest or as enemy. Hospitality, hostility, *hostpitality*'.[35] Timon is 'undone by goodness', by doing 'too much good', and Flavius asks the crucial social question: 'Who then dares to be half so kind again?' (IV. ii. 38, 40).

The play descants upon the theme of friendship as the commonwealth of Athens disintegrates into 'a forest of beasts' (IV. iii. 347), while Timon's misfortune draws him near to the pathologically disaffected Apemantus. His low opinion of mankind is affirmed by the procession of parasites that visit him in his isolation. The Painter and the Poet revert to type, and will exchange their devalued aesthetic currency, their empty promises, for gold: 'Promising is the very air o' th' time; it opens the eyes of expectation' (V. i. 22–23). But this drives a sinister wedge between language and action that demarcates the courtier from a 'simpler kind of people':

> Performance is ever the duller for his act and, but in the plainer and simpler kind of people, the deed of saying is quite out of use. To promise is most courtly and fashionable; performance is a kind of will or testament which argues a great sickness in his judgement that makes it. (V. i. 23–8)

Timon's discovery of 'gold' in nature (IV. iii. 25), a quantity of which will make 'Black white, foul fair, wrong right, / Base noble, old young, coward valiant' (IV. iii. 28–9) recalls the ambivalence of 'nature' in *Romeo and Juliet*. And it is greed and self-interest that attracts the Senators who seek to placate Timon on behalf of the Senate:

> They confess
> Toward thee forgetfulness too general gross,
> Which now the public body, which doth seldom
> Play the recanter, feeling in itself
> A lack of Timon's aid, hath sense withal
> Of its own fall, restraining aid to Timon,
> And send forth us to make their sorrowed render,
> Together with a recompense more fruitful
> Than their offence can weigh down by the dram,
> Ay, even such heaps and sums of love and wealth,
> As shall to thee blot out what wrongs were theirs,
> And write in thee the figures of their love,
> Ever to read them thine. (V. ii. 28–40)

The tortuousness of the rhetoric betrays their hypocrisy, and the absolute venality that it seeks to obscure. The friendship they offer (in the face of the military threat to Athens from Alcibiades) is 'vulgar and customarie' to use Montaigne's terms, full of distrust to the point where it resembles Aristotle's 'Oh you my friends, there is no perfect friend'.[36] Indeed, at the root of the problem is the radical perversion of the mechanisms of the process of exchange as they are articulated in the rituals of friendship and hospitality. It is competitiveness, and commodification, encouraged by a fundamentally antisocial individualism, that are at the heart of the Athenian republic itself and that contribute to its growing precariousness and susceptibility to military threat, and to Timon's misanthropy. The social, the political and the psychological are all woven into the figure that is Timon.

The Athens of Shakespeare's (and Middleton's) play is portrayed as a self-contained city state, but at its heart is a series of contradictions, including potential for corruption. The dominant mood of the play, and its emotional force, is 'anti-acquisitive' in the sense deployed by L. C. Knights in his book *Drama and Society in the Age of Jonson* (1962). Karatani argues that in the case of 'absolute monarchies, as their mercantilist policies demonstrate, it is self-evident that we are dealing with a union of capital and state – in other words, that the state and capitalism are inseparable'.[37] We might measure this observation against the anticipatory claim made by Nicos Poulantzas that 'we should clearly recognize that though the state has a global function of cohesive factor in the unity, this does not mean that for this reason it always maintains the dominant role in a formation, nor that when this dominant role is held by the economic, the state no longer has this function of cohesive factor'.[38] In all of the plays we have looked at, what we might call 'the state' (i.e. the institution that combines the juridical – law – and political – the management of class antagonism) is in trouble. The source of that trouble is the disruptive force of money, which threatens to destroy traditional relations of exchange, friendship and hospitality, the three pillars upon which the order of society rests. Timon departs from his household and retreats from a society now fuelled by usury into nature and becomes, literally, 'un-accommodated man'. But ironically he also finds in the earth 'gold' that has the capacity to assist in perverting social, (and aesthetic) relationships. If, as Poulantzas argues, the function of the state is to prevent 'classes and "society" from consuming themselves' and that the deployment of the term 'society' 'indicates that it prevents the social formation from bursting apart',[39] then in these plays this is exactly what we see, whether it be Verona, Venice or Ancient Greece. Perhaps we need to see this disturbance of the social order as a particular feature of a republicanism that is rather different from the 'monarchic republic' of the English variety described by Patrick Collinson,[40] but that operates from the household outwards. The characterization of money as the token par excellence of exchange, therefore becomes a metaphor for the radical transformations that confronted early modern society; a society that sought to cope with the gradual erosion, over a long period of time, of social relationships at all levels that were built upon traditional hierarchy and obligation.

John Drakakis is emeritus professor at the University of Stirling, and was for 6 years a visiting professor at the University of Lincoln. He is the general editor of the Routledge *New Critical Idiom* series, and he is the general and contributing editor to the forthcoming revision of Geoffrey Bullough's *Narrative and Dramatic Sources of Shakespeare*. He has recently edited Shakespeare's *The Merchant of Venice* for Arden (Third Series), and he has contributed a number of book chapters and journal articles on Shakespearean subjects. He is the editor, along with Dale Townshend, of *Gothic Shakespeares*, and *Macbeth: A Critical Reader* for the Arden Early Modern Drama *Guides* series. He is on the editorial board of a number of scholarly journals and he has guest-edited volumes for the *ESSE* journal and *Poetics Today*. He is a Fellow of the English Association, an Honorary Fellow of Glyndwr University and he holds an honorary PhD from the University of Clermont-Auvergne. He has recently been elected as an Honorary Fellow of the British Shakespeare Association.

Notes

1. Karl Marx, *A Contribution to the Critique of Political Economy*, trans. S. W. Rayazanskaya (Moscow, 1977), 27.
2. Aristotle, *The Politics*, trans. T. A. Sinclair and revised by Trevor Saunders (Harmondsworth: Penguin Books, 1992), 82. All citations of *The Politics* are from this edition. *The Politics* was published in an English translation in 1598, around the same time as the appearance of some of Shakespeare's Mature Comedies.
3. Ibid., 79.
4. Ibid.
5. Ibid., 87.
6. Ibid.
7. Kojin Karatani, *The Structure of World History: From Modes of Production to Modes of Exchange*, trans. Michael K. Bourdaghs (Durham, NC: Duke University Press, 2014).

8. Marx, *Critique of Political Economy*, 41.
9. Karatani, *Structure of World History*, 40.
10. Ibid., 37.
11. Ibid., 6.
12. Ibid., 37–38.
13. Ibid., 49.
14. Ibid., 82–83.
15. Karl Marx, *Capital Volume III*, trans., David Fernbach (Harmondsworth: Penguin Books, 1981), 447.
16. Karatani, *Structure of World History*, 83.
17. Ibid., 83–84.
18. Ibid., 84.
19. William Shakespeare, *Romeo and Juliet*, ed. René Weiss, Arden Third Series (London: Bloomsbury, 2012). All citations to this text are from this edition.
20. Cf. David Hawkes, *Shakespeare and Economic Theory* (London: Bloomsbury, 2015), 14. The isolation of land and labour as commodities is emphasized by the characterization of the usurer as the consumer of land and patrimony.
21. David Bevington, ed., *Troilus and Cressida*, Arden Third Series (Walton-on-Thames: Thomas Nelson, 1998), 194 fn.61.
22. Aristotle, *Oeconomica*, trans. G. Cyril Armstrong, vol. II (Cambridge, MA: Harvard University Press, 1977), 345.
23. Giorgio Agamben, *The Sacrament of Language*, trans. Adam Kotsko (Cambridge: Polity Press, 2010), 70.
24. David Hawkes, *Shakespeare and Economic Theory* (London: Bloomsbury, 2015), 15.
25. Thomas Nicolls, trans. *The history written by Thucydides the Athenian of the warre, whiche was between the Peloponnesians and the Athenyans* (London, 1550), fol. Liiii^v.
26. See John Jowett, ed., 'The Life of Timon of Athens' in *Thomas Middleton and Early Modern Textual Culture: A Companion to the Collected Works*, ed. Gary Taylor and John Lavagnino (Oxford: Oxford University Press, 2013), 704–5.
27. Cf. Karatani, *Structure of World History*, 168ff.
28. Aristotle, *The Ethiques of Aristotle, that is to saye, precepts of good behauiour and perfighte honestie, now newly re-stated into English* (London, 1547), sigs. P1^v–P2.
29. Jacques Derrida and Anne Dufourmantelle, *Of Hospitality*, trans., Rachel Bowlby (Stanford, CA: Stanford University Press, 2000), 109.
30. Ibid., 135ff.
31. John Florio, trans., *Montaigne's Essays*, 'Of Friendship', vol. I (London: Everyman, 1965), 201.
32. Ibid., 203.
33. Joyce Oldham Appleby, *Economic Thought and Ideology in Seventeenth-century England* (Princeton, NJ: Princeton University Press, 1980), 201.
34. Hawkes, *Shakespeare and Economic Theory*, 72.
35. Jacques Derrida and Anne Dufourmantelle, *Of Hospitality*, 45.
36. Florio, *Montaigne's Essays*, volume 1, 203.
37. Karatani, *The Structure of World History*, 169.
38. Nicos Poulantzas, *Political Power and Social Classes*, trans. Tomothy O'Hagan (London: Verso, 1973), 56.
39. Ibid., 50.
40. Patrick Collinson, 'The Monarchial Republic of Queen Elizabeth I', *The Bulletin of the John Rylands Library* (1987), 394–424.

Chapter 3

Offshore Desires
Mobility, Liquidity and History in Shakespeare's Mediterranean

Rui Carvalho Homem

In the opening pages of his *Shakespeare in the Present*, the late Terence Hawkes memorably discusses the set of conditions under which, in our time, we confront texts from the past. As he describes it, reflective readers have faced, in the critical environment of the late twentieth and early twenty-first century, a sustained call for historicizing their object of inquiry while hardly proving able to let go of their 'situatedness' as a determinant of the 'selections and suppressions' that regulate our dealings with the past.[1] This chapter is emphatically grounded on a sense of contingency defined both by the challenge posed by the Shakespearian text's 'temporal and cultural alterity',[2] and an awareness that (again in Hawkes's words) 'we can only see the past through the eyes of the present'.[3] From this dual perspective I want to claim the relevance of re-reading the 'mouldy tale'[4] of *Pericles* and the farcical extremes of *The Comedy of Errors* to

Notes for this section begin on page 65.

probe the ability of different strands within the Shakespeare canon to provide imaginative resources with which we can both confront the otherness of the past and respond to the 'urgency of now'.[5]

The phrase 'the urgency of now', when critically enlisted, stresses an imperative to respond to one's circumstance that is pointedly temporal. Additionally, however, the 'now' that it urges us to act upon is also conceptual (our tools of inquiry can only be those afforded by our moment in intellectual history) and spatial (involving the contexts, the global and local dynamics that have shaped both the objective circumstance and the framework of inquiry). Indeed, this chapter is grounded on a rather emphatic acknowledgement of a 'place of reading'[6] concomitantly defined by several factors. These certainly include the critical mores that have prevailed in western academia – the tension, signalled above, between the urge to historicize, and the assumption that 'the critic's own situation in our cultural present' is 'a resource' rather than an 'impediment' to a sound critical exercise.[7] Beyond this, however, the factors that delineate my 'place of reading' have to include the formative particularity of my location on a western European, Atlantic but quasi-Mediterranean periphery (Portugal) with a cherished memory of the country's expansionist early modern past;[8] but also the specificity of addressing, from a liminally Atlantic locale whose language gave Early Modern English drama words for currency such as 'portagues' and 'crusadoes',[9] the importance of mobility and money in the imaginative processing of the Mediterranean by an English playwright whose work has generated a global academic industry.

Such factors will largely be taken for granted in the following pages, and yet the geopolitics of academic inquiry are anything but irrelevant to this chapter's double critical remit: (i) to discuss how Shakespeare, central as he was to the imaginative production of an early modern London with a growing mercantile and Atlantic maritime economy, represented a range of human transactions that he displaced to an ancient Mediterranean world of seaports and trading cities; (ii) to consider how such representations can arguably resonate with current concerns over human mobility and global socio-economic dynamics. The relevance of this link between early modern circumstances and current crises indeed increases when we realize that Shakespeare was engaging in such imaginative dislocations against a historical backdrop of considerable geopolitical change. Indeed, his work emerged from the period that witnessed what Braudel influentially called the 'northern invasion' of the space of Mediterranean commerce by northern European ventures, which signalled the historical shift of a sense of centrality from the Mediterranean to the Atlantic.[10]

These geopolitical implications acquire an additional cogency in light of the growing attention to perceptions and representations of space that has marked the humanities and social sciences since the 1980s, sometimes under the name of 'spatiality studies' – drawing on prior contributions ranging from phenomenology and existentialism through structuralism to theories of post- or late modernity. Despite the variousness of their intellectual and ideological leanings, the combined effect of such contributions to the recent focus on space has been to emphasize that places obtain their meanings from a discursive and relational process. As proposed by the editors of an influential collection, 'If places are no longer the clear supports of our identity, they nonetheless play a potentially important part in the symbolic and psychical dimension of our identifications'. And they add: 'How ... does space become place? By being named. ... Place is space to which meaning has been ascribed'.[11] The argument that this process is verbally constructed, and based on the dynamics of mutually defining relationships, rescues the 'spatial imagination' from the conceptual constraint of an association with stasis, and indeed binds it (as suggested by David Harvey) to a dual temporal design, articulating retrospection and anticipation: 'The preservation or construction of a sense of place is ... *an active moment* in the passage from memory to hope, *from past to future*'.[12]

Such remarks propose an integration of historiographic and geographic perspectives that neatly assists the immediate critical framework for a discussion of how Shakespeare represents the mobility of people and money against scenarios that challenge linear understandings of time and place. In the two plays discussed below, this happens by dislocating to Antiquity discourses and concerns that characterized the rising commercial capitalism of early modern London. What I am describing as the immediate critical framework primarily consists of the substantial scholarly tradition that has focused on Shakespeare, money and the economy, a tradition that in the final quarter of the twentieth century fostered the so-called 'new economic criticism', and, more recently and topically, included responses to the global financial crisis that has unfolded since 2008.[13] Parallel to such scholarly responses, intersections of Shakespeare and finance have obtained a range of representations on stage and screen:

productions of *Timon of Athens* exploring the topicality of the post-Lehman Brothers crisis, such as Nicholas Hytner's for the National Theatre in 2012, promptly come to mind; but 'corporate Shakespeare' predated the events that marked and followed 2008, and included Michael Almereyda's film *Hamlet* (2000), set in a rarefied New York hi-tech corporate environment. Such productions refract a sense of *agon* and crisis through recent financial frameworks, and they pursue this strategy by relocating the time and action of Shakespeare's plots to western present-day (or imminent future) scenarios – the London City, Wall Street. They endorse perceptions of such locales as the epicentres of an ultra-advanced but ultimately crass finance found to hinge on a well-known paradox: the uncertainties of individual decisions (a singularity magnified, in such productions, by the generic framework of tragedy) are suffered by millions in myriad elsewheres.

Rather than engaging with such western and fast-forwarded displacements, in the pages below I will consider the imaginative and expressive footholds that present-day audiences and readers, as witnesses and victims of global financial and social crises, can derive from Shakespeare's own arguable relocations – in his case, eastern and regressive – of the early modern world of mobility and exchange.[14] I am also opting out of that focus on individual pathos which is proper to the generic framework of tragedy to emphasize rather the communality of comedy, and how it can be modally inflected by romance and satire. I am interested in addressing how in *The Comedy of Errors* and *Pericles* Shakespeare (partly determined by his sources) dislocates transactions observed in the mercantile and monetary world around him from his western and Atlantic there and then to the Ancient world, and hence to that world's defining locales in the eastern Mediterranean, 'the geographical and economic birthplace of risk'.[15] Further, I am interested in the referents that are activated, for present-day audiences, by representations of personal aspiration and acquisitive desire that the playwright dramatically embeds in ventures associated with seascapes that have recently acquired an uncanny topicality.

Indeed, in the two plays in question a series of hazardous sea crossings, real or presumed drownings, quasi-miraculous rescues at sea, and the uncertainties of hospitality versus hostility in coastal, mercantile cities are explicitly bound to place names from Antiquity: Ephesus, Epidamnum, Pentapolis, Antioch, Tyre, Tarsus, Mytilene.[16] For Shakespeare's original audiences, such place names may have carried the imaginative resonance Harley Granville-Barker once attributed to the toponymic litanies of *Antony and Cleopatra* (with its particular 'spacious[ness]'),[17] besides suggesting, through their association with navigation and trade, that the voyaging and mercantile concerns of the new economy of exchange had a long lineage behind them.[18] However, this general perception could combine with a more specific recognition: the coastlines against which the plots of *The Comedy of Errors* and *Pericles* unfold had by the late sixteenth century become newly familiar to Elizabethan audiences because of the opportunities English merchants were then seizing in the Mediterranean: for some English commercial sailing, 'a typical itinerary might include Livorno, Zante, Scandaroon (the port of Aleppo, also known as Alexandretta), Smyrna, Chios, and Constantinople'.[19]

Conversely, present-day audiences may be startled into an awareness of that topography and toponymy as strangely current because of the predicaments that have made them feature on the world's screens and front pages all through the second decade of the twenty-first century. Ephesus, the ancient city near present-day Selçuk in Asia Minor, in the province of Izmir (former Smyrna), invoked by Shakespeare for both *The Comedy of Errors* and the ultimate reunion scene in *Pericles*, is today one of the main archaeological attractions in Turkey, for which in recent years operators were promising a money-back guarantee for all who were not '100% satisfied'[20] – but, as widely reported, its appeal to visitors has suffered from its closeness to one of the most hazardous coastlines in the recent migrant crisis.[21] This has been the case even more in the recent circumstances of another location of *Pericles* – Mytilene, on Lesbos, much discussed in 2016 for the poignant support that local populations then gave to refugees, despite their disruptive effect on their main source of income.[22] But the associations between the places and place names of Shakespeare's Mediterranean and historically recent crises of human mobility are, in fact, temporally broader than the latest developments: Epidamnum, evoked by Egeon in *The Comedy of Errors* as one of the trading cities of his former mercantile ventures, is present-day Durrës, in Albania, the site of a migrant crisis that, back in 1991, first acquainted readers and viewers worldwide with images of a type that have more recently become all too common.[23]

Seeking in Shakespeare imaginative resources for representing and better understanding the plight of migrants and refugees is hardly new, as made clear (for example) by reports of improvised productions on refugee camps.[24] Rather than charting such initiatives, however, I am interested in highlighting that the expressive range of the plays includes an imagination and rhetoric of disaster associated with the coastlines of Antiquity that resonates in the dismal scenarios of the present-day crises of human mobility. All of the routes evoked in the two plays concern an area of the world marked by an ambivalence that may affect other geo-economies, but has in the eastern Mediterranean recently become evident: the same sea that is coveted and crisscrossed by affluent and willingly displaced tourists, from the middle-class amenities of crowded cruise ships to the yachts of the super-rich, has become the setting for the most serious crisis of human displacement, involving the utter disruption of community and family, impossibly risky crossings and mass drownings. The intense global reporting, filming and photographing of the migrant and refugee crises has added ethical complexities to the discussions that the topic has obtained in western media, its emotional ballast often maximized by images of young children (culminating in the controversial publication of photographs of drowned Alan Kurdi, the three-year-old Syrian boy found dead in September 2015 on a beach in Bodrum, recognized as having impacted, in a variety of often contrasting ways, election campaigns and government policies in the west[25]).

The reactions of public opinions and electorates to such events and their substantial coverage have been far from uniform, but they have in broad terms confirmed the intensity with which the recent crises of human mobility are challenging long-cherished assumptions about the structuring values of materially advanced societies – from Europe to America, Asia and Australia. Outside the more volatile ground of the global media and the instant responses they have obtained, public institutions have produced substantial overviews of such challenges, sometimes resorting to academic formats and venues to consolidate the conceptual apparatus with which to confront them.[26] And indeed, prior to the disasters that have marked the second decade of the new millennium, academic and critical confrontation with the phenomena of human displacement and their broader role in shaping history and culture had already been intense, fostering pleas for the development of 'mobility studies' such as Stephen Greenblatt's in *Cultural Mobility: A Manifesto*.[27] In an earlier, online version of his opening argument, Greenblatt asked rhetorically: 'what if mobility were understood to be the constitutive condition of culture, not its disruption?'[28] This general claim was pondered in the collection with regard to the determining power that emplacement or displacement may have as regards identities, and aimed at an understanding of recent and current predicaments: 'We need to understand colonization, exile, emigration, wandering, contamination, and unintended consequences, along with the fierce compulsions of greed, longing, and restlessness, for it is these disruptive forces that principally shape the history and diffusion of identity and language, and not a rooted sense of cultural legitimacy'.[29]

Such claims, and the ways in which they bear on our circumstance, can and should be brought to bear as well on our ability to address past representations of human displacement to shed light on current disasters – all the more so when the representations in question are part of 'the centre of the canon'.[30] And, for my reading of Shakespeare against the perplexities posed by the current combination in the same space (the eastern Mediterranean) of leisure and disaster, huge wealth and utter dispossession, I will be exploring the operative potential of two words with an ironical, indeed crass cogency, at the intersection of the literal and figurative: mobility and liquidity. Besides the evident primary relevance they have when the topic is displacement by/across stretches of water, both words have socio-economic and financial acceptations that very much apply to the critical human displacements of recent years. Sociologically, and according to the *Oxford English Dictionary*, mobility refers to 'the ability or potential of individuals within a society to move between different social levels', 'horizontally' or 'vertically', and, more specifically, to 'the ability or potential of a workforce to move from place to place'; in financial parlance, 'mobility' also applies to a consideration of 'assets' that can be displaced with a view to obtaining a material advantage, resources that can be 'mobilized' and made to circulate in order to generate more wealth. This is where some of the implications of 'mobility' partly overlap with those of 'liquidity', that quality of assets or 'securities' that are 'capable of being promptly converted into cash', that will be all the more 'liquid' if they can be 'categorized as near money'. The *OED* also clarifies that mobile/mobility and liquid/liquidity, in these understandings of the terms, find their first occurrences in the second half of the nineteenth century – reflecting, in sum, the socio-economic and financial processes and discourses proper to the heyday of the industrial age.[31] Arguably at the other end of an historical process, the mobility crisis experienced in recent years by individuals and groups set afloat in the liquid element of the Mediterranean can hardly be separated from the broader vistas of the liquidity crises (the phrase becomes sinisterly ironical), and other financial disasters, that have disrupted the world's economies especially since 2008, even when the centres of (in)decision that have determined the wayward flows of capital within the global financial order are oceanic distances (also digital distances) away.

The opening scene of *The Comedy of Errors* can arguably offer a first vindication of the cogency of these reflections, as the tone for the play is set by the old merchant whose name (Egeon), although he hails from Syracuse, is homophonous with the arm of the Mediterranean that stretches between Greece and Turkey. Prompted by the Duke of Ephesus, who is personally sympathetic but judicially intransigent to this mercantile interloper from an enemy city, Egeon narrates a history that spans much of the region. The blend of mercantile and personal fortunes in Egeon's narrative leaves no room for distinctions between love and money that other moments in social history might expect to find discursively kept apart but here seem mutually validating and enhancing.[32] Hence, the 'joy' with which Egeon credits his married life shares a verse line with his account of how 'our wealth increased / By prosperous voyages' (I. ii. 40–41)[33] between Syracuse and Epidamnum, the comma between 'joy' and 'our wealth' allowing for both distinction and *in*distinction. Mobility becomes a key issue for such conflated personal and business fortunes: challenged by the consequences of 'my factor's death', Egeon gives priority to 'the great care of goods at random left', merchandise that has to be made mobile again, set afloat in the liquid element, in order to generate wealth (or liquidity) – and he removes himself 'from kind embracements of my spouse' (42–44). His pregnant wife rejoins him and unburdens herself of the yield of their marriage – which compounds her husband's efforts to secure the yield of his trade. Both, however, are scattered by the hazards of mobility, since the family finds itself on a ship abandoned by the crew and 'sinking-ripe' (78) (a paradoxical image of loss and fruitfulness), and then 'splitted in the midst' (104), with husband and wife and the two sets of twins symmetrically divided between ships from Corinth and Epidaurus. Again, toponymy performs the dual task of signifying dispersal and inscribing Egeon's tale against the geographical span of the main arms of the eastern Mediterranean.

This general spatial breadth, the appeal of exotic place names, and maritime disaster were recurrent traits in romance, and the favour that (when appropriated by early modern drama) they enjoyed with audiences was famously confirmed by Sidney's sneers in the *Defense of Poesie* at plays 'where you shall have Asia of the one side, and Afric of the other, and ... many other under-kingdoms', and where 'by and by we hear news of shipwreck'.[34] I want to focus on shipwreck: from what otherwise would be the archaizing haze of tales of families divided and miraculously reunited, of love interrupted and many years later resumed, shipwreck stands out as a disaster with an impact on the English literary and theatrical imagination that the geographic conditions of an insular culture and the long-distance voyaging of early commercial capitalism largely explain. Materially, as Peter Grav notes, 'One of the greatest ... economic dangers faced by sixteenth-century merchants was the loss of a fully laden ship at sea';[35] imaginatively, shipwreck provided a focus for the terrors of drowning, of dissolution in the liquid element, manifested even in plays that ostensibly have little to do with the mercantile. One has only to remember the haunting imagery of Clarence's dream in *Richard III*, with its visions of 'the tumbling billows of the main' and 'a thousand fearful wracks', its imaginings of '[the] dreadful noise of water in mine ears', and 'sights of ugly death within mine eyes' (I. iv. 20–24).

Having glimpsed but escaped such fate, made imminent by the unrest of 'the always wind-obeying deep' (I. i. 64), and endowed with additional pathos by the 'piteous plainings of the pretty babes' (73), Egeon remains mobile along the coastlines of the Mediterranean, determined no longer by the 'prosperous voyages' (41) of earlier times, but rather by his quest for a lost son. That this mobility no longer generates liquidity is made evident when the formerly affluent merchant proves unable to bail himself out by paying the sum of 'a thousand marks' (22) exacted in Ephesus as ransom for an enemy alien. The elements of pathos in Egeon's tale could be construed as outliving its archaic framework: parental grief for children who might drown, or be abruptly snatched from them, finds obvious correspondences in the globally circulated images of recent sufferings. Hence, it could be read as one of the elements in *The Comedy of Errors*, Act I scene i, the reception of which (four centuries later) seems to validate Terry Eagleton's claim that human suffering is the great trans-historical constant – or rather, that there are 'aspects of our existence which are permanent structures of our species-being .... And among these is the reality of suffering'.[36] However, Egeon's representation of paternal grief is made problematic, perhaps archaized and hence othered, by the perception that one of the pairs of twins on board that sinking ship were enslaved children, bought and taken from 'exceeding poor' parents, made into mobile assets and endangered on the high seas – and possibly posted beyond the pale of Egeon's grief for 'the pretty babes' with their 'piteous plainings' (I. i. 7, 63): did these include the Dromios? This doubt arguably qualifies, for a present-day audience, the pathos of Egeon's lot when a price is (likewise) put on his life; as it may qualify perceptions of his helplessness when abandoned with wife and children by sailors behaving with the callousness of latter-day people smugglers.

Between the pathos of Egeon's sentencing in Act I scene i and his ultimate rescue as part of the recomposition of his family in Act V, the plot and imagery of romance are largely suspended by the structural dynamics of a comedy modally inflected by satire against an urban landscape, rather than maritime vistas.[37] Nonetheless, the play is dominated by representations of circulation and flow, of the mobility of agents and assets with a view to generating liquidity.[38] These plot features are magnified into a laughable obviousness by the recurrence in the text of words for trade and finance – beginning with 'money', which has in *Errors* the highest number of occurrences (twenty-two) in any Shakespeare play. 'Money' is complemented by a rich lexicon that includes 'goods', 'confiscate', 'buy[ing]', 'statute[s]', 'expense', 'wealth', 'credit' – and, of course, 'gold', the word count for which shows *Errors* to come second only to *Timon of Athens*. On its own, the play's lexical range might not have an overwhelming importance, but this level of insistence becomes conspicuous in a play that has the shortest text in the Shakespeare canon, amounting to a verbal percussion that presses home the city's obsessive concerns. Such lexically marked obsessiveness becomes a trademark of the urban space; its deployment grows in inverse proportion to the characters' dwindling ability to get intention and effect to match; and their hopelessness grows in direct proportion to their frantic mobility around the town. Ensuring that monetary anxieties are never out of one's mind, that lexical recurrence becomes also a gauge of failed agency, of utter loss of control on the part of merchants otherwise overconfident in their management of their goods, capital, trade language, and the space within which they incessantly move and talk, committed to a business rhythm which becomes increasingly that of farce.[39]

The process is punctuated by the beatings suffered by the two Dromios, the objects of the famous pun on 'the thousand marks' (I. ii. 81ff). The passage links the name for a currency, hence for financial value, and the debasement of ill-treating a bondsman;

even if the lot of the battered slave is denied any pathos through the emotion-suspending effect of slapstick, the pun shows money and the human at their de-humanizing interface.[40] This is further emphasized by the monetarization of the closest of human relations: one of the inferences to be drawn from Luciana's remark, 'If you did wed my sister for her wealth, / Then for her wealth's sake use her with more kindness' (III. ii. 5–6), is that respect for money easily trumps other considerations. Further, the role and position of the Courtesan obtain a social acknowledgment that is fully compatible with the text's monetary logic.

If Dromio's pun on 'marks' is a nodal point for the deeper reflections prompted by what otherwise is light-hearted farce, Antipholus of Ephesus's gold 'chain' – successively misdelivered, inquired after and chased around the city[41] – becomes an epitome of the failed concatenations, the delusions of circulation and mobility in the proto-capitalist city.[42] Indeed, the pretensions of such a space are famously dismissed by Antipholus of Syracuse's diagnosis that 'this town is full of cozenage' (I. ii. 97). The intensity with which material quests are involved in derision and farce suggests that there may be an element of over-earnestness in Peter Grav's claim that 'from beginning to end, *Errors* represents Shakespeare's earliest sustained critique of societies built on economic foundations'.[43] Nonetheless, the play's satirical and farcical treatment of the cocky confidence of agents of business and finance, left helpless when their actions produce effects opposite to their intentions, is not just one of the long-standing attractions of *Errors* – but also one that finds a deeper resonance in current contexts of reception, marked as they are by a heightened awareness of financial crises and hence a high level of suspicion regarding self-proclaimed experts.

For western audiences, the 'eastern' setting, in Ephesus, of a plot so intensely resonant with the concerns of a monetary modernity could entail a sense of anachronism and anatopism. However, this perception can itself be rendered more uncertain by the higher levels of recognition that, as argued above, the recent mobility crises have imparted to the toponymy of the eastern Mediterranean. The link between the liquidity of capital that keeps businesses afloat and the liquid element that ensures the mobility of goods, but also drowns and disperses in the surrounding seas, is resumed in the closing scene by Aemilia, the Abbess. Aemilia's first query on reasons for mad behaviour, despite her own bereavement at the loss of son and husband at sea many years earlier, curiously concerns money rather than loved ones: 'Hath he not lost much wealth by wrack of sea?' (V. i. 49). Her remark reminds audiences not just of Egeon's tale in the opening scene, but also of two other passages in which maritime and liquid tropes had been employed to represent family disruption: Antipholus of Syracuse's self-description, 'I to the world am like a drop of water / That in the ocean seeks another drop, / Who, falling there to find his fellow forth, / Unseen, inquisitive, confounds himself' (I. ii. 35–38);[44] and Luciana's troping of supposedly indissoluble marital bonds: 'For know, my love, as easy mayst thou fall / A drop of water in the breaking gulf, / And take unmingled thence that drop again / Without addition or diminishing, / As take from me thyself, and not me too' (II. iii. 134–38). The closing scene of *The Comedy of Errors* evokes similar imagery but also, through evidence of the power designs of the commercial city, it foregrounds the prevalent mercantile ethos of Shakespeare's Ephesus; it binds the modes of romance and satire; it resonates with the topicality for which I have been presenting a case; and it provides me with a cue to move to a brief discussion of Shakespeare's other play of shipwrecks and mobility in the eastern Mediterranean.

The geographic vistas summoned by the text of *Pericles* through toponymy are broad but consistent – and fully in line with my earlier argument for their current visibility: Tyre, Antioch, Tarsus, Mytilene, Pentapolis and Ephesus. These points on the map of the eastern Mediterranean define a space that contains the hazardous sea crossings in the play; but this space is both archaized and magnified through the allegorical drift by which Gower construes the basin of the eastern Mediterranean as co-extensive with 'the world', since Pericles's 'careful search' is described as unfolding within 'the four opposing coigns / Which the world together joins' (III. 0. 16–18). Together with the abundant imagery of maritime disaster, this concurs towards the prevalence of pathos in a text insistently marked by 'the wayward seas' (IV. iv. 10) 'where, when men been, there's seldom ease' (II. 0. 28), by emotionally charged incidents such as a birth at sea during a storm (III. 0) followed by an (apparent) death on board and a sea burial (III. i.), and by allegorizations, as in Marina's summation of her fate: 'Born in a tempest when my mother died, / This world to me is as a lasting storm' (IV. i. 17–18).

Some of the tropes in *Pericles* that resonate with current perceptions of challenges posed by the topography featured in the play involve long-standing commonplaces with a striking longevity. A particular case comes up in Act I scene 4, when Pericles, on his arrival in Tarsus, addresses the governor and reassures him about his intentions. The dynamics of the scene hinge on the long historical perception, shared by early modern audiences, that seaborne arrivals more often than not involved predatory violence (plunder, rape, enslavement); hence, the assurance given by Pericles that, on the contrary, his ships bring relief to the starving city. He adds:

> And these our ships, you happily may think
> Are like the Trojan horse was stuff'd within
> With bloody veins expecting overthrow,
> Are stor'd with corn to make your needy bread,
> And give them life whom hunger starv'd half dead. (I. iv. 92–6)

Through one of the most ancient of tropes, Pericles acknowledges the fears of those starving in Tarsus, and stresses that he and his companions are not the Homeric Trojan horse.[45] The cultural conditions under which his statement can be received today, however, include conspicuous uses of that particular image to represent an antithetical situation: the fears of intrusion and disruption entertained by more prosperous communities wanting to wall themselves against the arrival of starvelings from the sea asking for their food. The trope has been explicitly used by vocal proponents of a 'fortress Europe' (or fortress America) attitude towards the feared encroachment of migrants. An article entitled 'The Trojan Horse of Refugees in Europe', posted in early February 2016 on an English-language Russian online journal, argued that 'countries either have to relinquish some of their universal values by disregarding some of the recognized human rights and freedoms, or the clashes between the two cultures will progress to tragic atrocities'.[46] Across the Atlantic, on a variety of occasions since late 2015, Donald Trump has concurred, declaring that Syrian refugees accepted for asylum in America are 'a Trojan horse', and arguing for the containment of refugees on Syrian territory that could be 'bought' for that purpose.[47] The trope has also been applied to the migrant and refugee phenomenon widely across the blogosphere.

If trade and money, with their attendant discourses, seemed to determine the representational range of *The Comedy of Errors* both in its romance framework of voyaging and in its satirical/farcical take on the modern urban space, in *Pericles*, however, the language and incidents of romance, their archaic import enhanced by the Gower choruses, are suspended to allow money to take a centre-stage position just for a couple of scenes in Act IV. In their language and circumstances, they offer as stark a contrast as they could to the rest of the play, since these are the notorious Mytilene brothel scenes – which remind us, in fact, that in Shakespeare 'the brothel [often] stands for all systems of commercial exchange'.[48] The transactions that occupy the three pimps offer a risible and brutal epitome of the dynamics of the proto-capitalist western urban space – even if nominally dislocated to the shores of Asia Minor. By comparison, the Courtesan's house in *The Comedy of Errors* is an abode of gentility.

In other terms: in *The Comedy of Errors* the coexistence of elements of romance and elements of an urban setting that is modern in the business-like manner of its socio-economic arrangements becomes laughable for their surprising compatibility; thus (as pointed out above), the Abbess, leader of a contemplative community, reveals a mindset so determined by the monetarized world of action that the prime reason that occurs to her for anyone to become deranged is financial loss. The rationale of exchange is so pervasive that there is a seamless movement between the various areas of life and experience. Thus, when Antipholus of Ephesus brings guests home for lunch he is doing business by other means, and his discomfiture at finding himself locked out of doors is explicitly construed as bad for business, since it harms his reputation and credit.[49] Visiting the Courtesan instead of having lunch with his wife appears as an alternative that is hardly transgressive: as a character in Massinger's *The City Madam* (1632) was to put it with regard to prostitution and marriage, 'The commoditie is the same' (III. i. 80–81).

In *Pericles*, however, the farcical import of the Mytilene brothel lies in its utter incompatibility with the circumstances and language of the rest of the play, marked by voyaging that at no point appears mercantile or materially acquisitive, and only in the 'relief' episode in Tarsus involves an explicitly material dimension. In stark contrast to this, in the harbour town of Mytilene hard-nosed business defines the dialogue of Pander, Bawd and Bolt, marked out by its bawdy prose from the blank verse of other scenes and the rhymed tetrameters of the Gower choruses. Pander's initial injunction – 'Search the market narrowly' (IV. ii. 3) – still employs the word in its physical, topographical sense; but the remark that follows – 'We lost too much money this mart' (IV. ii. 4) – already inflects the synonym towards a measure of abstraction, closer to that present-day usage we recognize when we are prompted to 'study the market' or 'compare the market'.

The boisterous laughter prompted by the low-life scene is qualified for present-day audiences by the fact that their trade is in human flesh. If this sets the scene at an ethical distance, the opening imperative to 'search the market' reflects a recognizable commercial crisis: the brothel suffers from lack of liquidity because it is running out of stock – their stock being also their human resources. As the Bawd candidly puts it, 'We were never so much out of creatures', and her brazen description materializes the problem as much as it renders it obscenely clear: the remaining 'poor three' whores 'with continual action are even as good as rotten', and there is thus an absolute need to invest in 'fresh ones, whate'er we pay for them' (IV. ii. 6–11). Deathly venereal disease is bluntly acknowledged and found to victimize foreigners – before the age of sexual tourism – by reifying them as dead flesh: 'The poor Transylvanian is dead that lay with the little baggage'; 'she made him roast meat for worms' (IV. ii. 19–22). The precariousness of their business may, incidentally, be represented in terms that evoke the play's prevalent seafaring dangers – 'The stuff we have, a strong wind will blow it to pieces' (IV. ii. 16–17); but the language of trade and money punctuates the dialogue with mock seriousness, as the Pander philosophizes that 'our credit comes not in like the commodity, nor the commodity wages not with the danger' (27–28).[50] Bolt buys Marina from the pirates (a case of ancient human trafficking); and this bit of business is enveloped in the practices and language of professional traders: the payment of a non-returnable deposit ('my earnest', 41) secures the deal, agreed for the total sum of 'a thousand pieces' (48), which the brothel expects to get back by auctioning her virginity in the market.

It is Marina's arrival that signals the irreconcilable nature of the romance and satirical strands in *Pericles*.[51] The first textual marker of this intractability is the couplet that Marina sets up against the bawdy and monetarized prose of Act IV scene ii, binding, through rhyme, an image of her defining marine origin with a vow of impregnable chastity: 'If fires be hot, knives sharp or waters deep, / Untried I still my virgin knot will keep' (IV. ii. 138–39). This assertion of essential worth comes to trump, in a risible way, the contingencies of the market as verbalized in the brothel – partly because of the pimps' ineptness. And yet Marina's success in keeping herself out of the sex market and its inexorable exchange nexus involves triumphing over the lust of increasingly distinguished customers, who describe with a ludicrous religious fervour how she converts them – 'I am for no more bawdy houses. Shall's go hear the vestals sing?' (IV. v. 6–7) – and indeed represent their conversion as a case of cancelling the mobility of desire: 'I am out of the road of rutting for ever' (IV. v. 9).[52]

Marina's ultimate triumph over the mobility of lust, however, coincides with her encounter with the governor of Mytilene himself. Lysimachus initially seems to dismiss her beauty in a casual-sounding remark that evokes the (stereotypical) undiscriminating lust of sailors: 'she would serve after a long voyage at sea' (IV. vi. 40–41). Lysimachus inquires in succession after her 'trade', her 'profession', her condition as 'a gamester' and 'creature of sale' (62, 68, 71, 74). However, their dialogue evolves from prose, proper to a trading relation, to verse, which the play's decorum associates with heightened values and, indeed, with the 'gold' with which the governor ultimately rewards her condition as 'a piece of virtue' (111), a phrase that echoes the brothel's previous purchase of her for 'a thousand pieces'. Towards the end of the scene, Bolt himself has become convinced of the practical wisdom of bailing the virgin out of the brothel for his personal profit as an extortionary impresario, pimping her talents rather than her body. And the conditions unfold towards a reunion and recognition scene, which, after a plot structured by voyages 'from bourn to bourn, region to region' (IV. iv. 4), the previous Gower chorus had pointed towards with the closing line: 'And think you now are all in Mytilene' (IV. iv. 51).

The final act, by opening with a sailor from Tyre meeting one from Mytilene, reminds audiences that this convergence at a (today notorious) seaport on Lesbos involves yet another sea crossing, but one that sees Pericles immobilized by grief at the supposed deaths of his wife and daughter. In *Errors*, Egeon was ransomed from execution by the social and material consequences of being reunited with his family; Pericles is rescued from stasis and stupor into the interpersonal dynamics of discourse and the mobility of normal living – and this happens through the agency of a daughter 'born at sea' (V. i. 147) and named after that accident, brought from Tarsus to Lesbos by pirates – and hence 'found at sea again' (V. i. 187). Marina's effect on Pericles, during the recognition scene, is also troped in maritime terms: 'this great sea of joys rushing upon me', threatening to 'o'erbear the shores of my mortality / And drown me with their sweetness' (V. i. 182–84).

The play's final sea crossing means that *Pericles* locates its scene of family reunion in Ephesus, the same location as *The Comedy of Errors*; and, again, a long-lost wife and mother is found to have survived under a contemplative guise – now a votaress of Diana. The outcome sees the characters ready to take yet again to the liquid element across their 'world' in the eastern Mediterranean – to Pentapolis for the wedding of Marina and Lisymachus, who will then sail on to Tyre, where they will 'reign' (V. iii. 82). The Ephesus of *Pericles* allows for the final conditions for utter bliss to be promised to all characters, but, unlike in the Ephesus of *Errors*, the happy ending is not ostensibly buttressed by a modern discourse of monetary wealth and civic reputation. And yet the chain that leads to *Pericles*'s happy ending of unqualified romance crucially includes the play's only spot where people and goods (people *as* goods) are brutally inserted in a mock replica of the proto-capitalist dynamics of exchange: the brothel. The Mytilene microcosm for 'continual action' is crucial for the happy ending: it is because she is brought as a saleable asset to the Mytilene market and faces the challenge posed by the brothel that Marina has to excel in her proselytism of virtue; it is because the virgin lives in the brothel that Lysimachus meets her and is captivated by her, thereby graduating from whoremonger to prince charming; it is because she threatens the pimps with ruin that Marina is allowed to reveal her exalted talents to all the worthies of Mytilene and be judged the mythical wise virgin who can cure a king. From this derives the recognition scene on board Pericles's ship, and later the second recognition scene and full family reunion in Ephesus.

Ultimately, in either play, though by different representational means, forms of mobility that directly or indirectly hinge on monetary dynamics (and either prior or ongoing sea crossings), prove decisive for characters to see their desires gratified; and this on locations that, today, are the unlikeliest venues to offer happy endings to those that land on their shores. This awareness does not cancel, however, the ability of these two plays to provide us with imaginative footholds for pondering and expressing the dismal geopolitics of our age; even if, in their final blissful scenes, the visitors or denizens of Ephesus in *The Comedy of Errors* and *Pericles* would surely be enough like today's satisfied tourists not to claim their money back.

Acknowledgements

Research for this chapter was supported by FCT (Fundação para a Ciência e a Tecnologia) through CETAPS (Centre for English, Translation and Anglo-Portuguese Studies – Ref.UID/ELT/04097/2013).

Rui Carvalho Homem is Professor of English at the University of Oporto (Universidade do Porto), Portugal. His publications include monographs, edited collections and articles on Early Modern English culture (with a particular focus on drama), Irish literature, translation, and intermediality. As a literary translator, he has published annotated versions of Shakespeare, Christopher Marlowe, Seamus Heaney and Philip Larkin. He is currently the Chair of ESRA, the European Shakespeare Research Association

Notes

1. Terence Hawkes, *Shakespeare in the Present* (London: Routledge, 2002), 2.
2. Cary DiPietro and Hugh Grady, eds, *Shakespeare and the Urgency of Now* (Houndmills: Palgrave Macmillan, 2013), 1.
3. Hawkes, *Shakespeare in the Present*, 2.
4. The phrase was memorably Ben Jonson's in 'Ode to Himself'; see C. H. Herford, Percy and Evelyn Simpson, eds, *Ben Jonson*, vol. VI (Oxford: Clarendon, 1948), 492.
5. As acknowledged by DiPietro and Grady (*Shakespeare and the Urgency of Now*, 2), the phrase was originally coined by Martin Luther King and has been much used since in a variety of public contexts.
6. The phrase is an extrapolation of what the late Irish poet Seamus Heaney called 'the place of writing', an acknowledgement of locales as determinants of our perceptions and inscriptions – Seamus Heaney, *The Place of Writing* (Atlanta, GA: Scholars Press, 1989).
7. Hugh Grady recollects how Hawkes and himself, as proponents of 'presentism', predicated it on the shared 'assumption that the critic's own situation in our cultural present is a resource for, rather than an impediment to, a productive and insightful reading of Shakespeare': see Hugh Grady and Terence Hawkes, *Shakespeare and Impure Aesthetics* (Cambridge: CUP, 2009), 236.
8. The traditional historical narrative of seafaring prowess and 'discoveries' has been challenged, contextualized and reconceptualized by more recent scholarship, but 'expansion' remains the centrepiece in the historiography of Portugal's early modern maritime and proto-imperial protagonisms. Concomitant to that narrative of Portugal's contributions to extending European knowledge of (and power over) the world, the country's particular situation within the European context has often been pondered, the best-known thesis about Portuguese geographic identity stressing that it is poised on the border between the Atlantic and the Mediterranean: see Orlando Ribeiro, *Portugal, o Mediterrâneo e o Atlântico: Estudo Geográfico* (Coimbra: Coimbra Editora, 1945). This (today, much favoured) argument for liminality has often been extended, as in descriptions of the country as part of 'the Mediterranean Atlantic' – Paul Butel, *The Atlantic* (London: Routledge, 1999), 45.
9. *The Jew of Malta* I. ii. 245; *Othello* III. iv. 26.
10. Fernand Braudel, *The Mediterranean and the Mediterranean World in the Age of Philip II*, trans. Siân Reynolds, vol. 1 (New York: Harper & Row, 1972), 615–42.

11. Erica Carter, James Donald and Judith Squires, eds, *Space & Place: Theories of Identity and Location* (London: Lawrence & Wishart, 1993), xii.
12. David Harvey, *Justice, Nature and the Geography of Difference* (Cambridge, MA: Blackwell, 1996), 306; my emphasis.
13. For a recent overview and in-depth discussion of the topic's various strands, see David Hawkes, *Shakespeare and Economic Theory* (London: Bloomsbury, 2015). Earlier studies that have proved inspiring to this chapter include: Douglas Bruster, *Drama and the Market in the Age of Shakespeare* (Cambridge: CUP, 1992); and Linda Woodbridge, ed., *Money and the Age of Shakespeare: Essays in New Economic Criticism* (New York and Houndmills: Palgrave Macmillan, 2003). Besides Hawkes's work, studies that reflect the post-2008 developments with a relevance to my argument include Richard Halpern, 'Bassanio's Bailout: A Brief History of Risk, Shakespeare to Wall Street', *SEDERI* 24 (2014): 27–45.
14. As particular cases of what Douglas Bruster has described as 'the tendency of the Renaissance theaters to collapse distance and difference': see Bruster, *Drama and the Market*, 32.
15. Halpern, 'Bassanio's Bailout', 31.
16. Ephesus is in Asia Minor and Mytilene on Lesbos (also off Asia Minor); Tyre is a port in present-day Lebanon, while Antakya and Tarsus are just to the north of it, in south-east Turkey; Pentapolis is associated with the coast of Cyrenaica, in present-day Libya.
17. Harley Granville-Barker, *Prefaces to Shakespeare* (1930; London: Batsford, 1958), vol. 1, 367.
18. For Peter Grav, 'reading Ephesus as the London that Shakespeare lived in – a city in which mercantile influence was pervasive in the 1590s – does not seem that large a stretch' – Peter Grav, *Shakespeare and the Economic Imperative: 'what's aught but as 'tis valued?'* (New York: Routledge, 2008), 33.
19. Daniel Vitkus, '"The Common Market of All the World": English Theater, the Global System, and the Ottoman Empire in the Early Modern Period', in *Global Traffic: Discourses and Practices of Trade in English Literature and Culture from 1550 to 1700*, ed. Barbara Sebek and Stephen Deng (New York: Palgrave Macmillan, 2008), (19–37), 26. Walter Cohen also points out that 'during the 1580s, England established consuls in leading cities of the Ottoman empire, including Aleppo, Alexandria, Algiers, Damascus, Tunis, Tripoli in Syria, and Tripoli in Barbary', and he argues that 'the pattern of allusion' of Shakespeare's geography 'produces almost a global feel' – Walter Cohen, 'The Undiscovered Country: Shakespeare and Mercantile 'Geography'', in *Marxist Shakespeares*, ed. Jean E. Howard and Scott Cutler Shershow (London and New York: Routledge, 2001), (128–58), 130, 132.
20. Ephesus Ancient City, http://www.ephesus.us/ (accessed 23 February 2017).
21. 'Refugee Boat Sinks near Izmir, 61 Dead', *Hurriet Daily News*, http://www.hurriyetdailynews.com/refugee-boats-sinks-near-izmir-at-least-20-dead.aspx?pageID=238&nID=29518&, 6 September 2012; 'Turkish Tourism Hit by Security Concerns', *Deutsche Welle*, 10 August 2015, http://www.dw.com/en/turkish-tourism-hit-by-security-concerns/a-18639199 (both accessed 23 February 2017).
22. *The Guardian*, 'Lesbos: A Greek Island in Limbo over Tourism, Refugees – and its Future, https://www.theguardian.com/travel/2016/mar/24/lesbos-greek-island-in-limbo-tourism-refugee-crisis-future, 24 March 2016; Lesvos Solidarity, http://www.lesvossolidarity.org/index.php/en/ (accessed 23 February 2017).

23. Migrants at Sea, https://migrantsatsea.org/2011/07/29/20th-anniversary-of-the-arrival-at-bari-italy-of-15000-albanian-boat-people/ (accessed 23 February 2017,); 'Thousands of Albanians Flee Aboard Ships to Italy', *The New York Times*, http://www.nytimes.com/1991/03/07/world/thousands-of-albanians-flee-aboard-ships-to-italy.html, 6 March 1991 (accessed 23 February 2017).
24. 'War, Migration and Revenge: Shakespeare is the Bard of Today's World', *The Guardian*, https://www.theguardian.com/commentisfree/2015/oct/30/war-migration-revenge-shakespeare-world-syrian-refugee-camps, 30 October 2015 (accessed 23 February 2017).
25. The impact of this event was discussed in major media outlets on the first anniversary of the drowning. See: 'Looking Back at Alan Kurdi and Other Faces of Syrian Crisis', *The New York Times*, https://www.nytimes.com/2016/09/03/world/middleeast/alan-kurdi-aylan-anniversary-turkey-syria-refugees-death.html?_r=0, 2 September 2016; 'The Death of Alan Kurdi: One Year on Compassion for Refugees Fades', *The Guardian*, https://www.theguardian.com/world/2016/sep/01/alan-kurdi-death-one-year-on-compassion-towards-refugees-fades, 2 September 2016; '"Photo of My Dead Son Has Changed Nothing", Says Father of Drowned Syrian Refugee Boy Alan Kurdi', *The Telegraph*, http://www.telegraph.co.uk/news/2016/09/01/photo-of-my-dead-son-has-changed-nothing-says-father-of-drowned/, 2 September 2016 (accessed 23 February 2017).
26. For example, the European Commission has published a 'policy review' entitled 'Research on Migration: Facing Realities and Maximising Opportunities' (2016), https://ec.europa.eu/research/social-sciences/pdf/policy_reviews/ki-04-15-841_en_n.pdf (accessed 23 February 2017); and a 'conference report', Understanding and Tackling the Migration Challenge: The Role of Research (2016), http://ec.europa.eu/research/social-sciences/pdf/other_pubs/migration_conference_report_2016.pdf (accessed 23 February 2017).
27. Stephen Greenblatt, ed., *Cultural Mobility: A Manifesto* (Cambridge: CUP, 2009).
28. Greenblatt, *Cultural Mobility*, http://isites.harvard.edu/fs/docs/icb.topic733185.files/Greenblatt.pdf, accessed 30 April 2016.
29. Greenblatt, *Cultural Mobility*, 2.
30. See Harold Bloom's famous epithet for Shakespeare: *The Western Canon: The Books and School of the Ages* (New York: Harcourt, 1994), 45.
31. All citations in the lines above refer to *OED Online*, http://www.oed.com/ (accessed 25 February 2017).
32. This mutuality of money and the emotions is often discussed as reflecting the 'troubled transition from an economy based around use-value to a society organized around the pursuit of exchange-value' – Hawkes, *Shakespeare and Economic Theory*, xiv. Theodore B. Leinwand also remarks on the rapport, in the period, between the language of 'credit, debt, mortgages, and venturing' and that of the emotions – Theodore B. Leinwand, *Theatre, Finance, and Society in Early Modern England* (Cambridge: CUP, 1999), 3.
33. All Shakespeare citations refer to the latest Arden editions of the plays in question.
34. Katherine Duncan-Jones, ed., *Sir Philip Sidney* (Oxford: OUP, 1994), 134–35.
35. Grav, *Shakespeare and the Economic Imperative*, 36.
36. Terry Eagleton, *Sweet Violence: The Idea of the Tragic* (Oxford: Blackwell, 2003), xii.

37. This combination of satire and the urban demonstrates 'the basic receptivity of late Elizabethan and early Jacobean audiences to the satiric strain as expressed in the materialist vision' – Bruster, *Drama and the Market*, 39.
38. For Peter Grav, '*The Comedy of Errors* seems at times to be as concerned with the vagaries of commercial exchange systems as it is with mistaken identities' – Grav, *Shakespeare and the Economic Imperative*, 28.
39. The characters' frantic dynamic is reminiscent of the working of a mechanism that is out of order but cannot be stopped – and hence of Henri Bergson's famous dictum on the 'mechanical rigidity' to which human mobility is reduced in order to generate laughter – Henri Bergson, *Laughter* (1900; Rockville, MD: Wildside Press, 2008), 6 and *passim*. The compulsive nature of movement in the play is matched by a compulsive deployment of language, and the language of money: David Landreth notes how semiotics has discussed 'the discursive character of money and the monetary character of discourse', and the process by which 'Mammon grows ever chattier over time' – David Landreth, *The Face of Mammon: The Matter of Money in English Renaissance Literature* (Oxford: OUP, 2012), 41. The farcical mismanagement of their best interests by the characters of *Errors*, as they try to go about their business, also becomes an illustration of what Bradley Ryner has called 'the tension between conceptualising the individual as controlling economic transactions and conceptualising the individual as controlled by impersonal economic forces' – Bradley Ryner, *Performing Economic Thought: English Drama and Mercantile Writing, 1600–1640* (Edinburgh: Edinburgh UP, 2014), 78; and Ceri Sullivan has pointed out that 'drama is at the heart of the genres produced by credit, fictions produced for financial effect where merchants regard their selves in instrumental terms', and that satirical laughter 'is an aggressive ranking device which indicates withheld credit' – Ceri Sullivan, *The Rhetoric of Credit: Merchants in Early Modern Writing* (Cranbury, NJ: Associated UP, 2002), 122.
40. The pun is a striking example of how 'the commodification of the personal marked the drama of this period with new energy' – Bruster, *Drama and the Market*, 42.
41. The chain becomes the objective focus for a strand of the plot that has featured prominently in the play's critical processing. Curtis Perry highlights, as regards the structural relevance of this prop, 'the connection between farce and commodity culture' – Curtis Perry, 'Commerce, Community, and Nostalgia in *The Comedy of Errors*', in *Money and the Age of Shakespeare*, ed. Woodbridge, (39–51), 49.
42. Cf Bruster, *Drama and the Market*, 75–77. Curtis Perry suggests, further, that the relative informality of earlier networks of credit, on the basis of forms of trust and financial interdependence, created the conditions for intense anxiety whenever any of the links in such networks proved problematic – Perry, 'Commerce', 40.
43. Grav, *Shakespeare and the Economic Imperative*, 53.
44. This passage is 'one of the few places in that play [*The Comedy of Errors*] that offers the kind of subjectivity effect we expect from Shakespeare' – Perry, 'Commerce', 39–40.
45. For Valerie Forman, *Pericles* posits an economy that 'rewrites the defensive categorizations in which poverty is foreign and wealth is native, thus defusing ... [a perception of] threats posed by foreigners ... by imagining contact with other countries as a source of productivity rather than as a form of violation' – Valerie Forman, *Tragicomic Redemptions: Global Economics and the Early Modern English Stage* (Philadelphia, PA: University of Pennsylvania Press, 2008), 20.

46. Ekaterina Ryzhkova, 'The Trojan Horse of Refugees in Europe', *New Eastern Outlook* http://journal-neo.org/2016/02/05/the-trojan-horse-of-refugees-in-europe/, 5 February 2016 (accessed 23 February 2017).
47. Maggie Haberman, 'Donald Trump Questions Whether Syrian Refugees Are a "Trojan Horse"', *New York Times,* http://www.nytimes.com/politics/first-draft/2015/11/16/trump-questions-whether-syrian-refugees-are-trojan-horse/?_r=0, 16 November 2015 (accessed 23 February 2017).
48. Hawkes, *Shakespeare and Economic Theory*, 104. The historically perceived homologies (and exchangeability) of people and money, through the materiality of the coin, are also noted by David Landreth: 'Situated between the material and the social worlds, the coin bears a strange, even parodic likeness to the human bodies among whom it changes hands' – Landreth, *The Face of Mammon*, 6.
49. Craig Muldrew has extensively argued the conditions under which 'the early modern economy was a system of cultural, as well as material, exchanges in which the central mediating factor was credit or trust' – *The Economy of Obligation: The Culture of Credit and Social Relations in Early Modern England* (New York: St Martin's Press, 1998), 4 and *passim*.
50. 'Shakespeare's usages of "commodity" allow us to observe the word settling into its modern meaning' – Hawkes, *Shakespeare and Economic Theory*, 99.
51. As pointed out by Bradley Ryner, 'a play's economic thought comes into particular relief when two genres run into one another or when a play draws attention to its own generic construction' –Ryner, *Performing Economic Thought*, 167.
52. Valerie Forman offers a sustained reading of the economic implications of *Pericles's* redemptive design, but she acknowledges that 'some of Marina's profit making in the brothel scene might seem hyper-redemptive and thus potentially parodic' – Forman, *Tragicomic Redemptions*, 83.

Chapter 4
Pity Silenced
Economies of Mercy in *The Merchant of Venice*

Alessandra Marzola

In a play so overtly steeped in economy, finance and credit as *The Merchant of Venice*, mercy and pity, the alleged virtues of the Christian merchants, have frequently been enlisted as beacons of spiritual hope. Whether they enlighten the threatening darkness of mercantilism, as they are supposed to do, is a dubious matter. Does Portia's famous address to the Jew's mercy in Act IV point to the Christian ways of forgiveness and redemption from the evil/devil of usurious exploitation? Is then the mercy Portia advocates the blazon of the Christian merchants in whose name she is pleading the Jew? Or is mercy instead a rhetorical construct, the cover of a mercilessness rooted in Christian and Jewish mercantilism alike? In fact, both questions could be answered in the affirmative, for the sublimating function of mercy and pity does not contradict their economic nature or their belonging to the play's economic transactions. Rather, precisely in so far as they transcend the economic mindset of the

Notes for this section begin on page 84.

play, these Christian virtues serve the purposes of the new economy which the play depicts in its tormented genealogy.[1]

Retracing such genealogy in light of mercy and pity is what I set out to do in the following pages. In looking at the ways the play construes mercy and pity as the allegedly spiritual validations of the Christian merchants, I will focus in particular on the overriding power of mercy over the cognate virtue of pity: a repression or suppression which – I submit – resonates with the Protestant effacement of Catholic manners. The generic Christianity of the forgiveness summoned by Portia relies in fact upon an all-inclusive mercy which qualifies as Protestant to the extent that it subsumes, incorporates and represses all traces of Catholic pity. The lingering presence of such pitiful traces – the spectral residua of averred Catholicism – points however, in the conclusion, to the fault lines of mercy, and to the shortcomings of its validating power.[2]

Mercy above all

Limited to three occurrences and to the Duke's passing mentions, pity makes its only appearance at the outset of Act IV, the justice-making tour de force of the play.[3] There, the Venetian establishment, led by Portia cross-dressed as Balthazar, invalidates the Jew's bond in ways that will drastically backfire. Not only is pity confined to a narrow role: it is also left unable to stand alone because invariably coupled with the master virtue of mercy. Without mercy, pity would not exist. Shylock – proclaims the Duke in addressing Antonio – is: 'A stony adversary, an inhuman wretch, / Uncapable of pity, void and empty / From any dram of mercy' (IV. i. 3–5). In his winning of Shylock's goodwill soon after, the Duke conjures up instead the image of a merciful *and* pitiful Jew: Shylock, he pretends, will soon dismiss his fashion of malice. He will take everybody aback by showing 'thy mercy and remorse more strange / Than is thy strange apparent cruelty' (IV. i. 21–22). He will in consequence glance 'an eye of pity' (IV. i. 29) on Antonio's losses, which boils down to losing the forfeiture (4.1.26) and forgiving a moiety of the principal (IV. i. 28). Confined as it is to these parallel and divergent addresses, pity, whether pronounced as defective or declared as sound, is no more and no less than the material manifestation of godly mercy among human beings. Akin to sovereign mercy, but as inferior in degree as human subjects are inferior to God, pity is thinned down to the charitable and practical deeds that accompany merciful forgiveness. And apparently, despite their vital role in relieving poverty, such pitiful deeds can only be evoked here, in these opening strategies of address. From now on, and throughout Act IV, mercy will instead submerge pity, subsuming its vital materiality within its extended spiritual capacities, as if its separate existence could threaten not only Portia's legal devices and cunning negotiations, but also, and above all, the Christian redemptive thrust of the play itself.

The aggrandizing of mercy in Act IV comes as no surprise in light of the purposes it so crucially serves. It is mercy that ultimately allows Venice to absorb the shock caused by the abrupt intrusion of the new market economy (or 'chrematistics') into the natural/good economy (the Aristotelian *oikos*) of Venice.[4] No matter how precariously, mercy helps to fill the breach which opens up in the 'natural economy' of Venice when the unfettered desire entailed in the art of moneymaking is given free rein. And mercy does so effectively, by dissolving the physical body that lies ominously in the gap; by presiding over its melting into a spiritualized soul. It is mercy that gives godly warrant to the process whereby Antonio's flesh, until then firmly lodged within the Old Testament letter of the common law, is swept up into the Pauline spirit of equity.[5] In authorizing such internalization of guilt, debt and flesh, mercy de facto upholds the enforcement of the legal measures that ensue. It is after all under the aegis and in the name of mercy, that Shylock is expelled, the wealth of the merchant prodigiously restored, and the financial stability of Lorenzo and Jessica granted. Coming in retaliation for the Jew's rebuttal of Christian mercy, Portia/Balthazar's casuistic conversion of Shylock's rights into life penalties eventually sanctions the unfolding of a highly questionable practice of mercy on the Christian side. Unlike the virtue extolled by Portia/Balthazar in her initial speech, the mercy finally rendered to Shylock is harshly conditional, cruelly exacting and utterly penalizing: life and half of the capital are forgiven, but under the provisions minutely listed by Antonio. And, under the circumstance, Antonio gives proof of unprecedented exactness: the fine is retracted for one half of Shylock's goods, provided that the Jew lets Antonio have the other half in captive use. The two further conditions – that he turns Christian and bestows money unto Lorenzo and Jessica as a gift after his death – tighten the belt of Antonio's mercy into a noose around Shylock's neck.

The uneasy violence involved in this final enactment of precisionist mercy comes at the end of a process in the course of which the unrestrained virtue advocated initially becomes the subject of increasing restrictions. It is a refashioning that qualifies mercy as exchange value, plus-value and interest, and thus roots mercy visibly within the chrematistic market economy of Venice. On the other hand, etymology itself points to the marketability of mercy, a noun, which, like 'merchant', derives from *merces* (in Latin), *merci* in Old French, and which Church Latin applies to the heavenly reward of those who show kindness to the helpless.[6] Far from being confined to heaven, however, the quality of mercy that Portia extols in her masterful speech is an exquisite blend of godly and temporal attributes which serve the pragmatic purposes of the new economy. Besides being the marker of godly and kingly power alike, mercy empowers those who demonstrate they possess it. It qualifies them as elected, by yielding in the process a blessing that is increased by redoubled interest: 'It is twice blest: / It blesseth him that gives and him that takes' (IV. i. 190–91). More importantly, in as much as it is interiorized as spiritual and thus made invisible, mercy can serve the essential purpose of mitigating, through forgiveness, the harshness of the law: 'And earthly power does then show likest God's / When mercy seasons justice' (IV. i. 200–1).

The seasoning of justice Portia advances here carries, in fact, nuances of meaning which have far-reaching implications, as Jacques Derrida has brilliantly demonstrated: seasoning is keeping the taste of justice, while affecting it, changing it without changing it, elevating it to heights higher than the royal crown, sublimating it and repressing it.[7] In proposing to translate 'seasons' as '*relève*' ('Quand le pardon relève la justice'), the French equivalent of the Hegelian *aufheben*, Derrida highlights the process at stake: 'Such a *relève* is precisely what is at issue here, in Portia's mouth (mercy *relève*, it elevates, replaces and interiorizes the justice that it seasons)'. 'What counts' – Derrida adds – 'is the resemblance, the analogy, the figuration ..., a sort of human translation of divinity ...'[8]

Marketable mercy

No matter how spiritualized, mercy remains steeped in the monetary market: 'We do pray for mercy', pleads Portia, adding hereafter, in a note of caution, 'And that same prayer doth teach us all to render / The deeds of mercy' (IV. ii. 204–6). While it clearly echoes Matthew 6: 2 ('And forgive us our debts as we forgive our debtors'), Portia's appeal, a parallel of the Duke's previous clue, 'How shalt thou hope for mercy, rend'ring none?' (IV. ii. 86), also evokes the fantasy of a mercy-for-mercy deal, an adaptation of the eye-for-eye, tooth-for-tooth passage in Leviticus 24: 20. Such a deal threatens retaliations on Shylock in the form of blackmail, a threat which forthcoming events will prove more than credible. The retaliatory quality of this liquid virtue adds to its monetary value. It soon becomes clear that mercy is priced as a valuable asset in the Venetian court, the setting of which adumbrates the Stock Exchange of modern times.[9] At the Belmont household, ahead of the trial, and before her impersonation as Balthazar, Portia had offered to pay off the 'petty debt' (III. ii. 316) of Antonio, a trifle in comparison with her fortunes, with nonchalant prodigality. Twenty times over was the disproportionate rate of interest she had lavishly put forth to settle the dispute that vexed Bassanio's dear friend. But no matter how multiplied, the money which Portia puts on offer here at Belmont has nothing to do with mercy. It is an investment in marriage, the high purchase price of her would-be husband, whom, as she briskly declares, she will in consequence treasure as a valuable commodity: 'Since you are dear bought, I will love you dear' (III. ii. 322).

Once cross-dressed as Balthazar in the Venice courtroom, Portia will apply her reckoning mindset to mercy with equal keenness, although in significantly different proportions. At stake here is after all her own patrimony, the liquid reserve of Venice, which, as he had done with his own estates, Bassanio threatens to fritter away, when, for the sake of beloved Antonio, he raises the purchase price of Shylock's mercy from twice as much the money originally owed, to the inestimable value of his own flesh, the flesh which Portia has just bought so dearly: 'If that will not suffice, / I will be bound to pay it ten times o'er / On forfeit of my hands, my head, my heart' (IV. ii. 214–16). Needless to say, the bargain – Bassanio's pound of flesh against Antonio's – is incompatible with the new market economy, as incompatible as the bond which Antonio has signed and which Portia/Balthazar has so laboriously been trying to deface. Exactly like Antonio's surrendering posture as 'a tainted whether of the flock, / Meetest for death' (IV. i. 116–17), Bassanio's self-sacrificing bid casts the looming shadow of a Christ-like figure, whose blood is not shed in redemption of mankind, but wasted instead on homoerotic love.[10] Portia's turnaround to moneyed mercy, and to the security of marriage that will ensue, comes as no surprise. The purchase price of mercy which she eventually sets is thrice the money owed to Shylock, a midline between twice as much and ten, the spread market value for the flesh of the merchant: 'Be merciful' – she ultimately pleads – 'Take thrice thy money, bid me tear the bond!' (IV. i. 238–39). While highly suggestive, the anachronistic analogy between the deals of mercy in the Venice courtroom and the trade of stocks in a modern Stock Exchange, fits only in part. Here, in fact, bids for the commodity of mercy are made among purchasers, but in the absence of a seller, the crucial counterpart of all financial deals. It would be tempting to argue that mercy to Shylock is not a commodity and hence not on sale. However, the bare truth is that he simply does not own the property or the propriety of mercy which is demanded of him. He is as alien to the Christian seasoning of justice, as he is an alien to Venice, a foreignness which Portia/Balthazar promptly exploits when she strikes back with her over-literal interpretation of the bond and appeals to the laws against aliens, thereby endowing Venice with its own patrimony of mercy to be rendered at pleasure. 'Down, therefore, and beg mercy of the Duke' (IV. ii. 374), Portia enjoins Shylock, in a tone which is as intimidating as her previous 'Then must the Jew be merciful' (IV. ii. 186), after enumerating the penalties for aliens who seek, either directly or indirectly, 'the life of any citizen' (IV. i. 362). Before he can barter the Christians' mercy on market conditions, Shylock is cast into the predicament of a pleader of alms, a refugee begging for humanitarian aid. By subsuming mercy and the market into justice, Venice pre-empts and undercuts any bargaining on his side. The Christian establishment has in fact already set, once and for all, its own severely conditional price for mercy, the full import of which amounts to sparing the bare life of the Jew, while ruling out his Jewishness.

It is hard to retrace, by the end of Act IV, the threads of the pity that the Duke had invoked at the outset as the charitable approach that follows from godly mercy. From the point at which Portia marks her entry as Balthazar the lawyer, prescribing rather than pleading mercy ('Then must the Jew be merciful', IV. i. 186), the virtue of mercy progressively enshrines itself into the merchants' hearts. It turns into their property/propriety. By so doing, it absorbs, and at the same time pre-empts and curbs the separate existence of pity. The charitable 'eye of pity' (IV. i. 28) is suppressed and supplanted by the pitiless allowances granted by moneyed mercy – a mercy which eventually blends with the justice that it was expected to season and to enliven. Whether we call it just mercy or merciful justice, the sentence eventually pronounced on Shylock, and proffered in the form of a pre-emptive graceful concession witnesses awkwardly, on the Christian side, to the incapability of pity assigned to Shylock in the first place.

Portia's deals of mercy, however, are not enough to settle accounts or to finalize deals. As the ring plot illustrates, the homoerotic love between Antonio and Bassanio lingers on as a barrier to the forming of marriage contracts, a threat which Antonio offers to prevent as he pledges his soul on Bassanio's forfeit of marital fidelity: 'I dare be bound again, / My soul upon the forfeit, that your lord / Will never more break faith advisedly' (V. i. 264–68).

The Sonnets: pity strikes back

We have no clues as to whether Antonio will ever lose the immaterial fortune he has pawned, but we know for sure that, should Bassanio break his marriage vows, Antonio would not be demanded to pay in cash, let alone in flesh. Having already dissolved the flesh of words, of vows and oaths, into the thin air of the soul, and having in the process crucially served the purpose of ethnically cleansing Venice, mercy will no longer be needed, not at least to such an overarching extent. In the newly idealized, albeit severely compromised, mercantile community that *The Merchant of Venice* foreshadows in the end, unbounded pity might regain its visibility. And we might even conjecture that, should Bassanio be drawn to expenditures of love with Antonio, Portia might appeal to her husband's pity in the mildly warning tone which we find in the final couplet of sonnet 1: 'Pity the world, or else this glutton be, / To eat the world's due, by the grave and thee' (13–14).[11] My reference to Shakespeare's sonnets is not coincidental, for here it is pity that, either as a social or a private shock-absorber, outdoes mercy in terms which seem to compensate for its silencing in *The Merchant*. Removed from God and steeped in the exchange economy of courtly poetry, pity is an all-purpose palliative. It is the temporary relief invoked of the addressee, so that he/she might conceal, soothe or even cure the wounds opened by the major or minor scars of guilt; the scandals and infidelities of the pleading poet. It is the remedy dispensed to mitigate the infecting censure that brands theatrical profession, as in sonnet 111: 'Pity me then, and wish I were renewed, / Whilst like a willing patient, I will drink / Potions of eisel 'gainst my strong infection' (8–10). Or, as in sonnet 112, it is the filling of the impression that vulgar scandal stamped upon the poet's brow, an anachronistic performance of plastic surgery carried out in love and pity, in order to 'o'ergreen the bad and to enhance the good' (4).[12]

As it fulfils these functions of relief, pity, much like mercy in *The Merchant*, also works as the currency of love exchanges, as in the opening bid of sonnet 140 addressed to the Dark Lady, where the disdainful beloved is threatened with dangerous retaliations in case she should deny the soothing comfort of her pity, no matter how fictitious: 'Be wise as thou art cruel, do not press/ My tongue-tied patience with too much disdain, / Lest sorrow lends me words, and words express / The manner of my pity-wanting pain' (1–4). The same cautionary inflection returns in sonnet 142: 'Be it lawful I love thee as thou lov'st those / Whom thine eyes woo as mine impòrtune thee: / Root pity in thy heart, that when it grows, / Thy pity may deserve to pitied be' (9–12). Whether curative or retaliatory, the pity which is either deferentially invoked or haughtily exacted in the sonnets, converts the Christian mercy which it subsumes and presupposes to a multifaceted range of benevolent acts. Once the ordeal of the Merchant's mercy is over, and once guilt is internalized, pity can in fact put mercy into communal practice and thereby meet the requirements of the double-standard, subtly hypocritical morality which merchants in Venice – and in London – so badly need.[13]

No matter how humanized, the pity in *The Sonnets*, exactly like the mercy in *The Merchant*, is steeped in the commercial web of traffics. It is the mundane reward expected of earthly power, in forgiveness of love and money forfeitures. Were these faulty demeanours not covered by the canopy of pity, the bare bones of the emerging capitalism – the absorbing rapaciousness of the market – would be exposed mercilessly and the view would shatter the shaky foundations of the chrematistic market.

Beware of pity!

Unsurprisingly, the money-fraught ambience of *The Sonnets* and of *The Merchant* does not contemplate pity as an emotion, a feeling or a passion. Whether silenced or voiced, the pity patterned here is so tightly pointed to the market as to prevent the vast range of alternative functions which it is shown to fulfil in Shakespeare's work as a whole.[14] As a matter of fact, *The Merchant of Venice* also crudely demonstrates, from its outset, that pity as a private concern is incompatible with the merchant's social status.

The pity which Aristotle described in his *Rhetoric* as, 'a feeling of pain caused by the sight of some evil ... which befalls one who does not deserve it, and which we might expect to befall ourselves ...',[15] is the sentiment that Salerio defuses as he ventures into a deeply sympathetic interpretation of Antonio's sadness. As he offers a formidable insight into the anxieties of the time over the precarious standing of the mercantile self, Salerio sets the foundations for the communal sharing of charged emotions (I. i. 9–14; I. i. 23–41). He actually poses here as a potentially pitiful subject, who is keen to identify with the other's lurking misfortunes because he suspects that they might befall himself. And yet, before it can sprout among the merchants, this embryonic pity is briskly uprooted by Antonio in an open disavowal of his role as the pitied subject. Entrenching himself in the self-assurance of the *oekonomos* merchant, Antonio will remain glued to his flat posture, clinging to the saddened role he claims as his invariable prerogative, stubbornly impermeable to the currents of affection: 'I hold the world, but as the world, Gratiano – / A stage where every man must play a part, / And mine a sad one' (I. i. 79–81). On equal grounds, Antonio also remains disconcertingly unaware of risks and perils, heedless of mishaps at sea or land, and, for that reason, ignorant of the deadly implications of Shylock's merry bond. Except for his outbursts of unconditional love for Bassanio at the opening and towards the close of the play, Antonio remains numbed by the humours of melancholy, as stony as his inhuman adversary. Not even in the imminence of death will Antonio abandon his fondness for fixed roles and his parallel mistrust of mutability. Since he does not contemplate any form of mitigation, public mercy remains as inconceivable as the private pity which would dodge him into the role of the pitied subject. Far from diminishing, the new victimized role in which Antonio indulges under the threat of death is, in fact, self-magnifying. In the tragic scenario he envisages as he urges the Duke to proceed to swift judgement, he, 'the tainted whether of the flock meetest for death' (IV. i. 166–17), stands as a Christ-like victim, whose meek resignation is proportional to the enraged fury of the usurer: 'I do oppose / My patience to his fury, and am armed / To suffer with a quietness of spirit / The very tyranny and rage of his' (IV. i. 11–14). Just as he had initially rejected the fond pity of friends, Antonio seems here to pre-empt Balthazar's/ Portia's imminent pleas for merciful justice. As he does so, he defies arousals of pity on and off stage.

And yet, Antonio's intolerance of mercy and pity cannot be dismissed as a generic resistance to being cast into the subordinate role of the pitied. It is, I believe, the specific spectre of poverty that haunts the would-be merchant as he so sternly disallows all forms of pity, or charity, on behalf of his Christian coterie at Venice courtroom. Wrecked ships, miscarried investments, and lost fortunes sound the knell of worthlessness – the 'even now worth this and now worth nothing' (I. i. 36–37) which Salerio had conjectured in tones of urgent empathy. Losses brand Antonio with the censorious stigma of a poverty which annuls all the entrenched privileges allowed by census, rank and class thereby tarnishing the signs of godly election which, not in Venice, but in London, would have enabled the status of a Christian Protestant merchant. In the late 1590s London merchants would in fact not have been expected to belong to the province of those in need of relief. According to the Act for the Relief of the Poor issued by London Parliament in 1597 in order to face the pressing matter of endemic poverty, merchants, just like landowners, were actually required to pour money into the newly established poor relief scheme.

Underpinning the poor relief programs and the English Poor Laws was of course the vision of Reformed Protestantism, which censured poverty as the mark of predestined damnation, and the offshoot of guilt-ridden sloth, and which conversely extolled wealth, success in worldly occupations, and profitable laboriousness as absolute signs of election.[16]

It is then not a matter of wonder that Antonio should ward off so emphatically the spectre of poverty and cherish instead the fantasy of romantic death. Better falling for love, than outliving one's wealth and 'To view with hollow eye and wrinkled brow / An age of poverty' (IV. i. 278–79). As he loftily pronounces his resolution against the dismal prospect of poverty, Antonio challenges at the same time the threat of incumbent misery and the no less ominous prospect of Shylock's pity on his losses. Antonio also effectively thwarts the possibility of deeds of charity which, at this stage, before Portia has placed her Christian mercy within the legal practice of Protestant merchants, would still retain the suspicious aura of Catholic intercessions. The pity which the Duke had sparingly invoked at the outset as the mere unfolding of the superior virtue of mercy, might in fact still find its own self-governing practices of charity, practices that embraced the divergent view of poverty held by Catholics in their own schemes of aid. Charity and almsgiving, the good works which guaranteed salvation, were the forms of support Catholics envisioned to soften the hardship of a condition which, in so far as it was viewed as the mark of grace, and of closeness to Christ, might as well have been permanent; to Shakespeare's audience the 'age of poverty' which Antonio fears more than death might then have referred not only to a time in his life, but also to a time in contemporary history when a resurgence of Catholic charity might ascribe losses to the blessed destiny of poverty, thus impairing the self-sufficient model of the merchant's thriving economy.

That anxieties about the drawbacks of Catholic charity and pity on the new market economy should be given voice even in such a worldly play as *The Merchant of Venice*, comes as no surprise. Here, as much as elsewhere in Shakespeare, hidden traces or echoes of suppressed Catholicism linger either as fearful avatars or as nostalgic reminiscences.[17] And while it may well be a stretch to surmise, as some critics have done, that Shakespeare here cryptically addressed Queen Elizabeth's hidden sympathy with English Catholics in order to invoke her merciful intervention in the trials of Puritan priest-hunters against Jesuits levied of treachery,[18] it does not seem far-fetched to read traces of Marian potency[19] in Portia's petition. Albeit tainted and diminished by promiscuous Reformed traits,[20] Portia's salvific intercession carries Marian undertones which will powerfully re-emerge at the end of Act V, when the pity which the play has silenced resurfaces quaintly in Portia's unconditional granting of the financial supplies to anyone allegedly in need.

Marian pity revived

A world of difference marks the distance between the pious Portia, reported to be kneeling at holy crosses, absorbed in prayers for 'happy wedlock hours' (V. i. 38), in the company of a hermit on her way back to Belmont, and the resourceful young woman cross-dressed as Balthazar in the Venice courtroom. It is as though, once the Jewish threat had been dealt with, a new time had come. A time for meditation on celestial and terrestrial harmony, no matter how short-lived; for lyrical celebrations of romantic love, no matter how ill-fated; for renewed oaths and for spiritual pledges, no matter how misplaced. In this refashioned climate denouements come in the form of amazing revelations, and the granting of wealth to the Christians entitled is announced in oracular manners which evoke heavenly deeds more than earthly devices. Having dismissed her masculine cross-dressing, the newly feminine Portia of Act V, is evidently keen to belittle the power of her wit as much as she is eager to silence the paths she has trodden to enforce her pitiless mercy. As she produces the anonymous letters which announce Shylock's substantial gifs and Antonio's wondrous turns of fortune, Portia presents herself as the mere executer of magic and/ or of heavenly estates. Whatever the provenance of their inspiration, the bountiful deeds which Portia gives way to do not drop like the insubstantial rain of mercy, but like manna, the godlike ladies' gratuitous gift onto starved people, which Lorenzo acknowledges in deferential gratitude: 'Fair ladies you drop manna on the ways of starved people' (V. i. 311–12). Lorenzo's Christian appropriation of the Jewish manna trope in Leviticus[21] brings here to the surface the uneasy subject of unfettered desire for money. For, just as the manna in Leviticus came to appease an appetite which the people of Israel could not possibly sate with their provision of herds and cattle, the manna in Belmont comes to placate the greed which still qualms starved Lorenzo, no matter how conspicuous Jessica's endowment of Jewish stolen money. On the other hand, and although he would never confess to any insufficiency, Antonio is evidently reputed to be also in need of more allowances than those he himself, Portia and the Duke have jointly carved out of Shylock's patrimony in Venice. And, although he silences his starving, the relief he voices at the hardly credible news that his ships are safely come to road – 'Sweet lady, you have given me life and living' (V. i. 302) – speaks loud, echoing, in a reverse parallel, the chrematistic despair Shylock had vented on the penalizing verdict of Venice: 'You take my life / when you do take the means whereby I live' (IV. i. 387–88).

In the much-needed happy closure of the play, the beneficiaries of Portia's providential largeness, no matter how impotent, or disabled, could never be classified as poor subjects in need of the relief that Reformed Protestants contemplated. They might figure instead as Shylockian would-be merchants expecting ever increasing financial support on the basis of an entrenched relationship of trust with their donor. Unconditional trust is what Portia concedes to Antonio in her newly fashioned Marian pity as she prodigiously reverses the dreaded 'but even now worth this, / and now worth nothing?' (I. i. 36–37) into 'but even now worth nothing and now worth this'. Admittedly, more than a suspicious deed of charitable pity, this allowance resembles an implausible bid on the worth of Antonio's asset, the speculative bubble of a bold investor. And no matter how reminiscent of the Holy Virgin is her pitiful demeanour, Portia seems here to retain the shrewdness of a Christian female usurer,[22] who is keen to ensure the worth of her main lender, in case the soul he has pledged on Bassanio's marital fidelity is imperilled by financial hardships. Is then the aura of Marian pity that emblazons shrewd Portia the cover which 'overgreens' the bad and allows the good, as in sonnet 112? Is it the filling of the impression which the vulgar scandal of marketable and pitiless mercy has left on the brow of the ethnically cleansed Venice as much as on the London of Shakespeare which the play adumbrates in its Venetian setting? This indeed might be the case. For, as they cast a silencing spell on the ways mercy and love, gender and marriage have been traded for the sake of the merchant, the traces of Catholic pity revived here are definitely put to the service of the Protestant world of gentile merchants, which the expulsion of the Jewish usurer has enabled and emboldened.

Mounts of piety

Be it as it may, the manna that is dropped in the still liminal space of Act V eventually crystallizes the vast range of meanings which the play has attached to the surfeit of assets awaiting equitable distribution among the would-be merchants at the outset: on the one hand, Portia's inheritance; on the other, the Jewish usurer's flowing cash that is needed to win it. Using an anachronistic metaphor, we might crudely claim that the manna Portia dispenses here issues from her shrewd and double-edged lobbying in the interest of Christian merchants, in self-interest, and against Jewish usury. A compound of tangible money and intangible credit, the manna asset is in fact mainly financed by the Jew's properties and proprieties, but also includes Portia's special-purpose reserve of money, estates and credit to be used solely and conditionally for the construction of her marital contract. What Portia eventually seems to set up then is the odd antecedent of a not-for-profit institution of cooperative credit, one which enlists exclusively white Christian merchants and which charges rates of moral interest.

A less anachronistic analogy, which accords with Portia's tinge of Marian pity and with the cryptic traces of Catholicism in the play, comes to mind, however, if we think of Mounts of Piety (Monti di

Pietà), the early form of Catholic organized charity set up in fifteenth-century Italy with the joint purpose of aiding needy subjects and of combating Jewish moneylending.[23] The name itself is of course revealing. For here it is pity – not mercy – that explicitly stands for the money that this institutional pawnbroker would loan to people in need (whether poor or impoverished) in exchange for an item of corresponding value at a predetermined rate of interest. And it was the alleged promise of God's salvation, not predestined election, that underpinned the donations which the affluent members of Italian communes originally allowed in order to build up that mount, or, in plain words, to accumulate the starting capital. The differences between the pawns and loans of Shakespeare's theatrical merchant and the traffics of the historical Italian Monti are undoubtedly stark.[24] However, I think there remains in Shakespeare's play the deep-seated analogy of an anti-Jewish crusade, which both systems devised as a fierce measure against the usury they both demonized and yet practised in vested manners. By the end of the sixteenth century the Monti had already justified the usury they had initially condemned as a reflection of actual costs. A double-standard morality steeped in hypocrisy seems to have policed the usurious pity of the Italian Monti as much as the Catholic pity which, with its flimsy blazon, covers Shakespeare's traffic of Protestant mercy in *The Merchant of Venice*.

We have no conclusive evidence, of course, as to whether Shakespeare could ever have known about the Italian Monti di Pietà, but that should not prevent us from further inquiries into the ways moneyed pity, and interest-driven aid move across competing religious and political camps under changeable guises and ever-shifting shapes – as shifting indeed as is Shakespeare's Portia. Her vertiginous wheeling from the tradeable mercy of Protestant merchants to the Marian-like pity of bounteous manna, places before our eyes the unremitting spectacle and the unlimited power of vested interest.

Alessandra Marzola, professor of English Literature now retired, has taught at the universities of Bergamo, Torino and Parma. She has published and edited books on Shakespeare; twentieth-century British Theatre; 'Englishness' in the twentieth century; and literature, war and violence in twentieth-century Britain. Her books on Shakespeare include: *L'impossibile puritanesimo di Amleto* (1986), *La parola del mercante* (1996), *Otello: Passioni* (2015), and, as editor: *L'altro Shakespeare* (1992) and *The Difference of Shakespeare* (2008). She is also the co-author, with Davide Del Bello, of *Shakespeare and the Power of Difference* (2011).

Notes

1. My re-reading of mercy takes stock of relevant contributions in the field of New Economic Criticism. See in particular: Marc Shell, '"The Whether and the Ewe": Verbal Usury in *The Merchant of Venice*', in Marc Shell, *Money, Language and Thought: Literary and Philosophic Economies from Medieval to the Modern Period* (Berkeley, CA: University of California Press, 1982), 47–84; Lars Engle, *Shakespearean Pragmatism: Market of his Time* (Chicago, IL: Chicago University Press, 1993), 77–107; Linda Woodbridge, ed., *Money and the Age of Shakespeare: Essays in New Economic Criticism* (New York: Palgrave Macmillan, 2003), 143–201; Peter Grav, *Shakespeare and the Economic Imperative: 'What's Aught But As 'Tis Valued?'* (New York: Routledge, 2008), 83–108 ; Peter Grav, 'Taking Stock of Shakespeare and the New Economic Criticism' , *Shakespeare* 8, no. 1 (2012): 111–136. A seminal essay on which I rely for my presuppositions is Renè Girard's, '"To Entrap the Wisest": A Reading of *The Merchant of Venice*' in *Literature and Society*, ed. Edward Said (Baltimore, MD: Johns Hopkins University Press, 1978), 100–19. A philosophical essay to which my reading is largely indebted is Simon Critchley and Tom McCarthy's, 'Universal Shylockery: Money and Morality in *The Merchant of Venice*', *Diacritics* 34, no. 1 (Spring 2004): 2–17.
2. For the influence on Modern Welfare of different religious approaches to poverty relief schemes see Siegrun Kahle, 'The Religious Roots of Modern Poverty Policy: Catholic, Lutheran and Reformed Protestant Traditions Compared', *European Journal of Sociology* 46, no. 1 (2005): 91–126.
3. All quotations from *The Merchant of Venice* are from the following edition: William Shakespeare, *The Merchant of Venice*, ed. Leah S. Marcus (New York: Norton Critical Edition, 2006).
4. For a thorough discussion of the difference between *oikos* and chrematistics in Greek society see David Hawkes, *Shakespeare and Economic Theory* (London: Bloomsbury Publishing, 2015), 3–17. Aristotle's inquiry into this issue (Aristotle, *Economics*, trans. E. S. Forster (Oxford, 1920), 1343a, 21–24) is also addressed in Jacques Derrida, *Given Time: 1. Counterfeit Money*, trans. Peggy Kamuf (Chicago, IL: The University of Chicago Press, 1992), 158.

5. The issue of judicial equity and common law in *The Merchant of Venice* has been the object of a large body of criticism. For a recent synopsis of relevant bibliography see Ethan H. Shagan, 'Religious Nonconformity and the Quality of Mercy: "The Merchant of Venice" in Reformation Context', in *The Oxford Handbook of the Age of Shakespeare*, ed. R. Malcolm Smuts (Oxford: Oxford University Press, 2016), 398–418, here 400n.
6. The mercantile etymology of 'mercy' in *The Merchant* has been often noted, albeit to different ends and with disparate implications. Frederick Turner, for instance, relies on the market roots of mercy to argue counterintuitively in favour of the intrinsic ecology and benevolence of the market. See Frederick Turner, *Shakespeare's Twenty-First Century Economics: The Morality of Love and Money* (Oxford: Oxford University Press, 1999), 88. For a divergent interpretation, which I would subscribe to here, see Simon Critchley and Tom Mc Carthy's 'Universal Shylockery', 4.
7. Jacques Derrida, 'What is a "Relevant" Translation?', *Critical Inquiry* 27 (Winter 2001): 196.
8. Ibid., 197.
9. For Stock Exchange settings of the play see the 1993 Royal Shakespeare Company production by David Thacker and the 2010 Public Theatre production by David Sullivan at Hollywood.
10. A largely shared view is that *The Merchant* puts on record the shift from reassuring male amity to homoerotic bonds potentially threatening for the economy of marriage in the new market. An inaugural essay is Alan Sinfield, 'How to Read *The Merchant of Venice* without Being Heterosexist', in *Alternative Shakespeares 2*, ed. Terence Hawkes (London and New York: Routledge, 1996), 122–39. For a perceptive reassessment see Steve Patterson, "The Bankruptcy of Homoerotic Amity in Shakespeare's *Merchant of Venice*', *Shakespeare Quarterly* 50, no. 1 (1999): 9–32.
11. All references to Shakespeare's sonnets come from the following edition: William Shakespeare, *The Sonnets*, ed. G. Blakemore Evans (Cambridge: Cambridge University Press, 1996).
12. For an insightful discussion of Sonnet 112 in light of pity see David Punter, *The Literature of Pity* (Edinburgh: Edinburgh University Press 2014), 45–46.
13. I am not arguing of course in favour of a narrative of mercy and pity that runs from *The Merchant* into *The Sonnets*, a conjecture which goes against accepted chronologies of Shakespeare's works. However, no final evidence exists to deny that individual pity sonnets, above all those addressed to the Dark Lady, may have been written later than the major bulk of sonnets, at a time which might as well have been coterminous with *The Merchant*. On the controversial issue of dating see Katherine Duncan Jones, ed., *Shakespeare's Sonnets: Revised* (London: Arden, 2010), 1–27.
14. For an engaging, albeit partial treatment of this issue see Punter, *Literature of Pity*, 24–35.
15. Aristotle, *Rhetoric*, trans. W. Rhys Roberts (Mineola, NY: Dover Publications, 2004), 77.
16. For a view of different religious and political approaches to poverty in early modern England and Europe see Paul Slack, *Poverty in Tudor and Stuart England* (London: Longman, 1988); Brian Pullan, 'Catholics, Protestants and the Poor in Early Modern Europe', *The Journal of Interdisciplinary History* 35, no. 3 (2006): 441–56.

17. On Shakespeare's – hidden or overt – Catholic connections and heritage see, amongst many others: Alison Shell, *Catholicism, Controversy and the English Literary Imagination, 1558–1660* (Cambridge: Cambridge University Press, 1999); Stephen Greenblatt, *Hamlet in Purgatory* (Princeton: Princeton University Press 2001); Maurice Hunt, *Shakespeare's Religious Allusiveness: Its Play and Tolerance* (Burlington, VT: Ashgate, 2004); Richard Wilson, *Secret Shakespeare: Studies in Theatre, Religion and Resistance* (Manchester: Manchester University Press, 2004). For an historically revisionist approach to the Protestant Reformation see Eamon Duffy, 'The English Reformation after Revisionism', *Renaissance Quarterly* 59, no. 3 (2006): 720–31.
18. See John Klause, 'Catholic and Protestant. Jesuit and Jew: Historical Religion in *The Merchant of Venice*', in *Shakespeare and The Culture of Christianity in Early Modern England*, ed. David Beauregard and Dennis Taylor (New York: Fordham University Press, 2003), 180–221.
19. Marian imagery in early modern drama is discussed in Regina Buccola and Lisa Hopkins, eds, *Marian Moments in Early Modern British Drama* (Aldershot: Ashgate, 2007). For insights into Shakespeare's employment of both Catholic and post-Reformation views of the Marian cult, see Ruben Espinosa, *Masculinity and Marian Efficacy in Shakespeare's England* (London: Routledge, 2016).
20. Espinosa, *Masculinity and Marian Efficacy*, 75.
21. On this issue see Lara Bovilsky, '"A Gentle and no Jew": Jessica, Portia and Jewish Identity', *Renaissance Drama* 38, New Series (2010): 47–76; 70.
22. The case for Portia as a usurious moneylender has been convincingly argued in Natasha Korda's 'Dame Usury: Gender, Credit and (Ac)counting in the Sonnets and *The Merchant of Venice*', *Shakespeare Quarterly* 60, no. 2 (2009): 129–53.
23. For a description of the Monti di Pietà see Vittorio Meneghin; *I Monti di Pietà in Italia: dal 1462 al 1562* (Vicenza: L.I.E.F., 1987). On the relationship between the Monti di Pietà and Jewish moneylending in Italy see Maria Cristina Muzzarelli, 'Pawnbroking between Theory and Practice in Observant Socio-Economic Thought', in *A Companion to Observant Reform in the Late Middle Ages and Beyond*, ed. James Mixson and Bert Roest (Leiden: Brill, 2015) 204–30.
24. For remarks on the differences between the Italian Monti di Pietà and Protestant charity see Pullan, 'Catholics, Protestants and the Poor in Early Modern England', 446, 454.

Chapter 5
'Love Merchandized'
Money in Shakespeare's Sonnets

Manfred Pfister

The state of our national, European and global economies is of a kind to strike headlines every day on toppling markets, monetary imbalances or dubious financial transactions and thus puts the question of money, its nature, value and uses, into high relief. There are, of course, a number of plays in the Shakespearean canon that offer themselves immediately when it comes to exploring the nexus between his theatre and financial transactions and, in particular, the role that money plays in the dramatic negotiations of his plots: *The Merchant of Venice* is surely one of them, and *Timon of Athens*, not by chance Karl Marx' favourite Shakespearean play, another. Marx in his *Economic and Philosophic Manuscripts* of 1844 uses it to analyse the 'power of money' in a capitalist market society:

> By possessing the property of buying everything, by possessing the property of appropriating all objects, money is thus the object of eminent possession. The universality of its property is the omnipotence of

Notes for this section begin on page 95.

its being. It is therefore regarded as an omnipotent being. Money is the procurer between man's need and the object, between his life and his means of life. But that which mediates my life for me, also mediates the existence of other people for me. For me it is the other person.[1]

And, commenting on Timon's apostrophe to gold (*Timon*, IV. iii), he further explores its impact on the self in its interactions with others and society at large:

If money is the bond binding me to human life, binding society to me, connecting me with nature and man, is not money the bond of all bonds? Can it not dissolve and bind all ties? Is it not, therefore, also the universal agent of separation? It is the coin that really separates as well as the real binding agent – the chemical power of society. ... The distorting and confounding of all human and natural qualities, the fraternization of impossibilities – the divine power of money – lies in its character as men's estranged, alienating and self-disposing species-nature. Money is the alienated ability of mankind.[2]

If Marx is right in his analysis that money does not remain external to man's subjectivity and intersubjective interactions, we should find it also in the texts that are particularly dedicated to the emotions of love, although these are apparently furthest removed from the cash-nexus of economic and pecuniary interactions. And this is precisely what I shall try to do in my brief and cursory reading of Shakespeare's sonnets: to reveal the close imbrication or interpenetration of the erotic with the economic going on within them. My project of looking for money in love sonnets may appear to be wilfully paradoxical at first sight, but I hope I will be able to illuminate Shakespeare's sonnets in more relevant ways than with further speculations about who's who in the sonnets.

They were written, as Marx already intuited and more recent economic historiography has confirmed, at a time when modern marketing conditions and with them the national and international circulation of goods and money, both coin and paper, took on new dimensions in England and particularly in its rapidly growing capital with its flourishing entertainment industry. Though there was not yet a 'Bank of England' – it was only founded in 1695 – the sixteenth century had already seen a massive extension of private banking facilities, which were run, after the expulsion of Jewish merchants under Edward III, by mainly Italian companies: the 'Lombard merchants', for example, specializing successfully in pawn shops; the Ricciardi family of Lucca; and later the Frescobaldi of Florence, who financed the ventures of many royal houses across Europe and whose financial conquest of England signalled, according to Fernand Braudel, the greatest achievement of the Florentine firms, 'not only in holding the purse-strings of the kings of England, but also in controlling sales of English wool'. English institutions emerged at the same time: notable examples include the Court of the Exchequer lending money on mortgage; the Office of the King's Exchanger, which held its Exchange in Lombard Street, not far from London's printing shops; and various companies, in particular the companies of goldsmiths and of moneyers and the Society of Merchant Adventurers.

It seems significant in this context that Shakespeare as a playwright and member of a shareholding company depending on capital investment for its theatrical productions was deeply involved in the financial transaction of raising capital and making a profit. Even his life outside the theatre was marked by money matters; and, indeed, it seems to be telling that nearly everything we know about his personal life bears a pecuniary imprint. In the scarce documents relating to it we read about his mother pawning her estate and his father proving unable to redeem it and fined for not going to church; we read about various assessments, small fines and real-estate transactions, among them the acquisition of a high-value town house at Stratford and a conveyance of land and a copyhold for a cottage there, about payments to the Lord Chamberlain's Men for performances in the provinces and at court, an allowance of four yards of red cloth for him to wear in James's coronation procession, his obtaining a one-seventh share in the Second Blackfriars Theatre, and about several deeds, minor actions in court to collect money, down to his testament, in which he oddly and famously bequeathed his 'second best bed' to his wife.[3]

No wonder then that even Shakespeare's most personal poems, *The Sonnets*, speak so often the language of pecuniary and economic transactions. His soiled 'dyer's hand', which the speaker of his sonnets bemoans (sonnet 111), is dyed in the colours of lucre invested and made in the market place of the public theatre and the literary profession. This first brief quotation from the sonnets may also serve as an instance of how Shakespeare writes the economic context into his love poetry: it is by way of metaphors drawn from the world of trade and finance. This is one of the ways in which he disrupts and defamiliarizes the traditional poetic discourses of love and brings them up to date, in tune with the economic dynamics of an early capitalist and mercantilist society.

The extent to which he does this has been largely disregarded so far: Even Stephen Booth's monumental and meticulously detailed commentary on the sonnets, though exploring at great length the sexual connotations and bawdy allusions running through the text, fails to recognize its economic and financial leitmotifs.[4] Helen Vendler, in her otherwise admirable study of *The Art of Shakespeare's Sonnets*, makes do with a mere summary: 'Shakespeare is unusually rich in his borrowings of diction and formulas from patronage, from religion, from law, from courtship, from diplomacy, from astronomy, and *so on* [my italics]; there is no social discourse which he does not interrogate'.[5] And the 'Oxford Shakespeare Topics' introduction to the sonnets, though attempting to single out the 'Concerns of the Sonnets', comes up with no more than 'Time, Image, and Verse', 'Desire', 'Language of Sexuality' and 'Black Beauty' as their 'connecting interpretive threads' or 'dominant themes ... revisited and reinvented throughout all 154 of them'.[6] Only recently – actually this year – has it been taken note of in any systematic way, in Michael Tratner's contribution to the monumental *Cambridge Guide to the Worlds of Shakespeare*, which points out its presence and underlines it statistically: 'One place where commercial language appears extensively in Shakespeare is in the sonnets: fully a third of the sonnets refer to payments, credit, usury, or even mortgages'.[7]

Shakespeare almost completely discards the traditional cognitive 'metaphors we live by'[8] ingrained in our human consciousness – 'love is war', 'love is a game', 'love is music', 'love is a journey'... – and the metaphors inherited from Platonic or Petrarchan traditions, which impose on erotic desire notions of sublimation, alchemistic transubstantiation and the ascent from the bodily to the spiritual. These, though showing up every now and then, are more often than not exposed to a sobering critique. What strikes one, in contrast, is the unprecedented presence of metaphors thematizing the erotic in terms of usury (sonnet 6), borrowing, lending, loan (sonnet 6) or leasing (sonnets 13, 18), legacy and bequeathing (sonnet 5), saving and spending (sonnets 4, 9, 76), loss and gain (sonnets 42, 88, 119), parsimony, thrift and generous largesse (sonnets 4, 9), banking or exchanging goods, or traffic (sonnet 4), storing or converting (sonnet 14), use and abuse of credit or 'accounting' (sonnets 2, 30) – in other words, metaphors of taking stock of one's growing or dwindling means or possessions, of wealth, worth, riches, treasures, pearls and so on, to mention but some of them.

This monetary and economic leitmotif is introduced with a volley of images relating to treasures and abundance, summing one's account, usury or unthrift in the first movement of the sequence. From the first introduction of the beloved young men, characterized in terms of economical behaviour in a triad of strikingly paradoxical compounds – 'unthrifty loveliness', 'beauteous niggard', 'thriftless usurer' (sonnet 3, 1, 5, 6) – it is never completely lost sight of later on and surfaces again prominently in the 'rival poet' sonnets. In sonnet 6, already it takes the banking spirit so far as to actually calculate the extraordinary usurious 'interest' of a thousand percent to be expected from a loan – a form of 'amatory arithmetic', which J. B. Leishman has referred to in his study of the poetry of Andrew Marvell and related back to a tradition in Roman love poetry:[9]

> That use is not forbidden usury
> Which happies those that pay the willing loan;
> That's for thyself to breed another thee,
> Or ten times happier, be it ten for one:
> Ten times thyself were happier than thou art,
> If ten of thine ten times refigured thee: (sonnet 6, 5–10)[10]

The reference to banking and the ongoing debate about interest rates in relation to the Mosaic prohibition of *usura* is quite explicit here, and so is the use of a number of terms directly taken from the language of banking or business transactions, such as '(ac)count' (sonnets 30, 58, 62, 86, 90, 176), 'bankrupt' (sonnet 67) or 'audit' (sonnets 4, 49, 126). As some of these are of Italian derivation (*conto, banca, bancarotta* or, mediated via Middle French, *credit*) – as is the entire terminology relating to banking, marking its Italian origins in most of the European cultures – this metaphorical complex of love in terms of monetary or economic investment and exchange constitutes a second, though not yet sufficiently appreciated, link between Shakespeare's sonnets and Italian medieval and early modern culture – next to the form of the sonnet itself and the Petrarchan discourse of love's sublimations. This link runs so deep that an affectionate word like 'dear', which permeates the whole cycle, assumes the status of a 'metaphor we live by' and reverberates with the erotico-economic double sense of the friend as 'beloved' and 'expensive', who eventually proves 'a prize so dear' (sonnet 48, 14), 'the prize of all-too-precious you' (sonnet 86, 2), and 'too dear for [his] possessing' (sonnet 87, 1). Similarly, 'credit' (sonnet 138) reverberates both with the economic meaning of the early modern mercantilist 'culture of credit'[11] and ethical connotations of praiseworthy reliability and loving trust.

The beauties and virtues of the beloved are a 'treasure' (sonnet 2, 6; sonnet 136, 5); they are like 'stones of worth ... / Or captain jewels in the carcanet' (sonnet 52, 7–8). But they are not a treasure to be 'up-locked' by its rich possessor to gaze at it with ecstatic pleasure in his own privacy (sonnet 52, 1–4) – as Volpone does with his hoarded gold at the very beginning of Ben Jonson's comedy of acquisitiveness and greed. Such 'storing' (sonnets 14, 37, 64) would be a 'waste in niggarding' (sonnet 1, 12) and only create 'famine where abundance lies' (sonnet 1, 7). Only when put to 'use' (sonnet 2, 9) in the right way will it be able to partake in the natural 'increase' of living creatures (sonnet 1, 1; sonnet 11, 5). The 'surplus value' it will then produce is that of a natural growth, not that of a financial interest on capital transactions of lending and borrowing. The latter would be not use, but, like 'unused' wealth (sonnet 4, 13), an 'abuse' (sonnet 4, 4) or 'forbidden usury' (sonnet 6, 5) that sinfully makes money out of money and thus makes dead matter grow against the divine law of natural order. A Renaissance model for such un-usurious use, for such a natural surplus value, was highlighted for his and for our own late capitalist present in Ezra Pound's *Cantos* (XLII–LXIII): the bank of Monte dei Paschi di Siena, founded in 1472 to promote and support local business activities on the financial basis of the natural yield in wool, milk and meat of the rich pastures on the hills, the fertile *paschi*, surrounding the city.

To hoard and store one's treasures only to take stock of them or count and audit them, is as much an abuse as making them increase *contra naturam* in usurious financial transactions. The latter does not apply to sexual consummation as part of that noble work of procreation to which the speaker exhorts his beloved. This is the very point of the last verse of the enigmatic Sonnet 20, which concludes the 'procreation' sequence: 'Mine be thy love and thy love's use their pleasure'. It makes a distinction metaphorically based on a distinction operative in banking and the monetary market: the love he wants to make his own is the capital or principal, the main part or value of his beloved's love; the sexual pleasure to be derived from it by women – its *use* or *interest*.[12] Here, for once, there is a clear hierarchy of value, which contrasts a higher and sexually disinterested love with heterosexual passion. The surplus value gained in the former is the creative inspiration to beauty, virtue and poetry, and in the latter it is sexual pleasure and procreation. And both entail an economic aspect: sexual consummation and procreation have a dynastic value in promoting the future of the family and its property, and the poetry inspired by love serves the poet's self-fashioning, enhances his prestige with the cognoscenti and with that his 'cultural capital'.[13]

Sonnet writing is, not unlike economic interactions, a competitive game, in which you can – by lending, stealing or borrowing, bequeathing or inheriting – lose or gain. The competitors in this field can be both your antecedents (the poets of the past), or your contemporaries. The latter are at the thematic centre of the 'rival poet' sequence (sonnets 76–86) about the 'modern quill[s]' (sonnet 83, 7), which draw attention to themselves with new highly competitive marketing strategies of out-bidding the rivals in the business. Where our poet is aware of the indebtedness of all he writes to his beloved and to what he has already written about him – in financial terms, 'spending again what is already spent' (sonnet 76, 12) – he, unlike his rival, refuses to inveigle the reader with the spurious riches fashioned by 'new-found methods and ... compounds strange' (sonnet 76, 4). The apparent surplus value here is based on theft, dishonestly obtained and dishonestly reinvested:

> ... what of thee thy poet doth invent
> He robs thee of, and pays it thee again.
> He lends thee virtue, and he stole that word
> From thy behaviour; beauty doth he give,
> And found it in thy cheek: he can afford
> No praise to thee but what in thee doth live.
>   Then thank him not for that which he doth say,
>   Since what he owes thee thou thyself dost pay. (sonnet 79, 6–14)

The beauty such a poet's pen offers is 'second-hand' and as such it does not create any surplus value; he is only interested in increasing his own visibility and market value and is incapable of capturing and canvassing the uniqueness of the young man whose praises he sings. The true poet, in contrast, writes with the awareness that the friend's 'worth' or 'riches' (sonnets 82, 83, 87) cannot be increased by the 'strainéd touches rhetoric can lend' (sonnet 82, 9); 'it did exceed / The barren tender [the payment offered] of a poet's debt' (sonnet 83, 3–4). And in those self-critical moments, which his poetic rival goes totally without, he himself confesses bitterly to have sometime 'gored himself' and 'sold cheap that is most dear' (sonnet 110, 3). Even he, that is, has not managed to liberate his love entirely from the self-alienating effect of the cash-nexus.

Love, like all 'nature's riches' needs to be 'husband[ed]' (sonnet 94, 6), not marketed. The word 'husbandry' (sonnet 3, 7; sonnet 13, 10) Shakespeare uses here is the English equivalent to Greek οικονομία, from which our modern word for the science of economy derives. The early modern English word 'husbandry', however, still retains the notion of a household, an οικος, or farm, and the loving care that is needed to make it prosper and flourish. And this is the alternative erotic economy of Shakespeare's sonnets – an ecological economy that stays aloof from the financial dynamics of commerce and marketing and financial transactions.

The sonnets as written by Shakespeare are in themselves an instance of this: they were circulated freely in manuscript, which, it seems, have been valued and treasured, and some of them have been set to music soon.[14] None of them, though, have survived to become an expensive object in today's growing market for auratic autographs. In this they also show their disdain to capitalize on the love they celebrate:

> I love no less, though less the show appear.
> That love is merchandized whose rich seeming
> The owner's tongue doth publish everywhere. (sonnet 102, 3–5)

'Love merchandized' is the core-metaphor for this dark, capitalist shadow of self-alienated love. It is for this reason that I have chosen it to provide the title for my chapter, the subject of which is the catastrophe of love in the sonnets as a loss of credit. The notion of catastrophe culminates in the final phase of the sonnets, in those that involve the 'dark lady'. Here, the speaker painfully learns that the lady does not merit the credit he bestows upon her: 'Simply, I credit her false-speaking tongue' (sonnet 138, 7). 'What is desire?' he asks now, rejecting his passion for her as lust, defining 'lust in action' in a metaphor that brutally conflates the economical with the physiological: 'the expense of spirit in a waste of shame / Is lust in action:' (sonnet 129, 1–2). In a last invocation of the language of money and finance, he calls her an 'angel', alluding in this to a gold coin circulating in Tudor currency. She, however, proves a 'bad angel', an angel debased in value and not to be credited, so that he fears that 'my bad angel fire my good one out' (sonnet 144, 14). What this phrase suggests is not only the moral psychomachia of good and evil, but an economic theory of Shakespeare's time that has come to be known later as Gresham's – or Copernicus' – law': 'bad money drives out good'.[15]

Manfred Pfister was professor of English at the Freie Universität Berlin and guest professor at the universities of Vienna, Gdansk, Dartmouth College, Sussex, East Anglia and the Cuban International School of Film and Television, and is a member of the Berlin-Brandenburgische Akademie der Wissenschaften. He was co-editor of the *Shakespeare Jahrbuch* and *Poetica* and author of *Das Drama: Theorie und Analyse* (Munich 1982; Cambridge 1988). Among his more recent book publications are *Laurence Sterne* (2001), *A History of English Laughter* (2002), *Performing National Identity: Anglo-Italian Transactions* (2008), *Shakespeare's Sonnets Global, A Quatercentenary Anthology* (2009, 2014), *Dialoge zwischen Wissenschaft, Kunst und Literatur in der Renaissance* (2011), and *Heroen und Heroisierungen in der Renaissance* (2013); other works include editions of Bruce Chatwin's *In Patagonia* (2003), Samuel Butler's *Notebooks* (2005), Shelley's *Zastrozzi* (2009) and Sir Thomas Brownes' *Urne Buriall and Selected Writings* (2014). He is also a translator and as such one of the German voices of Robert Lowell (1982) and Ezra Pound's *Cantos* (2012). Together with linguist Ekkehard König, he has just published a book on interfacing linguistics and literary studies (2017). Since his retirement, he has spent half of his time in the Italian Maremma, where he pursues, among others, Anglo-Italian crossways.

Notes

1. English version taken from: https://www.marxists.org/archive/marx/works/1844/manuscripts/power.htm (accessed 1 March 2018).
2. Ibid.
3. My random list is compiled from the collection of documents and the 'Shakespearean Chronicle' in Stephen Greenblatt's 'General Introduction' to *The Norton Shakespeare* (New York: W. W. Norton & Company, 1997). For a detailed discussion of the finances of Shakespeare and his theatre company see Andrew Gurr, *The Shakespeare Company, 1594–1642*, and for his financial biography Robert Bearman, *Shakespeare's Money: How Much Did He Make and What Did This Mean?* (Oxford: Oxford University Press, 2016), and David J. Baker, 'Shakespeare's Money', in *The Cambridge Guide to the Worlds of Shakespeare: vol. I: Shakespeare's World, 1500–1660*, ed. Bruce R. Smith (Cambridge: Cambridge University Press, 2016), 631–35.
4. Stephen Booth, *Shakespeare's Sonnets: Edited with Analytic Commentary* (New Haven, CT: Yale University Press, 1977).
5. Helen Vendler, *The Art of Shakespeare's Sonnets* (Cambridge, MA: Belknap Press/Harvard University Press, 1997), 2.

6. Paul Edmondson and Stanley Wells, *Shakespeare's Sonnets* (Oxford: Oxford University Press), chapter 6, here 63.
7. Michael Tratner, 'Trade and Commerce: Mercantilism' in Smith, *Cambridge Guide*), 625–31 here 629.
8. George Lakoff and Mark Johnson, *Metaphors We Live By* (Chicago, IL: University of Chicago Press, 1980).
9. J. B. Leishman, *The Art of Marvell's Poetry* (London: Hutchinson, 1966).
10. *Shakespeare's Sonnets* are quoted throughout from Katherine Duncan Jones' Arden edition of the sonnets (Thomas Nelson and Sons, 1997)
11. Craig Muldrew, *The Economy of Obligation: The Culture of Credit and Social Relations in Early Modern England* (Houndmills: Palgrave, 1998).
12. See the note in John Kerrigan, ed., *Shakespeare, The Sonnets and A Lover's Complaint* (Harmondsworth: Penguin), 201.
13. See Stephen Greenblatt, *Renaissance Self-Fashioning: From More to Shakespeare* (Chicago, IL: Chicago University Press, 1980).
14. For single-sheet manuscripts of the sonnets, sonnets in manuscript miscellanies, and sonnets set to music, see Kerrigan, ed., *Sonnets and A Lover's Complaint*, 441–43.
15. See Tratner, 'Trade and Commerce', 630.

Chapter 6
Timon of Athens in the Downturn

James Tink

London in the summer of 2012 provided an unusual test case for studies of Shakespeare, adaptation and national culture. The opening ceremony of the London Olympics, which sought to idealize British identity for the global media audience, became a unique experiment in the power of 'the Shakespeare myth'.[1] It was probably inevitable that it would borrow something from the national bard; perhaps predictable that it should select the wonderment of *The Tempest*. In the event, Sir Kenneth Branagh, quoting Caliban in the guise of Isambard Kingdom Brunel, inaugurated a surprising TV spectacle: a celebration of the industrial revolution in British history which also presented a defiantly social democratic vision of civil rights, multi-culturalism and post-war welfare as the signs of post-imperial British culture. In the same year, the Cultural Olympiad included the international Shakespeare 'Globe to Globe' Festival at the London Globe Theatre and, further up the Thames, a high-profile revival of *Timon of Athens* at the National Theatre, directed by Nicholas Hytner with Simon Russell Beale in the lead. Of course, the choice of *Timon* was

Notes for this section begin on page 107.

also an artistic response to the ongoing recession in the UK and EU following the credit crunch and bank crises of 2008. The mixture of national celebration and economic uncertainty brought an opportunity to reflect on the powers of Shakespeare in the national present.

William Shakespeare and Thomas Middleton's co-written and possibly unperformed experiment in satirical-tragedy is a notoriously challenging text to realize. John Jowett has described how the play divides violently into the satirical Timon in the city of Athens and the more poetic Timon raging in the woods, a partition which he also suggestively describes as the 'classical' and 'romantic' tendencies of the play.[2] This is a productive approach to the drama in that it helps explain how it seems to be built around a division: not only the two spaces of Athens and the wilderness, but also the two sides of Timon's character, as he transforms from host to misanthrope throughout the plot. Moreover, Jowett suggests something about the drama's historical trajectory in literary aesthetics, from a moral satire rooted in early-modern economy, to a more expressive presentation of modern human subjectivity under duress: a reading that endures into Modernist and Beckettian approaches to the play as a study in abjection.[3] The alleged modernity of the play has also been associated with the themes of money and capitalism, especially following the famous comments of Karl Marx about the putative foresight of Shakespeare in predicting the power of capital.[4] A production of *Timon of Athens*, then, provides an opportunity to think with Shakespeare about the role of money and consumption, while also posing a challenge in the search for artistic coherence. Of course, a production of this pedigree at the National Theatre was also an example of what Michael Bristol calls 'big-time Shakespeare', a high profile and prestigious project intended to provoke publicity and media comment.[5] This essay will discuss various details of the Hytner production so as to reflect on some complications of the play, and also to consider what this suggests about adapting Shakespeare as a means to comment on the current economic downturn.

Theatre has long had the artistic license to bring 'presentism' to Shakespeare, arranging texts to suit topical contexts, and so it was that the main device of this production was to set the drama in a recognizably contemporary London, contrasting the chic uptown décor of acts one to three with a derelict, urban building site for the remainder of the play. As such, Beale's *Timon* can be read in a tradition of modern productions that have used the play to represent the highs and lows of urban life. Terence Hawkes has analysed the first post-war British *Timon of Athens* (at the Birmingham Repertory Theatre in 1947) as a calculated response to the austerity and social ambitions of the immediate post-war period;[6] the play's Arden Third Series editors have also catalogued the uses of *Timon* to explore themes of social inequality.[7] In this case, Hytner, working with the National Theatre's dramaturg Ben Power, reworked the Folio text to further transform the fictional Athens into the setting of the UK in 2012, in recession and undergoing controversial austerity policies. In particular, Hytner drew upon the public image of the recent London Occupy protests against corporate greed that, emulating the Wall Street protests of 2011, were carried out in the City of London in the Winter of 2011–2012. Those protestors had decamped to outside St Paul's Cathedral, thereby drawing the Church of England into an argument about economic policy. This was arguably alluded to in the opening scene, when a silent tableau of tents suggestive of the Occupy protests was replaced by a backdrop reproduction of El Greco's painting *Christ Driving the Traders from the Temple*. This was labelled 'The Timon Room', as we began watching Act 1 Scene 1 un-fold as a party in an art gallery. The combination of social exclusion and high society, and the allusion to the patronage of the arts, was thus symbolically suggested from the outset. Moreover, the play's formidably masculine line-up of masters, servants and soldiers were rewritten for a more mixed cast of executives, employees and the destitute, notably in the change of Flavius the steward into Flavia, Timon's personal assistant (played superbly by Deborah Finlay) and the transformation of Alcibiades from a wronged soldier to a megaphone-carrying protest leader. The subplot about military fealty in 3.6 was removed, while some unspecified lines from Shakespearean drama were apparently interpolated as his slogans (as discussed below).[8] Using naturalistic acting styles to familiarize the Jacobean text to a contemporary idiom, the Athenian scenes were then played for some class-conscious English satire in the tradition of city-comedy: Apemantus was a rumpled, world-weary academic-type; the creditors a mixture of smarmy bankers and power-dressed politicians. At a time when popular British TV shows have contrasted the *nouveau riche* county of Essex with the well-heeled and 'trustafarian' London neighbourhood of Chelsea, the painter and the jeweller spoke in demotic estuary (Essex) English, while the posh-but-dim Ventidius (in a comic role expanded to take over that of Lucius, the second creditor) spoke with the fashionably high rising terminals of upper-class, British English 'upspeak', where spoken indicatives sound like interrogatives. In an enjoyably pungent touch, when Timon finally turns against the Athenians at his second banquet (3.7), the steaming water mentioned in the Folio became dog turds thrown spitefully over his nauseous dinner guests.

In this context, the character of Timon was made sympathetic and vulnerable. Much of this was owed to Simon Beale's quiet, unassuming stage presence. Timon was not shown, as he might have been, as a playboy figure, but rather as a shy, slightly awkward person. For example, when the (female) jeweller attempted to flirt with him in scene one, he backed away in embarrassment, complaining 'Well mocked' (1.1.176).[9] As Timon's 'magic of bounty' (1.1.6) included the public patronage of the arts as well as to his private friends, his ruin might seem intended to elicit some sympathy, not least from audiences sitting in the corporate-sponsored institution of the Royal National Theatre. His subsequent self-banishment, swapping his suit for a donkey jacket and woollen hat, and scavenging for left-over food from pizza boxes, seemed more grimly destitute than ascetic. Moreover, the interaction with Flavia was revealing: irritable, but betraying an affection. When he tells the senators to pass on advice to his countrymen ('And tell them that to ease them of their griefs, / Their fear of hostile strokes, their aches, losses / *pangs of love...*' (5.2.83–5; my italics), the last phrase seemed to be ruefully aimed at his loyal assistant, suggesting a thwarted inner life. The production thus sought to humanize Timon, whose misanthropy, it was implied, stemmed from some emotional illiteracy and the effects of bad company.

Such attempts at psychologizing Timon as a victim, however, cannot entirely explain the ferocity of his outrage, or indeed the underlying theme of reciprocity, money and ethics that the play explores. To analyse the production, we need to consider the political implications of the original text and its distinct dramatic form. Historicist critics have debated whether Shakespeare and Middleton may have provided a pre-emptive critique of the emergent capitalist market and usury or sought to satirize in particular the aristocratic culture of gift-giving and excessive hospitality that abounded in the early Jacobean court.[10] This could also be Middleton's territory as much as Shakespeare's: if Middleton has been seen by Margot Heinemann and others as a tough-minded, even puritan, author of 'city tragedy' stressing 'personal responsibility for sin', then Timon's complaint that 'No villainous bounty yet hath passed my heart – / Unwisely, not ignobly, have I given' (2.2.172–3) might be read as incriminatory proof that he lacks the self-awareness to judge his bountifulness *as* ignoble.[11] In fact, it seems that the play is less concerned with the topic of usury *per se* than with the condition of excessive expenditure and debt. As Flavius/ Flavia points out to Timon, 'The greatest of your having lacks a half / To pay your present debts' (2.2.143–4). This was reinforced in this production by the omission of the sequence in which the Fool discusses usury (2.2.47–119). Timon's reversal of fortune and explosion of misanthropy reflected instead a horror of impoverishment and the experience of debt in itself. This was a self-evidently topical subject, not least for thinking about the actual state of Athens, the debt crisis of Greece, and the problems facing the European economy during the current downturn. Indeed, at least one conservative reviewer of the play associated Timon's ruin with the folly of 'mad Keynesianism' and the Greek socialist government.[12] However, this was not the overt artistic choice of this production that took aim instead at modern Britain in its Olympic year. Nevertheless, this production raised important questions about how local or national contexts could overlap with more global aspects of contemporary Shakespeare reception, as will now be examined.

In the text, Timon's rejection of Athens can be seen as a partly pastoral mode of criticism. At his initial appearance in the wood, for example, he contrasts the simplicity of the soil with the hypocrisy of society:

> Raise me this beggar and deject that lord:
> The senator shall bear contempt hereditary,
> The beggar native honour.
> It is the pasture lards the rother's sides,
> The want that makes him lean. Who dares – who dares
> In purity of manhood stand upright
> And say, 'This man's a flatterer'? If one be,
> So are they all, for every grece of fortune
> Is smoothed by that below. The learned pate
> Duck's to the golden fool. All's obliquy,
> There's nothing level in our cursed natures
> But direct villainy. Therefore be abhorred
> All feasts, societies and throngs of men!
> His semblable, yea himself, Timon disdains.
> Destruction fang mankind! Earth, yield me roots. (4.3.12–23)

At this point, the drama might seem to suggest a binary divide of pastoral to urban, *otium* to *negotium*.[13] However, the cumulative effect of Timon's misanthropic speeches is to render the potentially green world of the Athenian wood into a form of ruthless antipastoral. For example, Timon's accusation to Apemantus, 'Wouldst thou have thyself fall in the confusion of men and remain a beast with the beasts?' (4.3.322–3), results in a litany of bestial allegories:

> A beastly ambition, which the gods grant thee t'attain to. If thou wert the lion, the fox would beguile thee; if thou wert the lamb, the fox would eat thee; if thou wert the fox, the lion would suspect thee when peradventure thou wert accused by the ass; if thou wert the ass, thy dullness would torment thee, and still thou lived'st but as breakfast the wolf; if thou wert the wolf, thy greediness would afflict thee and oft thou should hazard thy life for thy dinner. (4.3.326–34)

Unable to find solace in nature, Timon withdraws from all human contact, and it falls to Alcibiades to avenge the ingratitude of Athens by his eventual military conquest of the city.

The London production reinforced the anti-pastoral tone through its choice of an urban, London setting. Moreover, the discourse of animality and disgust proved timely in less expected ways. The philosopher Yannis Stavrakakis has recently critiqued the ways in which the official discourse of global finance – which once encouraged economies such as Greece to raise public spending and spread a credit-based, consumer-led economy, but now demands debt repayment and austerity – has pathologized Greek society as villainous, infantile and even animalistic: the IMF did after all label Greece as one of the PIIGS Of Europe. Stavrakakis's objection is to how the contemporary rhetoric of debt and austerity has replaced a language of civility and political respect with a 'zoomorphic' language 'devoid of humanity, rationality and dignity', whereby the citizen is degraded to the level of a beast.[14] The reduction of the human into the animal is of course also the thrust of Timon's misanthropy, aimed in his case at his creditors, but extending into an appalled vision of the world as a great robbery of human values: 'And what a beast thou art already that sees not thy loss in transformation!' (4.3.344–5). This language of debasement provides a more disquieting topicality or 'presentism' for the play, well beyond its satirical swipes at pretentious Londoners, one that suggests this sudden crash of Athenian social values to the level of animals is also a breakdown of civic discourse.

In fact, the idea of extremism is, as Jowett notes, the signature tone of the drama, whereby 'Timon's remorseless excess of generosity followed by his aggressive antihumanitarianism is the play's distinctive form of passion'.[15] It is useful to consider further what that form of passion might be. An important tradition of modern *Timon* criticism has sought to relate Timon's zeal and ferocious misanthropy to his disappointed relationship to some idea of a cosmic order, or, in more psychoanalytical terms, his relation to a cultural symbolic order and an idea of the Other which breaks down. These criticisms have included: the power of money to sever the real value of natural essences (Marx); G. Wilson Knight's infamous 'pilgrimage of hate' against an ungrateful universe; a psychosexual fantasy of an unfaithful, maternal bounty; and, according to Ken Jackson, the desire to encounter a sacred *tout autre* as the alternative to material exchange.[16] In all these approaches, the play is said to explore a sudden catastrophic loss of a social bond. Again, this notion could make the London production seem timely. The philosopher Slavoj Žižek, in his book *The Year of Dreaming Dangerously*, argues that the contemporary figure of the sociopath, whether in art, popular culture or even real life, displays the perverse logic of modern society and allows for a critique of the symbolic order, by using 'a true sociopath as a social revolutionary effectively questioning the basic coordinates society's big Other'.[17] One example of his, curiously enough, is Shakespeare's Coriolanus (more specifically, Ralph Fiennes 2011 film version) in which his pride and betrayal of Rome is commended as an act of resistance.[18] Could Simon Russell Beale's Timon be added to this idea of the sociopath as one who exposes the fraudulent order? Certainly, the character presents us with a furious, if self-destructive, figure of resistance that the London production garbed in the colours of contemporary anti-capitalism. Nevertheless, Beale's sympathetic performance, and the production's overall mood of modern naturalism, seemed to bring to a liberal humanist, psychological plausibility to the character. Arguably, the more destructive potential of the literary character was downplayed, although it remained latent.

The other challenge of updating the politics of the play to the present was in Hytner's interpretation of Alcibiades and his followers. This character, although rather underdeveloped, is arguably presented as the dramatic counterpart to Timon in that he also has to cope with ingratitude and rejection; moreover, he also provides the closure to the final scenes of the play after the removal of Timon. Recently, the critics Hugh Grady and Kiernan Ryan have separately proposed that the drama promotes a redemptive aesthetic and Utopian notion of the future. This is said to be variously through Timon's own eventual transformation into an epitaph to posterity ('Here lie I, Timon, who alive all living men did hate, / Pass by and curse thy fill, but pass and stay not here thy gait' (5.570–1).) which thereby, according to Ryan, secures his presence as a form of textual promise answerable to the future, or, in Grady's reading, because the eventual intervention of Alcibiades as a type of Machiavellian legislator restores the republic of Athens and 'Make war breed peace, make peace stint war, make each / Prescribe to other, as each other's leech' (5.581–2), on the behalf of the posthumous Timon.[19] Whether through a transmission of pathos or an interventionist act of civic renewal, the play is claimed to provide a potentially recuperative form of closure through the intervention of the military leader. Yet in this production, the denouement was revised in keeping with the changes to the status of Alcibiades. After Timon's departure and offstage suicide in 5.3, scenes were drastically truncated into a series of short, TV-like bulletins of Alcibiades' protests, culminating in his final appearance in a business suit to sit down at a press conference table and report Timon's death in an offhand and distracted tone while the senators ruffle through their notes. Crucially, his final line was interpolated from *As You Like It*: 'Now go we in content / To liberty and not to banishment' (1.3.134–5). The implication seemed to be that counter-cultural protest movements against power are destined to sell out; a cynical, if rather glib, way to impose some meaning onto the Folio's admittedly problematic and underwritten denouement. Moreover, the addition of Celia's line from the comedy, with its sarcastic use of 'liberty' as a politician's platitude, implied another sense of the anti-pastoral, whereby the promise of a green world turns out to be politics as usual. This could perhaps be understood as simply a dig at the UK Coalition Government and a suspicion of politicians in general, but it also seemed like an attempt to force the drama towards a sardonic and in some ways reassuringly familiar sense of an ending: we expect politicians to sell out, so nothing changes.[20] Perhaps this is also a measure of our distance from the Jacobean past; the heroic scenario Grady refers to, whereby Alcibiades could reinvigorate Athens by restoring it to virtue, seems a long way off from the norms of modern European democratic regimes.

A similar ambiguity of the production was in its reworking of the demotic impulse of the original play. By reinventing Alcibiades and his comrades as what the cast list called 'rebels', and keeping their presence as noises-off for much of the play, the suggestion was that this underclass or opposition was the excluded other of the moneyed, corrupt Athenian class we were watching: the 99%, as the Occupy slogan would have it. The brigands and rebellious soldiers of the Folio text became the economically and politically subordinate, closer in fact to the spirit of the Greek *demos*. This was not just implied metonymically though costume, but also in inference. For example, in the Folio, the thieves take the gold from Timon because it seems to be in keeping with their venal nature (4.3.399–401); the mob that scrambled for gold here did not necessarily present a better picture of civility (and maybe provided a topical allusion to the widespread suburban looting in London during summer 2011), but they also served to represent an idea of a wider political community within the plot. Their complaint that 'We cannot live on grass, on berries, water, / As beast and birds and fishes' (4.3.417–8) riles Timon but can after all be understood as a legitimate statement of political need. The production invited the audience to identify with the rebels against the complacency of the senate, but even with the revisions to the text it could not develop the crowd in a more profound or sympathetic way, which might also explain the truncated and sour denouement. At this point the desire of the directors to translate the text into contemporary idiom seemed at its most strained; the desire to find a contemporary, liberal and democratic nuance in the play a step too far. Shakespeare and Middleton's notion of an Athenian commonwealth remains too distant from consumer democracy.

Ultimately, these problems of the production also revealed the difficulties of introducing Shakespeare as a commentary on the contemporary credit crunch. The promise of this production, which is also partly the promise of presentism, was that our anxieties about the current downturn could somehow be addressed through the power of Shakespeare (and, by implication, Middleton). Their satirical-tragedy presented audiences with an unflattering, comic portrait of Athenian decadence and a relatively sympathetic account of the man who the middle of humanity never knew, but the extremity of both ends (4.3.300). Yet the Jacobean moral economy of the play, in which money is related to the individual vice of profligacy, is not identical to our developed capitalist economy dependent on maximizing profit, no more than the text's curt impression of the Athenian commonwealth could fully resemble contemporary mass democracy. Instead, the drama persists as a form of early-modern fable, censuring its audience (then and now) on the dangers of gold and the horror of impoverishment. A sign of this is the text's own indication that it follows a *de casibus* tradition of tragedy as the fall of great men to fortune. In the opening scene, the poet gives a rather traditional explanation of tragic fortune that turns out to be a foreshadowing of the entire plot:

> When Fortune in her shift and change of mood
> Spurns down her late beloved, all his dependents,
> Which laboured after him to the mountain's top
> Even on their knees and hands, let him slip down,
> Not one accompanying his declining foot. (1.1.86–90)

The eventual design of *Timon of Athens* as a drama may derive from this notion of time and fate as a tragic condition of fortune. Yet in the twenty-first century, are our general expectations of capitalist boom and bust, prosperity and recession, investment and default, popularly understood as essentially tragic? It might well be claimed instead that modernity comprehends the fluctuations of economic cycles as the sign of a risk culture that is not seen as inherently tragic.[215] In other words, Timon's ruin may elicit pathos, but his generosity may not really work as an effective allegory of the downturn. This suggests a limitation of using Shakespeare's seventeenth-century anti-capitalism as if it was our contemporary. Moreover, the production also exposed some of the conditions of the local and the global in contemporary, international Shakespearean performance. For the production comprehended the conflict in the drama by familiarizing it to contemporary London, but, almost despite itself, it could not fail to evoke a wider set of contemporary associations – to trans-national protest movements, pathology, the allure of capital – that exceeded that context. In widening the scope of the play to try and examine the global downturn, the production drew attention to what was absent, that global dimension of the recession that has become part of everyday knowledge. Perhaps this marks a limitation of any topical, big-time, British-themed Shakespeare: that it is exceeded by the sense of the global. The sense of otherness and excess may also be a major literary legacy of this strange play about madness and disappointment, in which the tragic power of money and fortune ruins a fallible, well-meaning citizen. Audiences today might speculate in what ways our own experience of the allure, risk and *peripeteia* of the modern market economy is indeed our own experience of the tragic.

James Tink is Associate Professor in the Department of English Literature at the Graduate School of Arts and Letters, Tohoku University, Sendai, Japan. He specializes in early-modern literature, contemporary British fiction and literary theory. He is co-editor (with Sarah Bezan) of the volume *Seeing Animals After Derrida* (Lexington Books, 2018).

Notes

Originally published as James Tink, 'Staging Timon of Athens in the Downturn', *Shakespeare Review* vol. 50, issue 55 (2012), 155–170.

1. See Graham Holderness, *The Shakespeare Myth: essays in cultural materialism* (Manchester: Manchester University Press, 1988).
2. John Jowett, Introduction to *Timon of Athens*, by William Shakespeare (Oxford: Oxford University Press, 2004), 106–107.
3. Ibid., 97–99.
4. Karl Marx, *Early Writings*, trans. Rodney Livingstone and Gregor Benton (Harmondsworth, Penguin, 1992), 376–77.
5. Michael Bristol, *Big-Time Shakespeare* (London & New York: Routledge, 1996), 3–4.
6. Terence Hawkes, 'Band of Brothers', in *Presentist Shakespeares*, ed. Hugh Grady and Terence Hawkes (London & New York: Routledge, 2007), 14–18.
7. William Shakespeare, *Timon of Athens*, ed. Anthony B. Dawson and Gretchen E. Minton (London: Cengage Learning, 2008), 431–32.
8. The textual revisions to the play were notified (without any further details) in the programme notes for the production.
9. All citations are from *Timon of Athens* Arden Third Series, ed. Dawson and Minton.
10. On the idea of usury, see Hugh Grady, *Shakespeare and Impure Aesthetics* (Cambridge: Cambridge University Press, 2009), 113–14. On gift-giving, see Coppélia Kahn. '"Magic of County": *Timon of Athens*, Jacobean Patronage, and Maternal Power', *Shakespeare Quarterly* 38, no. 1 (Spring 1987): 34–57.
11. Margot Heinemann, *Puritanism & Theatre: Thomas Middleton and Opposition Drama under the Early Stuarts* (Cambridge: Cambridge University Press, 1980), 174.
12. See paragraph eighteen of Quentin Letts, '*Timon of Athens*: Greedy Greeks, huge debts... it's a Timon of our times', *Daily Mail*, July 19, 2012. https://www.dailymail.co.uk/tvshowbiz/article-2176204/Timon-Of-Athens-Greedy-Greeks-huge-debts--Timon-times.html
13. On the idea of *otium*, see Brian Vickers, 'Leisure and Idleness in the Renaissance: the ambivalence of otium', *Renaissance Studies* 4, no. 1–2 (1990), 1–154.

14. Yannis Stavrakakis, 'Debt Society: Greece and the Future of Post-Democracy', *Radical Philosophy* 181 (September/October 2013): 35. PIIGS was the journalistic acronym for Portugal, Ireland, Italy, Greece and Spain, the economies most at risk in the Eurozone crisis after 2008.
15. Jowett, Introduction to *Timon of Athens*, 106.
16. Marx, *Early Writings*, 375–79; G. Wilson-Knight, *The Wheel of Fire: Essays in Interpretation of Shakespeare's Sombre Tragedies* (Oxford: Oxford University Press, 1930), 227–262; Kahn, 'Magic of Bounty', 41; Ken Jackson, '"One Wish" or the Possibility of the Impossible: Derrida, the Gift, and God in *Timon of Athens*', *Shakespeare Quarterly* 52, no. 1 (Spring 2001): 34–66.
17. Slavoj Žižek, *The Year of Living Dangerously* (London: Verso, 2012), 124.
18. Ibid., 123.
19. Kiernan Ryan, '"Here's fine revolution": Shakespeare's Philosophy of the Future', *Essays in Criticism* 63, no.2 (2013): 121; this argument is also developed by Ryan in *Shakespeare's Universality: Here's Fine Revolution* (London: Bloomsbury, 2015), 109–128. Grady, *Shakespeare and Impure Aesthetics*, 128–29.
20. That the actor playing Alcibiades, Ciaráran McMenamin , spoke with a Northern Irish accent may also have evoked for some of the audience the situation of power sharing in Northern Ireland since the Good Friday Agreement of 1997.
21. The concept of capitalist modernity as a 'risk society' has been explored by Anthony Giddens and Ulrich Beck; see Philip Smith and Alexander Riley, *Cultural Theory: An Introduction* (Malden MA: Blackwell, 2009), 128–29.

Chapter 7
'Fill Thy Purse With Money'
Financing Performance in Shakespearean England

Tiffany Stern

If there was one thing that was a given about early modern players and playwrights, it was that they were poor – so much so that stories of their poverty were staples of anecdotes and jokes. One jest tells of a player who woke in the night to find thieves in his house. He was astonished: 'I wonder what you would finde here in the night, whereas I can finde nothing here in cleare day'.[1] Another explains how players – whether shareholders in their company (sharers) or hired by the day (hirelings) – depended on performance for money. If theatres were forcibly shut, as happened most summers, actors were destitute. As a result players were as 'afraid of the plague, as [...] a cowherd of a musket: for as death is formidable to the one, so is povertie and wants to the other'.[2]

Playwrights, likewise, were famous as much for their poverty as for their skill. They were often instantly recognizable simply by the pitiable state of their clothes: one jest calls a young playwright

Notes for this section begin on page 122.

a 'thred-bare contemned Urchin'; another depicts a pair of 'thred-bare' playwrights who are, it goes on, 'men that want [lack] mony more then wit'.[3] Nor were these descriptions confined to minor or would-be playwrights: recognized and established writers were, it was understood, doomed to poverty. Thomas Heywood, for instance, well-known for having a hand in over two hundred and twenty plays – including several sole-authored plays like *The Golden Age* – was mocked because 'Well of the Golden age he could intreat, / But little of the Mettal he could get'.[4]

Shakespeare, who was both an actor and a playwright, might therefore be assumed to have lived in the poverty that typified both his trades. And yet, as all biographies make clear, Shakespeare subsisted in comfort and retired with a sum of money healthy enough to buy the second largest house in Stratford-upon-Avon. His wealth will, of course, partly have stemmed from the money given him by his wily father, together with the additional money he seems to have received from his literary patron, Henry Wriothesley, the third Earl of Southampton. But as Shakespeare ploughed such money as he had acquired into his theatre, becoming a 'sharer' (an investor in his company) in 1594, and a 'housekeeper' (an investor in the theatres used by his company) in 1599, his ultimate wealth will have resulted not from inheritance, gifts – or playwriting or acting – but from receiving daily a cut of the entrance fees paid by spectators.

This chapter will consider Shakespeare as a sharer/householder for his company and will examine the financial priorities that came with his investment. It will explore the way Shakespeare's theatres, and all theatres of the time, were, because of the sharing system, focussed on making money as much as producing successful plays: food, drink, books, tobacco and personal adornments were sold in the theatrical precinct. What, it will question, did Shakespeare, a shareholder and housekeeper but also a writer and actor, feel about the incessant playhouse trading on which his financial success partly depended?

In 1594 Shakespeare made one of the greatest investments of his life. He gave a substantial down-payment to purchase a one-eighth share in the Lord Chamberlain's Men, the company for which he was acting and writing. No longer was his income reliant on revenue from performing or playwriting. Now it was dependent, instead, on audience revenue. This only intensified when, in 1599, he additionally became a housekeeper for the company. Now, through paying for maintenance of the theatrical buildings, he would receive an even greater share of the theatre's daily takings.

From 1594 onwards, then, Shakespeare will, play-by-play and day-by-day, have needed to care how much money his company was making. For *sharer* described not only the portion of money put into the theatre but also the portion taken out. As a contract for a different theatre, the Fortune, makes clear, it was usual that after 'evry day that any play [...] [was] exercised in the play howse' there would be a 'sharinge of the monies gathered and gotten att evry of the same'.[5] The money received from that performance's entrance fees would be pooled 'upon the shearing-board' (sharing table) and then 'parcel'd out', as Brome explains, to each sharer and housekeeper according to the quantity of investment initially put in.[6] That meant that each investor was reminded of the largeness or smallness of his original outlay every day. It also meant that each investor measured performances against one another in terms of the cash they yielded. Money seemed, at least to some sharers / housekeepers, more meaningful than details of the play that had produced it: 'the matter is not great what part the Player acts, whether of a begger or of a King; all the matter is, what share hee shall receive when the Play is ended'.[7]

Companies of the time, made up largely of investors, reflected sharers' and housekeepers' values.[8] They were dedicated to making money – through plays, of course, but also through other means. Trips to the theatre came to be, perhaps as a marketing strategy, associated positively with spending money. Whenever a 'restraint' closed the Rose theatre – a round theatre on the Surrey side of the Thames – petitions for it to be reopened concentrated on the positive value of the money expended in reaching it. Two surviving pleas from c.1592, which may be linked or may simply be representative, make this point.[9] One is by the theatre company; it argues that the 'plaiehowse on the Banckside, by reason of the passage to and frome the same by water, is a greate releif to the poore watermen'.[10] The other is by the watermen; they maintain that 'your [...] poore watermen have had muche helpe and reliefe for vs oure poore wives and Children by meanes of the resorte of suche people as come vnto the [...] playe howse'.[11] Both petitions were apparently organized by Philip Henslowe, financier of the Rose theatre; both are of course exploiting the plight of the watermen in the hope of getting the theatre reopened. Yet the documents also serve to remind the Privy Council, to whom they are addressed, that travel to theatres provided essential employment – and money – for attendant trades, and thus was economically good for the city and its environs. John Taylor, waterman and poet (known as 'the waterpoet'), makes a similar point. Describing why he petitioned the king 'that the Players might not have a play-house in London or in Middlesex', he explains that 'the Globe, the Rose, and the Swan' result in 'great concourse of people by water', and that the watermen will be made destitute if the players move.[12] Behind all such manipulative pleas is the understanding that part of the 'treat' of going to the theatre for the audience is the vehicular travel used to get there: spending money was an aspect of enjoying a day at the theatre.

So connected were playhouses and costly travel that when theatrical events did not go well, the spectators were as furious about the amount spent to reach them as they were about the poor entertainment. John Taylor writes of the time he hired the Hope playhouse for a poetic wit battle between himself and rival poet William Fennor. When Fennor did not turn up, leaving Taylor lamely reciting poems by himself, the spectators were outraged. The Hope, like the Rose, Swan and Globe, was situated over the Thames in Surrey, and to reach it from London spectators either had to pay a waterman to ferry them over the river or pay a toll to cross by land over London Bridge:

> Great cause they had to take it in offence,
> To come from their Affaires with such expence
> By Land and Water, and then at the play
> So extraordinarily to pay [...].[13]

The association between costly transport and a trip to the theatre continued to be made throughout the early modern period. Tellingly, London's private indoor theatres, though situated in liberties within the city (so getting to them did not involve a trip over the water) remained associated with expensive travel. The indoor theatre in which Shakespeare's company performed from c.1609, Blackfriars Playhouse, was, in particular, always 'Attended on with Coaches'.[14] Indeed, by 1631, the number and size of the vehicles going to Blackfriars had become so overwhelming that locals in the area mounted a petition complaining of *'Hindrance to the shopkeepers from the great recourse to the plays [...] of coaches'*.[15] Coaches broadcast the wealth and disposable income of the theatre-goers – and protected their fine clothes – but they also bolstered the idea that expensive travel was more than necessary for a trip to the theatre: it was a reason to go to the theatre in the first place. Travel, however, would not directly yield profit to the sharers / housekeepers, though it would put the audience in the right frame of mind for further expenditure. For investors to make serious money through the theatre, they had to make sure audiences would spend capital for and in the playhouse itself.

As was to be expected, the playhouse's door of entrance, public or private, was flanked by 'door-keepers' (sometimes also called 'gatherers' because they gathered coins) clutching pottery containers into which entrance fees had to be paid: playhouse and moneybox were thus met together. But, in a way that ensured that spending money remained a focus of the theatre trip, further money would need to be dropped into further moneyboxes if the spectator wanted to a good seat:

> whoever cares to stand below only pays one English penny, but if he wishes to sit he enters by another door, and pays anther penny, while if he desires to sit in the most comfortable seats which are cushioned [...] then he pays yet another English penny at another door.[16]

Over time the cost of entrance and internal fees for theatres increased, but the geography of place and payment remained the same: the playhouse, area by area, constantly asked spectators to pay, and repay, for the same event. Indeed, sections of the theatre, though sometimes named by their position or function – yard, box, gallery – were often described instead by the amount of money paid to reach them: the 'two penny gallery', the 'six penny room' and so forth. The layout of the theatre, understood in financial, as much as spatial, terms, reflected the values of the investors who collectively owned the spaces.

Money for entrance was not just a source of revenue for sharers and housekeepers, however. It also provided significant extra income for door-keepers. Famously untrustworthy, door-keepers were accused of collecting coins into their hands rather than their boxes; they would then 'scratch their heads where they itch not, and drop shillings and half-Crowne pieces in at their collars'.[17] Thomas Dekker, when praying that a new play goes down well, also prays that it acquires 'One Honest Doore-keeper'.[18] The very dishonesty of the door-keepers, however, testifies to the focus on money shared by theatre personnel. Money's look, sound and smell was part of the atmosphere of the playhouse, and everyone who worked for the theatre wanted it.

In order for theatres to do really well financially, whatever the quality of the play, companies provided an additional diversion – or, rather, a series of diversions – that could be guaranteed to be enjoyable and profitable to all concerned: shopping. For as long as spectators were in the theatre, 'hawkers' (travelling salesmen) sold them things to eat and drink. As Thomas Platter, a Swiss visitor to England in the 1590s, recalls, at London playhouses 'during the performance food and drink are carried round the audience, so that for what one cares to pay one may also have refreshment'.[19] A rich range of comestibles were available. To drink, one could buy water from 'a Water-bearer on the floore of a Play-house', as well as wine and ale in bottles: indeed, 'A base Mercenary Poet' (i.e. a poor and impecunious playwright) was said to hope, on hearing his play hissed, that 'bottle-Ale is opening'.[20] To eat there was, as shells excavated at the Rose playhouse attest, a variety of shellfish on offer, including cockles, periwinkles, crabs, mussels and oysters, which explains the 'Oyster-crying audience' complained of in *This Worlds Folly*.[21] There were, as husks at the Rose further reveal, walnuts and large quantities of hazelnuts available; that the sound of nutcracking sometimes overwhelmed the performance is attested by Edmund Gayton: 'at the Play-houses, betwixt the Acts, / The Musick Room is drown'd with these Nut-cracks'.[22] Additional snacks included other 'fruits [...] and nuts, according to the season' as well as dried fruits – seeds at the Rose suggest raisons and figs were popular.[23] Some playhouse food has left only textual (rather than archaeological) traces: a puny clerk is described by Overbury as someone who 'eats Gingerbread at a Play-house'; an obscene man is one who, '[b]eing at a Play in the Theatre', goes to 'those which sel nuts and apples, and other fruits' and 'taketh them away and muncheth them; and wrangleth about their price'; a lawyer's clerk is so penny-pinching that '[a]t a new play, he buyes his pippins [a *pippin* being a sweet or dessert apple] before he goes in, because hee can have more for mony'.[24]

It is the fresh fruit, however, that is most regularly referred to, probably because of the literal impact it had on performance: it was liable to be thrown at the stage at the beginning and end of plays. Edmund Gayton explains how, when 'the popular humour' had been unsatisfied by a drama, 'Oranges, Apples, Nuts, flew about most liberally'; and John Tatham wearily requests spectators to 'forbeare /

Your wonted custome, banding Tyle, or Peare, / Against our curtaines, to allure us forth'.[25] Clowns may even have had, as one of their jobs, the task of dealing with over-zealous fruit-hurlers (they might, of course, also have attracted them). Jestbooks record the responses of Richard Tarlton, the preeminent clown of the 1580s, when 'one from the Gallery threw a Pippin at him', and when hit by 'an apple [...] on the face'.[26] Nevertheless, particularly unpopular plays were regularly 'pippin-pelted from the stage'[27] – hence the punning term 'pelting comedies', meaning comedies that were on one level paltry, on another, likely to attract fruit.

Though records are sparse and frustratingly oblique, it seems possible that sharers and housekeepers, who allowed sellers of food and drink into the theatre, may also have organized them. John Heminges, a Globe sharer, seems to have owned a taphouse next door to the Globe so he could provide beer for audiences, and 'the odds are', opines Gurr, that he ran it on behalf of the company with 'the money being shared'.[28] If that is so, then hawkers, too, may have been dispensing drink and food for the company, further contributing to the sharers' profit. If that is not so, then hawkers will still have profited the theatre: they are likely to have paid at least a kickback to sharers / housekeepers in addition, of course, to paying entrance charges for, presumably, each area of the playhouse.[29] Most importantly, they supplied the audience with something it enjoyed and thus increased the sense that the theatre was a place in which pleasure could be acquired – for money.

Yet for Shakespeare, a writer – which was unusual in a sharer / housekeeper – as well as an actor, the theatrical sale of food and drink was probably a source of conflicted pleasure. Like other sharers, he will of necessity have had the theatre's financial interests at heart. Unlike them, however, he is likely to have had a predominantly artistic and intellectual investment in the plays his company mounted. The depictions above have shown how noisy and disturbing audience-trading will have been and how the sound, sight and smell of food will have provided distractions from the stage. As an author, Shakespeare seems to have been dismayed by the spectators diverted from performance by their own snacks. This is suggested when, in *Henry VIII*, the porter declaims against 'the youths that thunder at a Playhouse, and fight for bitten Apples' (3318–3319);[30] that same porter had earlier asked whether the 'rude Raskalls' are hoping to get 'Ale, and Cakes heere' (3267–3268). Other nuanced food and drink references – to, for instance, nuts ('thou wilt quarrell with a man for cracking Nuts' [*RJ*, 1449–1450]) – may also be traceable to this. Shakespeare, that is to say, may have thought one way as a sharer / housekeeper; another as an author.

Shakespeare may, too, have had an ambivalent approach to theatrical salesmen. When creating Autolycus, rogue salesman and thief in *The Winter's Tale*, he imagines a man who hawks ribbons, gloves and printed ballads together from the same tray; his 'Trafficke', he claims, 'is sheetes' (1691), seemingly conflating in one word printed papers and stolen bed-linen. Given that Henry Parrot maintains hawkers 'at Play-houses' are likely to add books to their trays to be 'mongst Pippins sold', Autolycus' mixed attitude and assorted goods are those of the theatrical tradesmen.[31] Staged in front of his 'real' counterparts (and perhaps engaging with them), Autolycus might have come across as a comment, a parody, a homage, a taunt – or some strange mixture of all of those.

At the same time, Shakespeare's company are likely to have done what they could to exploit the selling possibilities offered by hawkers. They may even have been involved in one of theatre's other major trades: bookselling. For the theatre, a place in which lovers of history, fiction and literature were gathered together, was naturally a location for selling printed literature – not least because spectators, who often arrived well before performance to secure themselves reasonable seats (there being no fixed seating in the early modern playhouse), tended to want lasting distractions with which to pass the time. William Fennor anticipates that his book *Fennors Descriptions* 'will hap into your hands, before a play begin, with the importunate clamour, of *Buy a new Booke*, by some needy companion', while Catchmey, the vicar in Cartwright's play *The Ordinarie* (3.5), details the wide range of publications to be found in a theatrical bookseller's tray:

> I shall live to see thee
> Stand in a Play-house doore with thy long box,
> Thy half-crown Library, and cry small Books.
> By a good godly Sermon Gentlemen –
> A judgment shewn upon a Knot of Drunkards –
> A pill to purge out Popery – The life
> And death of Katherin Stubs [...].[32]

As this list suggests, lurid tales that are short, rich in humour and hatred, but made 'allowable' by moral content, were theatrical staples; in terms of content, they provided the kinds of stories audiences were likely to see in plays anyway.

For Shakespeare, bookselling in the theatre had the potential to be awkward: what playwright would want his audience's attention diverted by books? On the other hand, he and his company may have exploited the opportunity / necessity. Thomas Middleton, who signs his own epistle to the readers before the 1611 edition of *The Roaring Girl* (suggesting he is involved in its publication) hopes his playbook will 'be allowed [...] Gallery room at the play-house'; as he expects it will be read there, he is likely to anticipate it will be sold there too.[33] Theatrical companies, whose 'release' of plays to the press has always seemed surprising, may have allowed some plays to be published in order to profit not only from the advertising they supplied, but also from the sales they would bring when retailed in the theatre. This is, of course, speculation. Yet it is instructive to consider the frequency with which 'residuals' of the dramas (this useful term is Bruce R. Smith's) were potentially generated by some of Shakespeare's plays. Bottom in *A Midsummer Night's Dream* refers to a ballad, *'Bottomes Dreame'*, to be sung at 'the latter end of a play' (1742–1743) – he may be gesturing at a lost song, but he may also be promoting a text that could have been hawked to spectators after performance; ditto Autolycus' 'very true' ballads which, having been sold in *The Winter's Tale*, could theoretically have been sold after it too. Certainly 'residual' texts about plays – particularly obvious for theatrical sale – were often printed, including a ballad about *Titus Andronicus*, a ballad about *King Lear* and a chapbook – George Wilkins's *The Painfull Adventures of Pericles Prince of Tyre* – about the play *Pericles*.[34] It is certainly worth reconsidering the relationships between book publication, the publication of 'residuals', theatre performance and theatre sales. They were, perhaps, mutually organized and mutually beneficial, rather than at odds with one another.

Even, however, if none of this is the case, the theatre will still have profited from theatrical booksellers. If the company did not control the books in the hawkers' trays, they may still have taken a share of their profits or received a retainer from them – in addition, again, to entrance fees. They will, too, have profited from the satisfaction, as well as the continued cash flow, of the audience brought about through books. If, by any chance, the play on stage was not going down well, books will have given spectators an alternative means of entertainment and another reason, beyond plays, to return to the playhouse.

Books, however, were only of interest to the literate. Not so another good that was sold in theatres: the newly-available drug that had taken the country by storm, tobacco. Tobacco was desired by all ranks of education and society so that, as Dekker wrote in 1609, the playhouse had become a place where 'your Stinkard has the selfe-same libertie to be there in his Tobacco-Fumes, which your sweet Courtier hath'.[35] Tobacco sales increased rapidly from the 1590s onwards, and by the time the playhouses were closed for the interregnum, going to theatres and taking tobacco were so closely linked that a pamphlet only half-ironically lamented the lot of '[t]he tobacco-man' – cheaters keen to make money, like so many other theatrical personnel – who 'used to walke up and downe, selling for a penny pipe, that which was not worth twelve pence an horse-load'.[36]

Shakespeare, conscious of theatrical sales of tobacco, may have used their effect. From 1609 onwards, he was writing plays for an enclosed space, the Blackfriars Playhouse, as well as an outdoor space, the Globe. And, while tobacco smoked outside will have dispersed into the air, tobacco smoked indoors will have lingered, affecting both smell and visibility. It is notable that Shakespeare's post-1609 plays, written partly with an indoor theatre in mind, contain lost people seemingly unable to see their way through a haze that is part-magical, part-mental – but perhaps also part-physical. In *The Tempest* Ferdinand 'hath lost his fellowes, / And strayes about to finde 'em' (560–561); his father, meanwhile, concludes 'Whom thus we stray to finde' is drowned, 'and the Sea mocks / Our frustrate search on land' (1524–1526); in *Cymbeline* '[t]wo Beggers told me, / I could not misse my way', says lost Posthumous, 'Will poore Folkes lye' (2089–2090). In a theatre in which the smoke of tobacco joined the smoke from candles, compromising visibility and making eyes smart, the environment was already miasmic. It is possible that Shakespeare was using as staging effect – or inspiration – the smoke trapped in the indoor theatre, and that the drowsy magic for which his later plays are prized might additionally emerge from purchases made in the playhouse itself.[37]

What furthers this possibility is the fact that Shakespeare seems to have exploited other Blackfriars sales in his plays. The Blackfriars playhouse was, like the whole Blackfriars district, renowned as a place in which to buy decorative feathers as an accessory. So in *Muses Looking Glasse*, two hawkers, Bird and Mrs Flowerdew, are depicted inside the Blackfriars theatre, 'the one having brought feathers to the Play-house, the other Pins and Looking-glasses'. Though they are Puritans and dislike plays, they have paid entrance to the theatre and are likely to have paid something more for the right to trade. Flowerdew is, however, so constitutionally averse to being in the playhouse that she starts to feel squeamish about the source of the money she will make:

Flowerdew	[...] it something pricks my Conscience,
	I come to sell 'em Pins and Looking-glasses.
Bird	I have their custome too for all their feathers:
	'Tis fit that we which are sincere Professors
	Should gain by Infidels.[38]

The Puritans, states Bird, will literally 'gain' from the purchasing theatre-goers; descriptions of feathered audiences at Blackfriars suggest they often did. Nathaniel Richards describes 'a Glitering Smocke Gallannt sitting at a Play' in Blackfriars who flaunts 'Hat and Feather', and another sitting 'yonder on the stage, / With the huge feather'; in *Notes from Blackfriars* Fitzgeffrey singles out an annoying audience-member as a 'plumed Dandebrat'.[39]

With feathers fastened to their hats by the pins they had also bought (the effect presumably admired in the mirrors additionally purchased), the audience at Blackfriars will have looked colourful, sumptuous and slightly absurd. Again, the feathered environment seems to be echoed in the late plays. In *The Tempest*, Ariel is befeathered when '*like a Harpey*' he '*claps his wings upon the Table*' (1583–1584). Time, the chorus in *A Winter's Tale*, takes it upon himself 'To vse my wings' (1583), again seemingly illustrating the transience of time with his feathers. In *Cymbeline* Jupiter appears to Posthumous bethroned, it seems, in feathers: he is '*sitting uppon an Eagle*' (3126–3127).[40] These references may reflect the ease of purchase of feathers in the Blackfriars district; but they may, too, be a way of confronting the spectators with their form and likeness – and turning it into something rich, strange and a little amusing.

Only one theatre purchase is utterly bleak. Prostitutes were, it was well known, available for sale in the theatres: indeed, the low reputation in which all theatres were held was partly connected to this. John Green in his *Refutation of the Apology for Actors* provides a list of those who 'runne madding unto playes' – he details 'the baudes to intice, the whores and courtesans to set themselves to sale'; Alexander Leighton even claimed that 'whoredome is sometimes committed at that place [the playhouse]' – which, again, would entirely divert attention from the stage.[41]

This trade may have been one to which the theatre simply turned a blind eye, while acknowledging that some audience members came with the intention of making a sexual purchase (without having to enter a house of sale). That means, however, that Shakespeare's prostitution, from the somewhat sympathetic portrayal of Doll Tearsheet to the dreadful bawd in *Pericles*, was depicted in front of trading women; stage prostitutes will have had an aggressive and disturbingly immediate and real metatheatrical side. It is of course also possible that theatres engaged more fundamentally in these sales. Certainly Philip Henslowe, financier of the Rose theatre, had investments in bawdyhouses: perhaps the two trades of theatre and prostitution were linked as taphouses and theatres seem to have been.

Whether selling was organized or simply sanctioned by theatrical companies, salesmen and women filled the theatres – meaning that audiences needed to come to plays with substantial sums of money. Money, then, became another audience preoccupation which, like the things it purchased, was liable to upstage the drama. Many jokes of the period, indeed, arise from the fact that plays were watched with an eye on the stage and another on one's purse: 'A Gsentleman at a Play sate by a fellow that he strongly suspected for a Cutt-purse, and for the probation of him, tooke occasion to draw out his purse [...] (but his eye watcht it strictly with a glance)';[42] 'A country gentleman suspecting himselfe at a play to be among some roring boyes who would cut his purse, put all his gold in his mouth'.[43] After George Peele, a playwright, had been robbed at a play, he returned to the theatre with fish-hooks sewn into his pocket; he 'seemed to affect the Play very well' and by so doing managed to entrap a thief who put his 'hand in George his pocket, and could not pull it out [...]. People thronged after to see this new Comedy, and so forsooke the other Play'.[44] It seems that plays, whoever they were by, were performed against a background of people burdened and regularly diverted by their own finances.

That makes Shakespeare's constant, and constantly ambivalent, concentration on money particularly interesting. He is fascinated by the way money diverts focus away from what actually matters. *The Merchant of Venice* is a story about the competing claims of money versus love, but that is a topic to which Shakespeare regularly turns. He also uses a fixation on money as a way of illustrating a character with bad values: Iago reveals his nature to the audience by enjoining Roderigo, on his own behalf, to 'Put Money in thy purse [...] put Money in thy purse [...] put Money in thy purse [...] put but Money in thy purse [...] fill thy purse with Money' (*Oth*, 692–699). *Troilus and Cressida*, too, argues Douglas Bruster, shows lapsed morality as a negative product of 'an entire system of commerce'.[45] In *Timon of Athens* Shakespeare goes a step further. The hero, reduced to penury, digs for something nourishing to eat – roots – and finds, instead, something that can yield no sustenance: 'Yellow, glittering, precious Gold' (1628). Thus Shakespeare makes visual the bible's metaphor that 'money is the root of all evil' (*1 Timothy* 6:10).[46]

This chapter has suggested that Shakespeare may have been disquieted by money and disturbed by the audience's constant spending. In this way he will have shared concerns with anti-theatricalists who were outraged about money 'lost' on fripperies in the theatre. William Prynne suggested that spectators may

> according to their severall qualities spend 2.d. 3.d. 4.d. [...] and sometimes 4. or 5. shillings at a Play-house, day by day, if Coach-hire, Boate-hire, Tobacco, Wine, Beere, and suchlike vaine expences which Playes doe usually occasion, be cast into the reckoning.[47]

Conscious that each non-play purchase set up a rival source of interest to the play on stage, Shakespeare may sometimes have attacked or parodied the acquisitive audience, and sometimes acquiesced to them; sometimes used them, and sometimes, particularly in his later plays, integrated their goods into his metatheatre. It is also possible that, over time, Shakespeare became more acquiescent or more reconciled to theatrical trading, or at least more subservient to the money he seems to have despised and wanted. He was, throughout his writing career, conscious of money's negative qualities – but this chapter has suggested that he found ways of confronting theatrical trade that were artistically, but still also financially, profitable.

Tiffany Stern is Professor of Shakespeare and Early Modern Drama at the Shakespeare Institute, University of Birmingham. She specializes in sixteenth- to eighteenth century drama, Shakespeare, theatre history, book history and editing. Her books are *Rehearsal from Shakespeare to Sheridan* (2000), *Making Shakespeare* (2004), *Shakespeare in Parts* (with Simon Palfrey, 2007) and *Documents of Performance in Early Modern England* (2009). She is co-editor of the New Mermaids and Arden Shakespeare Fourth series, and her current projects include a book on theatre and fairs, a book on documents beyond performance, and a new edition of *The Tempest*.

Notes

Originally published as Tiffany Stern, '"Fill thy purse with money": financing performance in Shakespearean England', *Shakespeare Jahrbuch* (2014), and is here republished by kind permission of the editors and the Shakespeare-Deutsche-Gesellschaft.

1. H. L, *Gratiae Ludentes* (London: Thomas Cotes for Humphrey Mosley, 1628), 180–181.
2. T. Gainsford, *The Rich Cabinet* (London: John Beale for Roger Jackson 1616), 116.
3. William Rowley, *A Search for Money* (London: Joseph Hunt, 1609), B3r.
4. *Choyce Drollery* (London: J. G. for Robert Pollard and John Sweeting, 1656), 6.
5. 'Lease of one thirty-second part of the Fortune, 1608' (not executed), in *The Henslowe Papers*, ed. by W. W. Greg (London: A. H. Bullen, 1907), 13.
6. Richard Brome, *The English Moor*, in *Five New Playes* (London: A. Crook and H. Brome, 1659), 86.
7. Richard Baker, *Meditations and Disquisitions upon the Lords Prayer* (London: Anne Griffin for Anne Bouler, 1636), 133.
8. For a description of the way players and entrepreneurs joined forces to fashion a theatre industry in London between 1560 and 1590, see William Ingram, *The Business of Playing: The Beginnings of the Adult Professional Theater in Elizabethan London* (Ithaca, NY: Cornell University Press, 1992).
9. Carol Chillington Rutter (ed.), *Documents of the Rose Playhouse* (Manchester: Manchester University Press, 1984), 63.
10. 'Petition from Lord Strange's Men', in Rutter (1984), 65.
11. 'Petition from Her Majesty's Watermen', in Rutter (1984), 65.
12. John Taylor, *The Watermens Suit Concerning Players* (c.1614), A2r, A3r.
13. John Taylor, *Taylors Revenge* (Rotterdam 1615), B3r.
14. Wye Saltonstall, *Picturae Loquentes* (London: Thomas Cotes for William Hope, 1631), G11r.
15. Undated Petition c. 1631 in *Calendar of State Papers, Domestic Series, of the Reign of Charles I*, vol. 5 ed. by John Bruce (London: Longman, Green, Longman & Roberts, 1860), 220.
16. Thomas Platter, 'Journal', in *The Journals of Two Travellers in Elizabethan and Early Stuart England: Thomas Platter and Horatio Busino*, ed. by P. E. Razzell (London: Caliban Books, 1995), 27–28.
17. *The Actors Remonstrance, or Complaint* (London: Edward Nickson, 1643), 6.
18. Thomas Dekker, *If It Be Not Good, the Divel Is In It* (London: J. T., 1612), A3v.
19. Platter (1995), 28.
20. Sir Thomas Overburie, *His Wife With New Elegies* (London: Edward Griffin for Laurence L'isle, 1616), G6r; John Stephens, 'A Base Mercenary Poet', in *Satirical Essays* (London: Nicholas Okes for Roger Barnes, 1615), 292.
21. Julian Bowsher / Pat Miller, *The Rose and the Globe: Playhouses of Shakespeare's Bankside, Southwark* (London: Lavenham Press, 2009), 148–153; I. H., *This Worlds Folly* (London: William Iaggard for Nicholas Bourne, 1615), B2r. For more on foods sold in early modern theatres, see Natasha Korda, *Labors Lost: Women's Work and the Early Modern English Stage* (Philadelphia: University of Pennsylvania Press, 2011), 146.

22. Edmund Gayton, *The Art of Longevity* (London 1659), 81.
23. Paul Hentzner, *A Journey into England by Paul Hentzner in the year 1598. Being a Part of His Itinerary*, ed. by Horace Walpole, trans. by R. Bentley (Twickenham 1757), 43.
24. Overburie (1616), I1r; Jo Healey, *Epictetus Manuall. Cebes Table. Thephrastus Characters* (London: George Purslowe for Edward Blount, 1616), L9v; Saltonstall, (1631), D3v.
25. Edmund Gayton, *Pleasant Notes upon Don Quixot* (London: William Hunt, 1654), 271; John Tatham, *The Fancies Theater* (London: John Norton for Richard Best, 1640), H3r.
26. Richard Tarlton, *Tarltons Jeasts* (London: J. H. for Andrew Crook, 1638), B2r.
27. Thomas Brande, address to Laud, 8 November 1629, quoted in G. E. Bentley, *The Jacobean and Caroline Stage*. Vol. 1 (Oxford: Clarendon Press, 1941), 25; *Foure Letters and Certaine Sonnets: Especially touching Robert Greene, and other parties, by him abused* (1592), 52.
28. Andrew Gurr, *The Shakespeare Company, 1594–1642* (Cambridge: Cambridge University Press, 2004), 25.
29. For more on refreshments as a potential source of housekeeper income, see Melissa D. Aaron, *Global Economics: A History of the Theater Business, the Chamberlain's / King's Men, and Their Plays, 1599–1642* (Newark: University of Delaware Press, 2005), 50.
30. William Shakespeare, *Henry VIII*, ed. by Charlton Hinman. The Norton Facsimile: The First Folio of Shakespeare (New York: W. W. Norton & Company, 1968). All quotations from Shakespeare are taken from the Norton Facsimile, using the Through Line Numbering of that edition.
31. Henry Parrot, *The Mastive* (London: Thomas Creede for Richard Meighen and Thomas Jones, 1615), A4v.
32. William Fennor, *Fennors Descriptions* (London: Edward Griffin for George Gibbs, 1616), π1v; William Cartwright, *The Ordinary* (London: Humphrey Moseley, 1651), 52. For more on book sales in playhouses, see Tiffany Stern, 'Watching as Reading: The Audience and Written Text in the Shakespeare's Playhouse', in Laurie Maguire (ed.), *How to Do Things with Shakespeare: New Approaches, New Essays* (Oxford: Blackwell Publishing, 2008), 136–159.
33. Thomas Middleton, *The Roaring Girle* (London: Thomas Archer, 1611), A3r.
34. Bruce R. Smith, 'Shakespeare's Residuals: The Circulation of Ballads in Cultural Memory', in *Shakespeare and Elizabethan Popular Culture*, ed. by Stuart Gillespie / Neil Rhodes (London: Thomson Learning, 2006), 193–217.
35. Thomas Dekker, *The Guls Horne-booke* (London: R. S., 1609), 28.
36. *The Actors Remonstrance, or Complaint* (1643), 7. For more on tobacco in playhouses see Ann Jennalie Cook, *The Privileged Playgoers of Shakespeare's London, 1576–1642* (Princeton: Princeton University Press, 1981), 199–201; and Bowsher / Miller (2009), 154–157.
37. For more on smoke and metatheatre, see Tiffany Stern, 'Taking Part: Actors and Audience on the Stage at Blackfriars', in Paul Menzer (ed.), *Inside Shakespeare: Essays on the Blackfriars Stage* (Selinsgrove: Susquehanna University Press, 2006), 45–46.
38. Thomas Randolph, *The Muses Looking Glasse* (London 1643), A2r.

39. Nathaniel Richards, *The Celestiall Publican* (London: Felix Kyngston for Roger Michell, 1630), L4v; Henry Peacham, *Thalia's Banquet* (London: Nicholas Okes for Francis Constable, 1620), D4v; Henry Fitzgeffrey, *Satyres and Satyricall Epigrams: The Third Booke of Humours: Intituled Notes from Black-Fryers* (London: Edward All-de for Miles Patrich, 1617), F2r.
40. For more on feathers in the theatre, see Stern (2006), 42.
41. John Green, *A Refutation of the Apology for Actors* (London: W. White for Thomas Langley, 1615), 55–56; Alexander Leighton, *Short Treatise against Stage-Playes* (n. p. 1625), 20.
42. H. F. Lippincott (ed.), *'Merry Passages and Jeasts': A Manuscript Jestbook of Sir Nicholas Le Strange* (Salzburg: Institut fur Englische Sprache und Literatur, 1974), 52.
43. William Drummond, *Ephemeris*. 2 vols. National Library of Scotland MS2060, 2: 36r.
44. George a Greene, *The Pinder of Wakefield* (London: G. P. for E. Blackamoore, 1632), B4v.
45. Douglas Bruster, *Drama and the Market in the Age of Shakespeare* (Cambridge: Cambridge University Press, 1992), 117.
46. That Shakespeare may have become more disturbed by finance as he became more involved in it is the argument of Peter F. Grav, *Shakespeare and the Economic Imperative: 'What's aught but as 'tis valued?'* (New York: Routledge, 2008).
47. William Prynne, *Histrio-mastix* (London: E. A. and W. J. for Michael Sparke, 1633), 322.

Chapter 8
Biography and Shakespeare's Money
Portraits of an Economic Persona

Paola Pugliatti

Biography and history

The relationship between biography and history has been an uneasy one since Antiquity. As Arnaldo Momigliano wrote in 1971 in the last paragraph of his book on Greek biography:

> The Greeks and the Romans realized that writing about the life of a fellow man is not quite the same as writing history. Perhaps we can do better. Perhaps we can absorb biography into history without any residuum. But we must not be too hasty. By keeping biography separate from history the Greeks and the Romans were able to appreciate what constitutes a poet, a philosopher, a martyr, a saint. They were also able to appreciate what remains human in a king or in a politician. That dim figure, Skylax of Caryanda, the explorer of the Indian coasts and the first biographer, has left us with a problem.[1]

Skylax of Caryanda, a Greek writer and explorer, lived between the end of the sixth and the beginning of the fifth century BCE. We know

Notes for this section begin on page 138.

about his writings (an account of his periplus of the Indian coast and a biography of Heraclides, King of Mylasa) from later mentions by Herodotus and Aristotle. Momigliano, who was probably the first historian to highlight and exemplify in an historical corpus of texts the uncertain relationship connecting, and dividing, history and biography, chose the 'dim figure' of Skylax as the emblem of this uncertainty. 'The first biographer has left us with a problem', he wrote; a problem which should not be solved by 'absorbing biography into history', but by defining what there can be, in biography, that makes us appreciate the stuff a poet, a philosopher, a martyr, a saint is made of. In other words, the problem with which Skylax has left us is that of defining the status of biography as a genre which 'personalizes' history, for writing about the life of a person is not the same as writing about the life of collective formations.

Nevertheless, both as an instrument of historical knowledge and as a literary form, biography continued to be described as ambiguous, uncertain, mixed, hybrid, a minor genre which has never solved its contradictions, and even an anti-historical genre. 'Of everything other than thought', Roger Collingwood wrote,

> there can be no history. Thus a biography, for example, however much history it contains, is constructed on principles that are not only non-historical but anti-historical. Its limits are biological events, the birth and death of a human organism: its framework is thus a framework not of thought but of natural process'.[2]

Furthermore, biography has also been considered embarrassing from the point of view of twentieth-century developments in historical research, as influenced by the École des Annales. The historical paradigm these historians elaborated further marginalized the singularizing perspective of biography. The *long durée* historiography they theorized and practised was in fact aimed at the study of cyclical oscillations and serial phenomena, and was thus radically averse both to the idea of 'person' as the maker of history, and the category of 'event' as constructed by traditional historiography; the kind of event which, in the words of Fernand Braudel, illustrates 'a short time span, proportionate to individuals, to daily life, to our illusions, to our hasty awareness – above all, the time of the chronicle and the journalist. ... the mediocre accidents of ordinary life'.[3] As Daniel Madélénat observed, the forms of history illustrated by the École des Annales and its extensions are hostile to biography, because:

their study employs quantitative, serial, statistic methods in which neither intuition nor sympathy for an individual can have a part. ... Biography is therefore confined to the condition of a living fossil (the 'history of great men'), or, at best, subdued as a deposit of facts which allow one to reach the collective dimension ... .[4]

But biography also appeared embarrassing as regards its literary pretensions as a narrative genre, for it is bound to ignore the revolution that the art of fiction has brought about, since the first decades of the twentieth century, by disrupting the categories of 'character' and 'time'. Biography cannot embrace this revolution, for it naturally looks for traces of coherence and completeness in the personage it describes, while it attempts to reconstruct the linear, sequential development of a life's temporal context; furthermore, when it deals with the other powerful twentieth-century paradigm that is psychoanalysis, biography does it with an amateurish outlook and amateurish instruments. In short, unaware of the dramatic changes that affected all fields of human thought in the twentieth century, biography has continued to mould its shape according to the basic dictates of the realistic novel.

But, however slighted and even despised, biography has never ceased to attract readers; and it has never ceased to make readers believe that, while reading, they are experiencing the 'real person'. As James Clifford writes:

> It is something of a mystery that so many biographies do in fact succeed in uniting a coherent personality. And the feat is particularly remarkable in a time and culture whose philosophers, psychologists, sociologists, and poets, cannot come to any real agreement as to what structures and practices add up to a 'person'. Biography, relying on little theoretical sophistication but placing its faith in the storyteller's arts, manages with surprising consistency to make us believe in the existence of a self.

This apparent paradox is perhaps explained precisely by the fact that, as Clifford later remarks: 'the biographer tends to be skeptical of abstract theories'.[5] Thus, in its essential, maybe naive claim, that of narrating the life of a person, biography has remained true to itself, ignoring the changed paradigms of nearby disciplines (history in the first place, but also sociology and anthropology), never disowning the cultural significance of the act of writing 'the history of kings and heroes' that had been discarded by historians.

But, if biography does not seem interested in justifying its existence and methods theoretically,[6] historians and sociologists have ended up by performing this task in its place, arguing that biography should not dissolve into either history or fiction, but remain as an independent form of historical knowledge with its autonomous methods, its own compositional rules and, above all, its own peculiar mission: if historians are not able to understand and transmit the complexities of human life, biography can perform this task for them.

Indeed, by the mid-twentieth century, social historians and sociologists had started to question the history of structures and the quantitative, serial approach that had dominated historiography. They felt that the history of the great cycles and structures developing within the *longue durée* was unable to transmit the complexity and richness of individual lives in a social and political context; and redirected attention to biography, to the qualitative, sociological study of individuals and events (what Jacques Le Goff called 'historical biography'[7]), which they considered a necessary component of the study of collective formations. The idea was that of reconciling two complementary points of view: if it is true that 'there are no individuals without a society', it is equally true that 'there is no society without individuals'.[8] In the words of Arnaldo Momigliano, 'No history, however bent on emphasizing collective decisions, can manage to get rid of the disturbing presence of individuals'.[9] Biography, then, started to be considered as a particular instrument of social research and historical knowledge; for the life of a person, as Jean Sagnes said, may 'disclose a whole society'.[10] What makes up the difference of biography, then, the residuum that, as the first Greek biographer reminds us, should not be dissolved, is its capacity to describe 'the general historical meaning of an individual's life'.[11]

The challenge of Shakespeare's lives

Let me now move on to Shakespeare and his biographers, to see how they have met the vicissitudes of biography as a genre; and, finally, further narrowing my perspective, how they have narrated and evaluated Shakespeare's involvement in economic affairs.

At a recent conference, James Shapiro started one of his comments by saying that there is no other aspect of Shakespeare scholarship that has been less theorized than biography. This is true, and it is even more remarkable that the quantitatively conspicuous and qualitatively rich corpus of texts that constitutes Shakespearean biography is simply ignored by the theoretical debate that has flourished since the 1980s.[12] Is this because writing a biography of Shakespeare is a self-justifying gesture? Or is it because the variety of approaches that these biographies embody discourages all forms of theoretical rationalization? If the first Greek biographer has left us with the problem of appreciating the 'residue' which makes biography a self-sufficient genre, William Shakespeare has left us with the near-impossible task of reconstructing events that do not allow reconstruction.[13] How can such a predicament be rationalized and discussed in a productive way?

To my knowledge, there is only a small handful of works that have reflected on these issues. In his 2009 book *Literary Biography*, Michael Benton devotes a chapter to Shakespeare biographies, and speaks of what he calls the 'inferential biography' that – he maintains – has produced a virtual kind of storytelling:

> These inferred Shakespeares, created from official records, historical extrapolations and traces found in unstable play texts, are little more than ghosts. Biography, along with portraiture ..., constantly strives to materialise the ghost and, in doing so, demonstrates the rules which govern the biographer's imagination and the virtual nature of the Shakespeares it creates. ... What, then, can biography do with an all but invisible subject?[14]

More important are a few writings by Park Honan, who, in his 1998 *Shakespeare: A Life*, shows full consciousness of the changed paradigms that I have been trying to illustrate in the first part of this chapter:

> Late in the twentieth century, attitudes to biography and history changed rapidly. Indirectly the ideas of the Annales school of historians in France, as well as works by America's new historicist critics and Britain's cultural materialists, ... expanded the territory of Renaissance studies. The 'documentary fact' seemed misleading without the social context which was a part of the fact to begin with; it could be argued, then, that Shakespeare's biographers had neglected Tudor and Jacobean society, interpreted documents in a near-vacuum, and neglected the poet's intelligence by explaining him as a 'miracle'.[15]

Honan returned to these issues over ten years later, in an article entitled 'To Change the Picture of Shakespeare Biography'. Discussing Gordon Ray's biography of Thackeray and Richard Ellmann's biography of Joyce, he writes that both authors

> recognized ... that narrow biographical forms had failed to accommodate 'social models' or adequate treatments of social history in close specific relation to an author. Ray and Ellmann respectively with

Thackeray and Joyce did get around difficulty; but Shakespeare's biographers had not done so, and instead relied on loosely attached or on fancifully evocative paragraphs of 'background', or, as in Samuel Schoenbaum's *Documentary Life*, they skimped on social contexts, though that work achieved other ends.[16]

A 'disintegrationist' new start?

One of the possible answers given to Park Honan's suggestion of a more structural negotiation with the social context in Shakespeare biography seems to be given by the recently changed attitude towards the biographical materials we possess; for instance, towards certain 'traditions' (as different from 'facts') which have probably been too hastily abandoned.

The basic factual information about Shakespeare's life is already present in Rowe's 1709 *Account*; but Rowe also included a few of the anecdotes or 'myths' that he collected from variously reliable sources (the deer-stealing episode and the consequent flight to London, the idea, or information, that Shakespeare was not a particularly good actor and that 'top of his performance was the Ghost in his own *Hamlet*', the retirement to Stratford only during the last years of his life, and so on).[17]

What shall we do with those unproved anecdotes? Are they really to be abandoned without further reflection on the peculiar kind of 'fact' they may represent? Do they not present a sort of tangential, oblique kind of 'truth', whose legitimacy may be found in their verisimilitude? These half-truths are, I believe, the verbal counterpart of the material items that are shown in all Shakespeare properties: items that *may have been* used in the Shakespeare household because they do not collide with plausibility: in other words, it cannot be proved that they were not.

Malone was the first to disown these traditions as inventions, inaugurating the biographical account based on 'facts' that found its most authoritative specimen in Schoenbaum's 1975 'documentary' biography.[18] Naturally, the way to a strictly documentary biography had been opened by Chambers in 1930; but even Chambers, commenting on the tradition that Shakespeare 'had been a schoolmaster in the country' says that 'the statement is not in itself incredible'.[19] Even to an historically minded biographer, therefore, certain traditions are acceptable because 'not incredible' – they are reported as fact, not mere speculation: in scientific parlance, they are 'falsifiable'.

In his biography of Luther, Erik Erikson reports an unverified anecdote about his protagonist and produces the following comment:

> If some of it is legend, so be it; the making of legend is as much part of the scholarly rewriting of history as it is part of the original facts used in the works of scholars. We are thus obliged to accept half-legend as half-history, provided only that a reported episode does not contradict other well-established facts; persists as having a ring of truth; and yields a meaning consistent with psychological theory.[20]

A similar evaluation of 'traditions', as opposed to 'facts' on the one hand and 'speculation' on the other, is made by Graham Holderness:

> In Shakespeare biography it is possible to view 'tradition' as in its own way authentic. ... Stratford neighbours, parish clerks, local gossips, actors and theatre managers of the seventeenth century – where else would we go for reliable information about the life of Shakespeare? On the other hand these 'traditions' are obviously telling a story as well as citing a fact, so the information they provide may well be both factual, and yet to some degree already partly fictionalized.[21]

Edmondson and Wells, in turn, in the Closing Remarks of *The Shakespeare Circle*, affirm:

> Across the chapters we have been made aware of the importance of tradition which can neither be confirmed or denied. But it remains important. One aspect of biography is its need to negotiate between the potentially conflicting natures of tradition and historical fact as evidenced in documentary records. ... Biography, like history, seeks the most reasonable explanation, but it is willing to admit tradition and informed speculation in order to achieve its goals. ... Among the many circles that make up an individual's life, oral history has an important place and currency, its own authority which needs to be analysed afresh as perspectives develop.[22]

Katherine Scheil, for example, has given substance to these claims in an article in which she discusses the narrative, inaugurated by Rowe, of Shakespeare's retirement from the London theatre scene to his native Stratford only at the end of his career versus the different narrative of a Shakespeare writing at least some of his plays in his comfortable Stratford house of New Place. Scheil does not take sides in favour of one or the other hypothesis, but discusses the less credited one, that of long working periods in Stratford, both on the basis of certain traditions and on that of recent archaeological findings following excavations at New Place.

In the case of Scheil's essay, the tradition being reconsidered is the diary of John Ward, vicar of Stratford and physician, who was based in Stratford roughly from 1662 to 1669. There is no reason, Scheil contends, to doubt the accuracy of Ward's entries concerning Shakespeare, although they were written long after Shakespeare's death; and the information he collected reinforces the hypothesis of a Shakespeare based mainly in Stratford.[23]

The informed re-evaluation of traditions is one of the critical gestures which mark the difference, on the one hand from 'documentary' biography and, on the other, from prevailingly speculative cradle-to-grave biographical narratives; and it is probably also by devoting attention to what is tangential and circumstantial that biography can reveal, to go back to my initial quote, 'what remains human in a king, in a politician or in a poet', thereby gaining a historical room of its own.

A more general tendency by whose means Shakespeare biography is looking for new ways to give substance to its object is the closer look some of Shakespeare's biographers are giving to comparatively neglected corners of his life, narrowing the scope of their research either temporally or thematically, and at the same time casting a more analytical look at specific issues. I refer to what Graham Holderness calls 'a kind of "disintegrationist" movement'.[24] His 2011 *Nine Lives* is an example which – in his own words – 'accepts that Shakespeare's lives are multiple and discontinuous, and yet they are facets of a single life';[25] but also other books give prominence to a more or less amplified contextual space: Shapiro's *1599: A Year in the Life of William Shakespeare* and his *1606: Shakespeare and the Year of 'Lear'*;[26] and, above all, Nicholl's *The Lodger Shakespeare*, a book which amplifies the context without sacrificing Shakespeare's role in and out of the story.[27]

Last in my list of 'disintegrationist' (or 'microhistorical') books comes *The Shakespeare Circle* edited by Paul Edmondson and Stanley Wells. This book contains twenty-five chapters, each devoted to particular members of Shakespeare's circle, that is, people and/or groups that he encountered (or must have encountered) in various periods of his life.

A further, all encompassing 'disintegrationist' field of research, particularly popular during the last twenty years, is the one which concerns Shakespeare as a collaborative writer, that places Shakespeare the writer more structurally, but also more problematically, within the context of his professional surroundings.[28]

It is evident that, while these developments have finally excluded the search for Shakespeare's life in his works, they are gaining ground at the expense of other practices, which are sacrificed and/or disintegrated: the continuous narrative, in the first place, but also the imposition of behaviouristic models of coherence and consistency. Naturally, the expansion of contexts and the various forms of negotiation with the environment have dimmed the sole focalization on William Shakespeare's 'self'. Indeed, both in Nicholl's *The Lodger Shakespeare* and in Edmondson and Wells's *The Shakespeare Circle*, Shakespeare becomes an almost marginal character, but a character illuminated by a light which, precisely because it is tangential, may reveal unexplored corners of his social being; a price to be paid if, as James Clifford says, we wish to direct 'our attention to the complex ways in which cultural patterns shape individual behaviour and experience'.[29]

Money in Shakespeare biography

The Shakespeare we want is not the man trivially attending to his worldly affairs instead of spending what time was not taken up by the composition of his plays and poems in contemplation and deep thought (or, as a different portrait would have it, in taverns and brothels); biographers, therefore, have given comparatively little attention to the issue of his economic negotiations. Those who are more interested in the issue of the money he made and how he made it are the anti-Stratfordians: however, the 'Shakespeare' they want is not different from ours: no less than ours he embodies the myth of the divine poet whose life cannot be soiled by worldly matters. Thus they have, so to speak, snatched from the adverse party the embarrassing theme of the poet's material affairs; there is, of course, no danger, for them, to soil the reputation of the poet, for – as Diana Price forcefully maintains in her *Unorthodox Biography*[30] – the man who was intent on accumulating material goods is for them a different person from the poet. Rather paradoxically, therefore, for both parties, moneymaking would obscure the literary achievement of the author of Shakespeare's plays and poems.

Understandably, early biographers are more interested in his social status than in his economic position (Nicholas Rowe mentions Shakespeare's properties in passing, simply stating that the estate he gathered was 'equal to his Occasion, and, in that, to his Wish').[31]

It is not until the end of the nineteenth century that we start finding evaluations of the issue of money. Halliwell-Phillipps's 1887 *Outlines of the Life of Shakespeare* is the first biography that can be considered 'documentary'. The biographer's general attitude is markedly anti-romantic, in that it is averse to any construction of a portrait, or to any judgement pronounced on the basis of actions, either derived from documents or from traditions, and even less inferred from the works. He says, for instance, that '[t]here are no external testimonies of any description in favour of a personal application of the Sonnets, while there are abundant difficulties arising from the reception of such a theory'.[32] When it comes to dealing with the money Shakespeare made, the biographer quotes Pope's famous line in *The First Epistle of the Second Book of Horace*, where he says that Shakespeare 'For gain, not glory, wing'd his roving flight',[33] thereby subliminally revealing his distaste for the topic. But the biographer abandons his factual attitude when he sweetens the act of purchasing the forty acres of land, by saying that 'he appears to have had a predilection in favour of Shottery' for '[i]t was in this village that he is generally believed ... to have met with his future wife, and hence has arisen the inevitable surmise that the inclination in favour of the particular investment emanated from recollections of the days of courtship'.[34] Moneymaking, in other words, although duly reported, is presented as an activity to be excused on the basis of imagined sentimental motivations.

Chambers published all the relevant documents, from those regarding Shakespeare's London residences as related to tax collection and other issues, to his will, and, throughout the whole of volume I of his *Study of Facts and Problems* – as in all other cases – his annotations are simply bibliographical.[35]

The general attitude of the following documentary biography, that of Samuel Schoenbaum (1975), is similar to Halliwell-Phillipps's. Schoenbaum devotes a chapter entitled 'A gentleman of Means' to Shakespeare's moneymaking; and he quotes Pope's line that in this case, too, give an implicit comment on the issue being treated. Also the decision to isolate and confine the theme of money within a dedicated chapter, as if it was not part of the chronological progress of the events and of the development of Shakespeare's personality, appears revealing: money is a foreign body to be set apart from the rest. What both Halliwell-Phillipps and Schoenbaum seem to imply is, in the final analysis, that – when it comes to Shakespeare's moneymaking – it would be better not to disturb the myth of personal coherence or evoke any cultural and social patterns that may have explained moneymaking as one of the many manifestations of Shakespeare's 'self': all 'self', however sublime, may after all have its own abject doppelgänger.

I will now approach a few twenty-first-century cradle-to-grave biographies and their treatment of Shakespeare's financial transactions with the help of Graham Holderness's *Nine Lives*. Life Four of the book is devoted to 'Shakespeare the Businessman'. Holderness remarks that '[a]lthough the commercial aspect dominates the documentary record, no commensurate prominence is given to Shakespeare the man of property in the biographies'.[36] He explains the marginalization of the financial aspect of Shakespeare's life by maintaining that biographers have always been reluctant to reconcile the businessman with the poet and to 'consider the possibility that Shakespeare might have been as enthusiastic about money and property and land as he was about plays and poems'.[37] Holderness then discusses what he considers the three most controversial issues in Shakespeare's financial engagement: his role in the Belott-Mountjoy lawsuit in 1612; the purchase of the Blackfriars gatehouse in 1613; and the Welcombe enclosure controversy in 1614. By examining the biographies of five authors (Wells, Bate, Greenblatt, Duncan-Jones and Ackroyd), he concludes that they end up by presenting several different portraits: Wells and Bate see Shakespeare as a Stratford citizen and family man who acquired property mainly to support his family; Greenblatt 'sees Shakespeare's financial acumen as to some degree akin to his artistic capabilities';[38] Duncan-Jones is the harshest on the issue of profit ('It does not need Katherine Duncan-Jones' systematic attempts to blacken Shakespeare's character to see the unattractive side of the man who bought a London house, but disinherited his wife from any promise of it; and who seems to have cared more about his own commercial interests than about the plight of his poorer Stratford neighbours'[39]). Holderness finally remarks that it is probably only Ackroyd, the professional writer untouched by academic prejudice, who in the end accepts 'that the twin roles of artist and entrepreneur might in fact have constituted a complex symbiotic life-story'.[40]

Rightly subtitled *An Alternative Biography*, *The Shakespeare Circle*, edited by Paul Edmondson and Stanley Wells, appeared in 2015. In twenty-five chapters by different authors, William Shakespeare, man and artist, is besieged by his family relationships, friends and neighbours, colleagues and patrons. The experiment is daring and interesting, and it displays an enormous body of fresh research.

In their General Introduction to the volume, the editors illustrate their attitude towards the use of facts, allusions and myth:

> Without wanting this book to be full of expressions such as 'he must have' and 'there can be little doubt that', we have not discouraged our contributors from going beyond narrowly documented evidence, relying on their familiarity with Shakespeare's life and times to exercise their imaginations in the attempt to illuminate obscure areas of his existence and experience.[41]

The theme of Shakespeare's money is mainly concentrated in Stanley Wells's chapter on the Combes, the one Stratford family, close neighbours and friends, who also had a prominent role in Shakespeare's affairs in his own city. Shakespeare's portrait as a businessman is here indirect, but what hints show through adumbrate the character of a respectful gentleman whose attitude towards money was neither lavish nor stingy, and, generally speaking, in harmony with the description the town's bailiff provided in 1605 as 'an honest gentleman their neighbour well respected'.[42]

Many of the essays in *The Shakespeare Circle* refer to recent archaeological investigations of New Place, and some suggest that further research into other persons, families and social groups, and further exploitation of these findings may provide fresh suggestions, if not fresh evidence.

What to my knowledge is the first financial biography of William Shakespeare, is a book by Robert Bearman entitled *Shakespeare's Money*. Bearman is a very historically minded scholar, particularly cautious about what cannot claim to be considered fact (a recurring expression in his book is 'it cannot be shown that': it is clear that Bearman gives no credit to traditions). In an article published in 2015, he advises caution even towards what we consider fact:

> our knowledge of what happened depends largely on accounts which have chanced to come down to us in the written record, with all the problems associated with whether we can trust what we are being told and having to accept that, even if all the protagonists had kept personal diaries, we might still have doubts about the reliability of the evidence. It follows that, in the sphere of what we might term strict historical investigation, we are dealing not with absolute certainty but with a balance of probabilities.[43]

Characteristically, given his general attitude, Bearman opens his book by explaining why a traditionally meant Shakespeare biography is, in his opinion, not possible:

> [I]t is not possible to write a biography of William Shakespeare within the normally accepted meaning of the word. One would hardly think so in view of the number of attempts which have been made, but the basic requirement for such an exercise simply does not exist – namely, a body of evidence allowing insight into the subject's feelings and views backed up with details of his or her day-to-day life and of the opinions of others on the subject's shortcomings, achievements, and appearance.[44]

The book's subtitle is: *How Much Did He Make and What Did This Mean?*; and indeed one of the merits of *Shakespeare's Money*, apart from the accuracy in the use of source materials, is that it also deals with the 'what did this mean' part of the issue, by systematically contextualizing Shakespeare's moneymaking and the consequent social status he achieved both in his London career and in his native Stratford.

Is it possible to infer from these recent endeavours the advent of a new ethos in Shakespeare biography? Is the practice of narrowing the areas of inspection and the closer focalization of issues and events, substantiated by the judicious re-evaluation of traditions, going to be further exploited with profit? Are the 'circles' surrounding Shakespeare's lives going to be expanded in different directions? And, more generally, are these recent ripples of the waters of Shakespeare biography apt to make us appreciate (to go back to my initial quote) 'what constitutes a poet'?

It is too early to reply to these questions with any confidence, and we do not even know whether these trends will continue and be further elaborated; but some assessments, mainly in the negative, may be advanced.

One of the procedures that appear to be no longer acceptable is the reading of Shakespeare's life, either of his 'self' or of his 'mind', through the examination of his works; the documentary biography, in turn, remains crystallized in its unique and indispensable function as reference work; and similarly the attractively novelistic cradle-to-grave biographies, even the most celebrated ones published during the last two decades, would now appear to be inspired by an old-fashioned intent, and therefore carrying an old-fashioned message. Other ways to bridge the documentary gaps and overcome the frustration of the scarcity of facts have started to affirm their right of citizenship.

There may be interesting developments in future lives.

Paola Pugliatti has written extensively on Shakespeare and early modern European culture and on modernist literature. Her present interests include biography and authorship studies. Her latest book-length studies are *Beggary and Theatre in Early Modern England* (2003) and *Shakespeare and the Just War Tradition* (2010). She is editor, with Donatella Pallotti, of *Journal of Early Modern Studies*.

Notes

1. Arnaldo Momigliano, *The Development of Greek Biography* (Cambridge, MA: Harvard University Press, 1971), 104.
2. R. G. Collingwood, *The Idea of History* (Oxford: Oxford University Press, 1961 [1946]), 304.
3. Fernand Braudel, 'History and the Social Sciences: The *Longue Durée*', in F. Braudel, *On History*, trans. Sarah Matthews (Chicago, IL: University of Chicago Press, 1980), 25–54, here 28.
4. Daniel Madelénat, *La biographie* (Paris: Presses Universitaires de France, 1984), 110. The translation is my own from the original: *leur étude fait appel à des méthodes quantitatives, sérielles, statistiques, où ni l'intuition, ni la sympathie pour un sujet n'ont leur part ... . La biographie se trouve ainsi renvoyée au statut de fossil vivant (l' 'histoire grands hommes'), ou, au mieux, vassalisée comme un reservoir de faits donnant accès au collectif.*
5. James Clifford, '"Hanging up Looking Glasses at Odd Corners": Ethnobiographical Prospects', in *Studies in Biography*, ed. Daniel Aron (Cambridge, MA: Harvard University Press, 1978), 41–56, here 44, 47.
6. With notable exceptions, the most conspicuous being the work of Leon Edel, the great biographer of Henry James. Among Shakespeare's biographers, Park Honan is one of the few who have reflected on biography writing; a chapter devoted to Shakespeare biographies is found in Michael Benton's book *Literary Biography: An Introduction* (Chichester: Wiley Blackwell, 2009). A good, substantially factual, summary is David Bevington's *Shakespeare and Biography* (Oxford: Oxford University Press, 2010).
7. Jacques Le Goff, 'Comment écrire une biographie historique aujourd'hui?', *Le Débat* 54, no. 2 (1989): 48–53.
8. Franco Ferrarotti, *On the Science of Uncertainty: The Biographical Method in Social Research* (Lanham, MD: Lexicon Books, 2003), xviii.
9. Momigliano, *Greek Biography*, 40.
10. Jean Sagnes, 'Écrire une biographie, pourquoi, comment? L'example de Napoléon III', *Historiens et Géographes: Revue de l'association des professeurs d'histoire et de Géograaphie* 413 (2011): 235–41, http://www.urbi-beziers.fr/articles/ecrire_une_biographie_pourquoi_comment_exemple_napoleon_III.pdf (accessed 27 April 2018). The translation is my own from the original: be *un révélateur de société*.
11. Le Goff, 'Comment écrire', 49. The translation is mine from the original: *la signification historique générale d'une vie individuelle*.

12. The first generation of these critics, active in the 1980s, included literary scholars who discussed mainly, in the wake of Virginia Woolf and her circle, what they called *biographie littéraire*, that is, the (literary) biographies of literary people, and formulated theories about a poetics of biography, a genre which aimed to combine historical truth and literary achievement. See, in particular, Madelénat, *La biographie*. The second generation has been active since the first years of the present century, and includes mainly (but not solely) north European social historians. The 'biographical turn' they are advocating aims at the construction of a perspective which views biography (and autobiography) as a distinct area in the humanities, and a methodology affecting not only history and literary studies, but also sociology, economics and politics. Chairs of biography studies and departments of biography have been established in a few universities (the University of Groningen is probably the most active research centre), and a number of associations and specialized journals are spreading knowledge of these new perspectives.
13. The last is, in a way, a commonplace statement. It is indeed true that we probably possess more evidence about the life of Shakespeare than about that of any of his contemporary writers. However, about Shakespeare, we would like to possess more.
14. Benton, *Literary Biography*, 67.
15. Park Honan, *Shakespeare: A Life* (Oxford: Oxford University Press, 1998), 422–23.
16. Park Honan, 'To Change the Picture of Shakespeare Biography', *Critical Survey* 21, no. 3 (2009): 103–6, here 104, doi: 10.3167/cs.2009.210308.
17. See *Some Account of the Life of Mr. William Shakespear*, http://archive.org/stream/someaccountofthe16275gut/16275-8.txt (accessed 26 July 2019).
18. Samuel Schoenbaum, *Wiliam Shakespeare: A Documentary Life* (Oxford and New York: Oxford University Press, in association with the Scolar Press, 1975). Other Shakespeare biographies which aim at being considered documentary are: Nathan Drake, *Shakespeare and His Times* (London: T. Cadell and D. Davies, 1817); and J. O. Halliwell-Phillipps, *Outlines of the Life of Shakespeare* (London: Longmans, Green, and Co., 1887, 1907 reprint, 2 vols).
19. E. K. Chambers, *William Shakespeare: A Study of Facts and Problems* (Oxford: Oxford University Press, 1930), 2 vols, vol. I, 22.
20. Quoted by Richard Ellmann, 'Literary Biography: An Inaugural Lecture' (Oxford: Clarendon Press, 1971), 10.
21. Graham Holderness, *Nine Lives of William Shakespeare* (London: Continuum, 2011), 8. Various kinds of information with different degrees of reliability about Shakespeare's life are categorized by E. K. Chambers as 'Records', 'Contemporary Allusions' and 'The Shakespeare Mythos'. E. K. Chambers, *William Shakespeare*, vol. II.
22. Paul Edmondson and Stanley Wells, *The Shakespeare Circle: An Alternative Biography* (Cambridge: Cambridge University Press, 2015), 331–32.
23. Katherine Scheil, 'Shakespearean Biography and the Geography of Collaboration', *Journal of Early Modern Studies* 5 (2016), 69–90, doi: 10.13128/JEMS-2279-7149-18083, http://www.fupress.net/index.php/bsfm-jems/article/view/18083 (accessed 26 July 2019).
24. Graham Holderness, 'Who Was William Shakespeare?', *Memoria di Shakespeare: A Journal of Shakespearean Studies*, 2 (2015): 61–79, here 75, doi: 10.13133/2283-8759-2, https://ojs.uniroma1./index.php/MemShakespeare (accessed 4 August 2018).

25. Ibid., 78. It has become fashionable to use the plural to express complexity: see William Leahy and Paola Pugliatti, eds, 'The Many Lives of William Shakespeare: Biography, Authorship and Collaboration' special issue, *Journal of Early Modern Studies* 5 (2016), http://www.fupress.net/index.php/bsfm-jems (accessed 4 August 2018).

26. James Shapiro, *1599: A Year in the Life of William Shakespeare* (London: Faber and Faber, 2005); James Shapiro, *1606: Shakespeare and the Year of Lear* (London: Faber and Faber, 2015). The idea of accompanying Shakespeare through a given period of his life was inaugurated by a booklet entitled *A Day with William Shakespeare* by Maurice Clare (pseudonym of May Clarissa Gillington Byron), published in 1913, and one of the sources of inspiration for Joyce's one-day narrative and Shakespeare fragments in *Ulysses*. Here, the author imagines and describes a day in 1599, beginning in the house of Christopher Mountjoy in Silver Street and ending late at night, with the protagonist watching the stars. The titles of Shapiro's books, as David Ellis suggests, lead the reader to think that what is being told is, step by step, what Shakespeare did in those years; on the contrary, the reader is offered 'something much more like a narrative of various important happenings in 1599, one of the years in which Shakespeare happened to be alive'. 'How to Write a Biography of Shakespeare', *Memoria di Shakespeare. A Journal of Shakespearean Studies* 2 (2015), 25–44, here 39, doi: 10.13133/2283-8759-2, https://ojs.uniroma1./index.php/MemShakespeare.

27. Charles Nicholl, *The Lodger Shakespeare: His Life on Silver Street* (London: Penguin Books, 2007). Nicholl's book is quoted as an example of 'microhistorical' biography by the social historian Matti Peltonen in his 'What is Micro in Microhistory?', in *Theoretical Discussions of Biography: Approaches from History, Microhistory, and Life Writing*, ed. Hans Renders and Binne de Haan (Lewiston, NY: Edwin Mellen, 2013), 157–78.

28. Information technology is also providing other instruments to the composition of the context(s) in which Shakespeare lived and worked: for example, a searchable and extremely detailed map of early modern London prepared by the University of Victoria, British Columbia, https://mapoflondon.uvic.ca/ (accessed 18 March 2017); and a particular section devoted to New Place excavations and findings (http://bloggingshakespeare.com/unearthing-shakespeare, accessed 18 March 2017), are providing different contextualizing instruments.

29. Clifford, '"Hanging up Looking Glasses at Odd Corners"', 42.

30. Diana Price, *Shakespeare's Unorthodox Biography: New Evidence of an Authorship Problem* (Westport, CT: Greenwood Press), 2001.

31. '*Some account*', http://archive.org/stream/someaccountofthe16275gut/16275-8.txt (accessed 12 March 2017).

32. Halliwell-Phillipps, *Outlines of the Life of Shakespeare*, vol. I, 174.

33. Ibid., 163.

34. Ibid., 162.

35. Chambers, *William Shakespeare*, vol. II, 87–180.

36. Holderness, *Nine Lives*, 81.

37. Ibid., 89.

38. Ibid., 84–5. Holderness also notes that different interpretations, in harmony with this basic evaluation, are also given to Shakespeare's retirement to his native town: while Wells and Bate see it in a positive light, Greenblatt sees it as 'a great falling off from the excitement and adulation of a life lived so close to the heart of the nation's cultural Renaissance' (ibid., 85).
39. Ibid., 89.
40. Ibid.
41. Edmondson and Wells, *Shakespeare Circle*, 5.
42. Stanley Wells, 'A Close Family Connection: the Combes', in Edmondson and Wells, *The Shakespeare Circle*, 149–60, here 150. Wells takes the quote from E. I. Fripp, *Shakespeare Man and Artist* (Oxford: Oxford University Press, 1938), 732.
43. Robert Bearman, 'William Shakespeare: What He Was Not', *Memoria di Shakespeare. A Journal of Shakespearean Studies*, no. 2 (2015), 81–107, here 87, doi: 10.13133/2283-8759-2, https://ojs.uniroma1.it/index.php/MemShakespeare/index (accessed 6 July 2018).
44. Robert Bearman, *Shakespeare's Money: How Much Did He Make It and What Did This Mean?* (Oxford: Oxford University Press, 2016), 1.

Chapter 9
Shakespeare and the Hybrid Economy

Sujata Iyengar

Introduction

Much critical ink has been spilled in defining and establishing the terms of discussion: appropriation, adaptation, tradaptation, offshoot, recontextualization, riff, remix, and so on have been used interchangeably or under erasure.[1] This chapter both examines the utility of such nice distinctions, and critiques existing taxonomies. It takes as its starting point the premise that scholars must carefully articulate our reasons for deploying particular terms, so that Shakespearean thinkers, readers, writers, and performers can develop a shared, even if contested, discourse. Ultimately, however, it suggests a new rubric or heading under which to consider Shakespearean appropriations: as transformations.

I suggest that Shakespearean appropriations potentially metamorphose or mutate culture, literary form, creativity, pedagogy, and, most provocatively, the market economy, in part because Shakespearean texts antedate current US copyright law and thus any use

Notes for this section begin on page 155.

we make of them is already 'transformative' (this is a version of the phenomenon that Julie Sanders has classified slightly differently by imagining Shakespeare as an 'open-source' creative repository).[2] In particular, Shakespearean appropriations, I will argue, *transform* creative production and intervene in contemporary commodity culture or the hypermediatized, monetized creative self. Transformative Shakespeares recreate Shakespearean and literary ontologies (What is Shakespeare? What is the literary?), genres and media (Where do we find Shakespeare? What elements do we consider Shakespeare?), motives and audiences (For whom and to whom is this Shakespeare?) and markets (Who is capitalizing from or on Shakespeare, and in what ways?). If we take even a single play such as *A Midsummer Night's Dream* we can find ventures that appropriate or transform it formally (the gay teen comedy-musical film *Were the World Mine* or the market-driven 'Graphic Novel' Shakespeares and the strange hybrid *Manga Shakespeare*); theoretically (present-day editions and the gender politics of editorial apparatus and line distributions); pedagogically (the use that teachers make of the play in my local public and independent schools in the Southeastern US); and creatively (the art and writing generated by so-called amateurs in 'Web 2.0' fora such as YouTube, Flickr, DeviantArt, GoodReads, WordPress, and other media).[3] All such examples return obsessively, I will suggest, to questions of originality and ownership, transforming Shakespeare in the process into the fungible fluid of currency.

Terms of Art and Terms of Law: Adaptation, Appropriation, Participation, Transformation

Many scholars have suggested that we can read Shakespearean appropriations as indices to late capitalist cultural production.[4] Many have also noted, that there exists no single 'original' or 'authentic' Shakespeare, but rather what Denise Albanese dubs, adapting Foucault's 'What is an Author?', a 'Shakespeare-function'.[5] Shakespeare *means* within a rich context in which instantiations and appropriations from different historical eras engage in a 'dialogic' conversation that generates relevance and import by working as a hermeneutic or interpretive system.[6] Interactive and social media networks have not only expanded access to Shakespearean works and enabled creative or cultural production but have also extended the reach of advertising and marketing into our personal lives and rendered creative or transformative professions of all kinds (teaching, music, writing, the fine and applied arts, theatre) increasingly precarious. So-called participatory cultures remake Shakespeare in venues such as YouTube (video) or WordPress (fanfic).[7] Current work in labour studies suggests that we are now all Shakespeare 'prosumers' who make and re-make Shakespeare in different commodity and cultural contexts.[8]

I would further like briefly to contextualize Shakespearean appropriation in light of the history of media and copyright law, in particular the doctrine of 'fair use' in the United States. Copyright itself in the US derives, as is well known, from English law, notably the so-called Statute of Anne (officially the 'Act for the Encouragement of Learning, by Vesting the Copies of Printed Books in the Authors or Purchasers of such Copies, during the Times therein mentioned', 8 Ann.c.21) in 1710, which limited the length of time under which publishers or stationers could print particular works but which also enabled the entrepreneurial printer Jacob Tonson 'to publish new editions, with new editors' so that he could through each editor theoretically extend his copyright in Shakespeare.[9] At the same time, those same editors 'inaugurated a scholarly examination of the text [...] and began the identification of an editorial role'; it is to Tonson's business acumen, which enabled him to pass on the profitable tradition of Shakespeare editing to his descendants, that we owe the industry of Shakespearean scholarship and the entire tradition of textual editing, as the literary critic James Marino and the intellectual property lawyer Jeffrey Gaba independently observe.[10]

Gaba, however, notes that the notoriously litigious Tonsons 'never went to court to protect their claimed copyright [in Shakespeare]', instead preferring to drive competitors out of business by 'flood[ing] the market' with cheap and small Shakespeare editions, as they did to counter Robert Walker's innovative 'penny parts' ('[a] single sheet, costing a penny, was published in a journal, and purchasers of the three or four of the sheets that constituted a play could bind them together for a copy of the play for a total cost of about four pennies').[11] If, as suggested by Gaba, 'claims of copyright had the effect more of limiting, rather than promoting, the dissemination of Shakespeare to the public', then it is easier to understand why Walker's competition resulted in 'copies of the Shakespeare plays bec[oming] accessible to a far larger public'.[12] Don-John Dugas has likewise argued that '[T]he availability of the Tonson single editions created a new kind of interest in and desire for straight Shakespeare plays', notably all of the plays, not just those that were most popular in performance.[13] Courts later in the eighteenth century upheld the statute of Anne against suits brought by booksellers, finding in Donaldson *v.* Becket (1774) against a perpetual copyright and asserting that after a copyright term expired, a work would fall into the public domain. Shakespeare thus entered the public domain, where he has remained and flourished ever since.

Thus the terms we use to discuss transformations of Shakespeare, 'adaptation' and 'appropriation', mean something very different in law and in literature. Broadly speaking, legally in both writing and in the visual arts, an 'adaptation' has been understood as subsidiary to an original copyrighted work, an 'appropriation' to be the theft of an original copyrighted work, both adaptations and appropriations to be 'derivative works' if taken from an original copyrighted source, and if you produce either one, somebody – the creator of the original, the copyright holder, the distributor, the performer, or all or some portion of these entities – might ask you for some money.[14] Where an 'adaptation' was understood to modify an original work to make it fit a new or altered situation, however, an 'appropriation' was understood to *re*-present the original work with few or no changes; its new meaning was thought to accrue from its recontextualization in a different time, space, or social environment.

In 1990, a highly influential *Harvard Law Review* commentary by Judge Pierre Leval clarified the US concept of 'fair use' and singled out the 'transformative principle' in copyright law.[15] Transformative use, he wrote, 'must be productive and must employ the quoted matter in a different manner or for a different purpose from the original'.[16] Returning to decisions from the eighteenth and nineteenth centuries, Judge Leval added:

> Quoting is not necessarily stealing [...] The first fair use factor calls for a careful evaluation whether the particular quotation is of the transformative type that advances knowledge and the progress of the arts or whether it merely repackages, free riding on another's creations [...] Factor One [the transformative principle] is the soul of fair use.[17]

Where Lawrence Lessig had worried in 2006 that fair use provided too fragile a pillar to support the edifice of intellectual freedom and what he called free culture, the strength of fair use doctrine has been buttressed by some recent rulings, in the suit of the Authors' Guild *v.* Google, Inc. (2005–13) and the US Supreme Court's refusal, in

April 2016, to reconsider a lower court ruling in favour of Google.[18] In the Google Books settlement of 2013, the Supreme Court laid out some of the effects they thought texts ought to have in order to be transformative. The court ruled that one of the most important aspects of whether or not a new work that quotes or is based upon a prior copyrighted work adheres to fair use is whether this new work uses the old in a manner that is 'transformative', that is, whether the new work creates something fresh from the old that is qualitatively different, transfigured, metamorphosed. In the Google Books ruling, the transformative principle outweighs the old heuristic under which publishers and creators could carefully control the proportion of a copyrighted work that was quoted. The old rule-of-thumb claimed that if you showed less than a certain percentage of a copyrighted work AND you were not interfering with its market value, you were in compliance with fair use. The transformative argument takes an entirely different set of premises, according to Kevin Smith, formerly of Duke University and now at the University of Kansas.[19] In sum, transformative works have to take you somewhere new. The old percentage standard (which was never really a standard), and the monetary argument are much weaker now, although publishers and media companies appear neither to have relinquished this control nor to have altered their own requirements for authors. Most publishers still demand permissions based on the *quantity* of material used, rather than whether or not the borrowing demonstrates transformative *qualities* (see: Routledge author guidelines, OUP, and CUP).

A couple of case-studies demonstrate the range and constraint of the fair use doctrine. While research, scholarship, and journalism were protected under the 'fair use' doctrine of copyright law, until recently an artist's strongest protection if she adapted a copyrighted work was the so-called 'parody' exemption. For example, when Alice Randall published her adaptation of Margaret Mitchell's classic *Gone With the Wind*, re-written from the point of view of the slaves at Tara, *The Wind Done Gone*, the Margaret Mitchell estate sued her, won the initial case, then lost the case on appeal because the court found the book to be parody. 'Parody' might seem to a lay-reader to offer an inappropriately facetious term for a serious book, whose strictures, implied and outright, against the disingenuous rosiness of Mitchell's fictional world were precisely what the Mitchell estate found objectionable. Legally, however, the parody exemption provided the best strategy to protect Randall's expression as a 'transformative' use; earlier courts had found 'satire', understood as a general critique of society, to be inadmissible as fair use and 'parody', understood as a specific commentary on an original text, to comprise fair use. The Randall settlement 'redefined parody by eliminating any requirement that parody include humor', observes Barbara Murphy, who pungently notes, however, that such a ruling 'seems to be an end-run around the fact that the copyright term [on *Gone With The Wind*] is much longer than it needs to be'.[20] One can also see how this situation played out in the visual arts in the United States with the success of Richard Prince's appeal in 2013 in Prince v. Cariou. In 2009 the photographer Patrick Cariou sued the artist Richard Prince over the latter's use in appropriation art of Cariou's photographs of Rastafarians in Jamaica, originally published in Cariou's book *Yes, Rasta*.[21] Appropriation art recontextualizes prior artefacts in new settings or situations in order to make a political point; it considers the mass circulation of images and treats them as a public or semi-public repository for future creativity, regardless of such images' provenance and authorship.[22] Prince resized, overpainted, collaged, and otherwise dramatically altered Cariou's black-and-white photographs for his 'Canal Zone' paintings, originally displayed at the Gagosian gallery in New York in 2008; the following year Cariou filed suit against Prince for copyright infringement.[23] Prince lost his case in 2011 (before the Google case), but in 2013, under appeal and the new standard, his appropriation was found to be transformative and thus protected, in all but five cases (Prince settled with Cariou in 2014 out-of-court with regard to those five). This was a huge victory for artists who mix/remix/sample/appropriate/adapt existing works, which is what artists and writers have always done to varying degrees.[24]

At the same time, copyright and creativity continue to collide. Consider the case of the suit brought by Marvin Gaye's family against performers Robin Thicke and Pharrell Williams for the hit recording 'Blurred Lines'. This case proved fascinating to anyone interested in copyright law and creativity for many reasons, not the least of which is that the suit was won on the basis of sheet music alone in an era when, suggests Jon Caramica, 'the arrangement of notes on a sheet of paper is among the least integral parts of pop music creation' and in which jurors were instructed to decide whether 'Blurred Lines' imitated the 'feel' and the 'sound' of Gaye's work (even though such a 'groove', observes Alex Sayf Cummings, is shared by any 'funky, winsome [...] late 1970s R&B').[25] Matthew D. Morrison's canny account of the case outlines the legal and musicological issues arising from the case, criticizes the jury's reliance on 'structural' musicological elements, predicts misgivings and a certain chilling effect among artists and performers, and perhaps indirectly anticipates Judge John A. Kronstadt's ultimate decision to reduce significantly the Gaye family's demand for damages and instead to award them a share of future earnings from the song.[26]

One of the reasons I am suggesting that we use 'transformation' for anything to do with Shakespeare is that what we do with him/it is *necessarily transformative*. As far as I can tell, the first person to use 'transformation' in a theoretical sense to discuss versions or modifications or adaptations of Shakespeare was Ruby Cohn in *Modern Shakespeare Offshoots*.[27] Cohn distinguishes between what she calls 'emendations' (the routine changes made to a play before it is performed on stage, changes that are, she writes, properly the province of 'theater history' rather than appropriation studies); 'adaptations' (more radical changes to Shakespeare on stage that change the language but nonetheless maintain large plot, structural, and characterological similarities) and 'transformations', where plot and structure from Shakespeare may be jettisoned altogether and Shakespeare's characters may appear in entirely new situations. I suggest that, punning on the transformative principle in law, we call all of Cohn's categories transformations. Whenever we do what we do to Shakespeare, we are transforming it. We don't have access to positivist historical truths and so we are reinventing it/him and ourselves with every iteration, appropriating it in the sense that we make it part of our own mental furniture and even our embodiment, our property.

And yet it is only 'property' in that it can be freely stolen, appropriated, made over. It is, suggests Graham Holderness, malleable and ductile, like gold.[28] Gary Bortolotti and Linda Hutcheon suggest that we should recuperate the term 'adaptation' in the sense of genetic adaptation to particular environments (this takes it closer to the sense in which we use 'appropriation').[29] But we cannot 'adapt' Shakespeare in a genetic sense: we lack access to its unmodified DNA, and moreover Shakespeare is (if we are going to stretch this metaphor) epigenetic. Or maybe Shakespeare is more of a *chimera*, a half-human-hybrid that bears in its manifestation in the world (in its material and textual forms) traces of other forms that it did not 'inherit' in a straightforward manner, a creature that has inherited two or more distinct and identifiable lineages or that has mutated during the process of growth or reproduction.

To sum up: legally, within the US, asserting either adaptation or appropriation transports one into a discussion of ownership and copyright. The freedom from copyright of classic authors such as Shakespeare, Jane Austen, and Charles Dickens has enabled the emergence of amateur and fan cultures that stimulate additional interest in the copyrighted derivative works as well as in the non-copyrighted texts. As Lessig, Henry Jenkins, Cory Doctorow and other writers on creativity have argued, one of the guiding principles of art is its tendency to generate MORE art: its plenitude, its *copia*. Jenkins has written about what he calls the 'convergence culture' where fan or amateur cultural production encounters professional work, and more recently (with Sam Ford and Joshua Green) about 'spreadable media', so-called because it is grabbable, shareable, mixable, and able to be recreated.[30] Shakespearean chimeras flourish because the texts are shareable or 'spreadable'.

Dandelions, Marble, and Honey

We find an added complication with regard to European requirements for transparency in publicly funded research. Such research must often be made available to the public free of charge, or published open-access. The difference in funding structures in the US and in Europe and Canada and also the shrinking of available reputable publishing outlets as major publishers have consolidated mean that despite the promise of digital technologies and Web 2.0 for the rapid and inspiring exchange of knowledge, research in the US is often siloed behind paywalls, since most public US institutions will not pay the open-access fees *necessarily required* by commercial publishers. And I say necessarily required: 'information doesn't want to be free', as Cory Doctorow's latest non-fiction book, which is not free, is entitled, nor is publishing, print- or electronic.[31] Doctorow's punning title distinguishes between two senses of the word 'free' in English that are helpfully demarcated in French. If something is *libre*, it is available without restriction or censorship, but not necessarily free of charge or free from cost (*gratuit*). Online open-access scholarly publishing presents a good example. Those of us who 'tag' essays for digital publication perform the labour of the typesetter or compositor, and those who build the software platforms on which that scholarship appears are the new punch-cutters or machine-tool operators, with skills as rare and highly specialized. Moreover, as Janelle Jenstadt and Brett Hirsch succinctly write, where print editions, once published, require minimal maintenance (they can be left untended, as long as they are kept from flood and fire),

> The digital editorial platform must adapt to changing technological specifications, redesign its interface periodically, plan for succession if the life of the project is to be longer than academic careers, check for 'link rot' and 'bit rot', and think about maintaining the functionality of digital tools that are built into the edition. Like a puppy, a digital edition is for life, not just for Christmas.[32]

Enabling information to be free (*libre*) sometimes means that that information cannot be free (*gratuit*).

How, then, to enable more recent, copyrighted creative works both to make money for their authors and to remain 'spreadable' and generative, given the draconian extensions to copyright law (in some cases, re-creating the state of perpetual copyright that existed prior to the Statute of Anne) under the Copyright Term Extension Act of 1998 (also called the Sonny Bono Act)?[33] Lessig developed the Creative Commons license, which allows creators to maintain some control over their work without demanding the full protection of copyright law.[34] The concept of Copyleft similarly lays out rights for the creator, but insists that users must continue to allow their own remixed material to be reused at liberty; its critics call it 'viral licensing', because it propagates itself.[35]

Shakespearean transformations model both the plenitude and the chimeric or hybrid nature of the emerging creative economy. Lessig anticipated the difficult birth of this hybrid economy, the awkward combination of a commodity economy and a gift culture. Both older models require expenditure, but the former is monetary and the latter is emotional. Where the barriers are clear there is an easy transaction. But (this is Henry Jenkins and Sam Ford): 'any viable hybrid economy needs to respect the rights and interests of participants within these two rather different systems for producing and appraising the value of transactions'.[36] Jenkins additionally suggests that we are encountering 'a growing recognition that profiting from freely given creative labour poses ethical challenges which are, in the long run, socially damaging to both the companies and the communities involved'.[37]

Doctorow has suggested what the current complex and convoluted situation with regard to copyright and creative expressions means in a frequently quoted metaphor that contrasts mammalian reproductive strategies with those of the dandelion. A mammal, Doctorow suggests, has one or two offspring that take a long time to mature, require significant parental attention, are significant, and take up space in the world. The dandelion, contrasts Doctorow, produces 2000 seeds: literally fluffy or insignificant, they cannot tell where they will travel; they are highly mobile and transportable; most will be ignored; a few will take root; some will flourish and form plants and seeds of their own. The key, Doctorow suggests, is not to think about individual sales but about royalties on the aggregate, commissions for directing others towards content (as on an Amazon Partners page, for example). Jenkins and Ford contextualize Doctorow's metaphor in light of the media theory of Harold Innis. Innis contrasted marble – slow, permanent, heavy, indelible, authoritative – with paper – fast, temporary, light, erasable, receptive, suggesting that while the former offered control over time and knowledge-dissemination, the latter offered control over space and knowledge-creation.[38]

Others in less academic realms have independently made these analogies among books, children, marble, in the context of our current digital media revolution. Popular journalist Joe Queenan makes this point colloquially in *One for the Books*, his recent homage to the approximately 6,128 books he estimates he has read during his lifetime:

> People who need to possess the physical copy of a book, not merely an electronic version, believe that the objects themselves are sacred. Some people may find this attitude baffling, arguing that books are merely objects that take up space. This is true, but so are Prague and your kids and the Sistine Chapel. Think it through, bozos.[39]

What does this have to do with Shakespeare? Implicitly, printed books are to digital media as marble is to paper. Shakespearean transformations in both legacy and emerging media offer models for these new economies and hybrids in part because of Shakespeare's 'spreadability'. It is an accident of copyright law and a function of iterability (the ability of Shakespeare to be performed over and over again, remade on stage and page and its subsequent ability to generate yet more art through every additional iteration). Shakespeare can model the engagement of community producers with consumers and the places where so-called hybrid economy seems to work. The difficulty is matching producers with consumers who would be willing to pay for their content: finding what economists call the 'long tail' of publishing, the half-life of books after they are first released.[40] Marketers also prize 'stickiness' in media, attributes and relationships that make consumers (readers, viewers, rewriters) return repeatedly to the source or inspiration or that viewers and readers remember and bring to mind even once the advertisement or cultural product has disappeared from their proximate screen or immediate line of vision.

Can we find examples of Lessig's hybrid gift and commercial economy in Shakespeare studies, or of Doctorow's metaphor of mammals versus dandelions? A search I made on January 8, 2016 of the top ten listing of Shakespeare's works on the US Amazon.com site showed seven out of the ten to be paperback Folger Library editions, an excellent example of this hybrid marketing with its combination of free digital, shareable, mashable, searchable texts online and commercial products (Simon and Schuster print editions). The other three were print versions of the notorious US series *No Fear Shakespeare*, also available freely online with additional content and context through the SparkNotes portal. The rest of the top *twenty* were ninety-nine-cent electronic Kindle Shakespeares, the Riverside Shakespeare (listed as both a rental or as a used copy), and James Shapiro's *Year of Lear*. So this list typifies Lessig's prediction ten years ago: it contains one single breakout best-seller (Shapiro) and then the literally low-rent *No Fear Shakespeare*, and a mid-list (Folger Shakespeare editions) that survives by knowing its market and by intensive outreach and having it partly available for free. Such titles are also indicative in a sense of how writers and scholars can monetize copyleft – derivative works, supplementary works on how to read Shakespeare, lectures, performances, readings, tasters for paid content.

We can all think of examples of such supplementary hybrid content: the website PlayShakespeare.com, which includes open-source and open-access texts and resources about Shakespeare, run by writers and journalists who are not professional academics but who successfully run along a para-Shakespearean track.[41] A more creative example of appropriation and an excellent example of both the 'long tail' in publishing and of how audiences, authors, and actors can collaborate in the imaginary playing space – perhaps we can call it an imaginary globe – would be the relationship between the young New Zealand theatre group The Candle Wasters and their Shakespeare web-series. Work-in-progress by Doug Lanier discusses their adaptation of *Much Ado About Nothing*, 'Nothing Much to Do', which takes the form of mock vlogs, iphone video, some shot as if *cinéma vérité* and some as though a student project (the very funny Dogberry and Verges sequences), so I will not discuss the content here but rather I will comment about how the troupe models for us how to get content to users.

The vlog has become a cult hit, and commenters on Tumblr who say they didn't know anything about Shakespeare claim that they went BACK to Shakespeare because of their interest in the vlog. This symbiotic interaction between producer and consumer appears vividly in Episode 45 of their sequel to 'Nothing Much to Do', 'Lovely Little Losers' (an appropriation of *Love's Labour's Lost*). In this episode, 'Whisper', the flatmates undergo a contest known as the 'whisper challenge', in which one character plays loud music via headphones in order to deafen another, while whispering a phrase to him, after which he in turn whispers it to his partner. The characters sign to each other to try to make each other understand over the music, while the spectators laugh at their misunderstandings. The scene is presented as comic. Some commenters on YouTube objected strongly to the representation of hearing impairment as a temporary comic relief, and also to the mockery of sign language. The company apologized, and asked the crowd whether they should pull down the offending episode or leave it there along with the commentary. A consensus emerged to leave the episode up, with a note acknowledging the offense inadvertently given, and to leave the commentary intact.[42]

Currently, the Candle Wasters are running a Kickstarter crowd-funding project, aimed at their established clientele, to produce a version of *A Midsummer Night's Dream* that picks up on the crowd's delight at their non-traditional cross-gender, cross-race, cross-sexual casting. Young viewers loved the bisexuality of the Don Pedro character in *Nothing Much to Do* and the mix of homo- and heteroerotic orientations in their web-series *Lovely Little Losers*. The Candle Wasters' version of *A Midsummer Night's Dream* looks from its trailer as though it too will employ cross-gender and color-conscious casting. In a sense we can see this transformation as the next phase from Gustafson's film *Were the World Mine*: in that film the gayness makes the comedy, but if this version turns out as planned the comedy will have to rely upon character, as in (arguably) its original conditions of production. This 'prosumer' or crowd-sourced or subscription model might include the film *Still Dreaming*, by Jillian and Hank Rogerson, an account of *Midsummer* as rehearsed and performed in a home for elderly actors, many of whom have Alzheimer's disease. After an initial screening of the rough cut at the Shakespeare Association of America, two Kickstarter campaigns, and intensive fundraising predominantly among that pre-selected audience, the completed film was shown at SAA 2016 in New Orleans. This is both a long tail and a long development: we could perhaps fancifully modify Doctorow's model to imagine dandelion seeds and plants as potential nourishment for your herbivorous mammal cultural product.

Plants finally take me to *A Midsummer Night's Dream* and to the transformations enacted upon the natural world through technology that seems, sometimes even to those who create it, magical. Bottom visually manifests the Shakespeare chimera. Many scholars, particularly those who have written about the persistence of the Apuleius myth of the Golden Ass, have characterized the play as a hybrid and Bottom as a figure for Shakespeare: half-human, half-ass, at the mercy of magical mischievous external forces, worshipped to insanity by some with superior powers and garlanded perforce by children, feared by mortals (non-academics) and yet nonetheless wistfully poetic even before he is translated. Shakespeare itself appropriates multiple sources: classical mythology, English fairy-lore, popular romance, even Englished Georgics or 'how-to' manuals such as Thomas Moffett's *The Silkworms and Their Flies*.[43] Hybrid or chimera Shakespeare is human, animal, faerie, mechanical. Like Bottom, it is a grotesque yet precious mammal, nourished on vegetable matter – not dandelions, but 'apricocks and dewberries [...] purple grapes, green figs, and mulberries' and of course a substance that is both 'spreadable' and 'sticky': honey.[44]

Holderness extends Descartes' metaphor of applying flame to beeswax and finding that, however it is melted, loses its shape, and is moulded and reformed, is still 'redolent of honey and pollen' by arguing that in a much-appropriated play such as *Hamlet* the critic applies the flame and Hamlet is the wax: endlessly mutable and yet somehow still redolent of honey and pollen, still capable of providing surprise and freshness.[45] Coincidentally, there are only five references to honey in *A Midsummer Night's Dream*, all of them surrounding Bottom, either when Titania bids her fairies steal for him 'honey-bags [...] from the humble-bees', or when he himself bids good Cobweb to 'bring [him] the honey-bag' and to 'have a care the honey-bag break not' and not be 'overflown with a honey-bag' or when Titania compares herself as she embraces him to the honeysuckle twining about the woodbine.[46] Preservative, sweetener, and antibiotic therapy, honey is one of the most ancient of foods and yet one that shows itself still to contain essential elements for a posthuman world.[47] So now I think that Shakespeare is not the wax: in a Web 2.0 environment, we do not need the flame to make Shakespeare sticky and spreadable. We do not need Shakespeare only to preserve our connections to the past and to sweeten the present but also to emphasize our entanglement in the messy, natural world even amid our technology. Shakespeare is no longer the wax but the honey.

Sujata Iyengar is Professor of English at the University of Georgia. In 2005, with the late Christy Desmet, she co-founded the first scholarly periodical devoted to Shakespearean afterlives, which she now co-edits with Matt Kozusko and Louise Geddes. She is the author and co-author of numerous volumes and scholarly articles on modern literature, Shakespeare on screens, twenty-first-century art and culture, and feminist art. She is currently working on two books, *Shakespeare and Adaptation Theory* (under contract with Arden) and *Shakespeare and the Art of the Book*. With Peg Pearson, she's also co-editing *Transformative Shakespeares*, a collection of creative and critical work surrounding Shakespeare.

Notes

Originally published as Sujata Iyengar, 'Shakespeare Transformed: Copyright, Copyleft, and Shakespeare After Shakespeare', in *Shakespeare après Shakespeare*, edited by Anne-Valérie Dulac and Laetitia Sansonetti (Paris: Société Francaise Shakespeare, 2017), and is here republished with kind permission of the editors and the Société Francaise Shakespeare.

1. There is a rich literature on Shakespearean adaptation, appropriation, 'tradaptation', borrowing, reworking, and so on towards which I can only gesture in this essay. On versions of Shakespeare as appropriations, see Christy Desmet and Robert Sawyer, eds., *Shakespeare and Appropriation*, London and New York, Routledge, 1999; Craig Dionne and Parmita Kapadia, *Native Shakespeares: Indigenous Appropriations on a Global Stage*, London and New York, Ashgate, 2008; Alexa

Huang and Elizabeth Rivlin, eds., *Shakespeare and the Ethics of Appropriation*, London and New York, Palgrave, 2014; as adaptations, see Margaret Jane Kidnie, *Shakespeare and the Problem of Adaptation*, London and New York, Routledge, 1999; as 'tradaptations', see Roshni Mooneeram, *From Creole to Standard: Shakespeare, Language, and Literature in a Postcolonial Context*, Amsterdam, Rodopi, 2014, p. 145; Jennifer Drouin, *Shakespeare in Quebec: Nation, Gender, and Adaptation*, Toronto, Toronto University Press, 2014, p. 22, p. 62, p. 89–110 *et passim*; as offshoots, see Ruby Cohn's classic *Modern Shakespearean Offshoots*, Princeton, New Jersey, Princeton University Press, 1976, reprinted Princeton, New Jersey, Princeton Legacy Library, 2015; as recontextualizations, see Daniel Fischlin and Mark Fortier, eds., *Adaptations of Shakespeare*, London and New York, Routledge, 2000, 2nd ed. 2014, p. 3, p. 5, p. 7; Douglas Lanier, 'Recent Shakespeare Adaptation and the Mutations of Cultural Capital', *Shakespeare Studies* 38 (2010), ed. Susan Zimmerman and Garrett Sullivan, Madison and Teaneck, Fairleigh Dickinson University Press, p. 107; as riffs, see Charles Marowitz, *The Marowitz Shakespeare: Adaptations and Collages of* Hamlet, Macbeth, The Taming of the Shrew, Measure for Measure, *and* The Merchant of Venice, New York, Drama Book Specialists, 1978 p. 9; Peter Erickson, *Citing Shakespeare: The Reinterpretation of Race in Contemporary Literature and Art*, New York and Houndmills, Basingstoke, Hampshire, Palgrave Macmillan, 2007; as remix, see Fran Teague, 'Using Shakespeare with Memes, Remixes, and Fanfic', *Shakespeare Survey* 64 (2011), 74–82. Work in progress further characterizes Shakespeare through the 'uses' to which amateur cultures and fan cultures put it (Louise Geddes and Valerie Fazel, eds., 'The Shakespeare User', edited collection in progress).
2. Julie Sanders, 'The Sonnets as an Open-source Initiative', *Shakespeare Survey* 64 (2011), 121–32.
3. References to the works of Shakespeare come from *Shakespeare's Plays, Folger Digital Texts*, edited by Barbara Mowat, Paul Werstine, Michael Poston, and Rebecca Niles, Folger Shakespeare Library, http://www.folgerdigitaltexts.org/?chapter=0&?target=about, last accessed May 17 2016. See also *Were the World Mine*, dir. Tom Gustafson, 2008; Richard Appignanesi and Kate Brown, *Manga Shakespeare: A Midsummer Night's Dream*, London, Self-Made Hero, 2008.
4. See, for example, John Drakakis, 'Ideology and Institution: Shakespeare and the Roadsweepers', in Graham Holderness, ed., *The Shakespeare Myth*, Manchester, UK, Manchester University Press, 1988, 24–41, p. 34; Michael Bristol, *Big-Time Shakespeare (Is Shakespeare Great? Or is it all just Hype?)*, New York and London, Routledge, 1996, p. 93, p. 113–114 *et passim*; Richard Finkelstein, 'Disney Cites Shakespeare: The Limits of Appropriation', in *Shakespeare and Appropriation*, *op. cit.*, 179–196, p. 193; and the essays in the collection *Shakespeare's Cultural Capital: His Economic Impact from the Sixteenth to the Twenty-first Century*, eds. Dominic Shellard and Siobhan Keenan, London, Palgrave Macmillan, 2016.
5. Stephen Orgel, 'The Authenic Shakespeare', in *The Authentic Shakespeare and Other Problems of the Early Modern Stage*, London and Abingdon, Routledge, 2002, 231–56; Michel Foucault, 'What is an Author?' in *Language, Counter-memory, Practice: Selected Essays and Interviews*, ed. Donald F. Bouchard, trans. Donald F. Bouchard and Sherry Simon, Ithaca, New York, Cornell University Press, 1977, 113–138; Denise Albanese, *Extramural Shakespeare*, New York, Palgrave Macmillan, 2010, pp. 5–6, 116–17, *et passim*.

6. Christy Desmet, 'Introduction', *Shakespeare and Appropriation, op. cit.*, p. 8; Terence Hawkes, *Meaning By Shakespeare*, London, Routledge, 1992.
7. Fran Teague, 'Using Shakespeare with Memes, Remixes, and Fanfic', *op. cit.*; Stephen O'Neill, *Shakespeare and YouTube: New Media Forms of the Bard*, London, Arden/Bloomsbury, 2014; Peter Holland, 'Spinach and Tobacco: Making Shakespearian Unoriginals', *Shakespeare Survey* 68 (2015), 197–209.
8. Christian Fuchs, 'Dallas Smythe and Digital Labor', in *The Routledge Companion to Labor and Media*, ed. Richard Maxwell, New York and London, 2016, 51–62, p. 57.
9. On the history of Shakespeare and copyright, see James Marino, *Owning Shakespeare, Owning William Shakespeare: The King's Men and their intellectual property*, Philadelphia, University of Pennsylvania Press, 2011, p. 1; Jeffrey M. Gaba, 'Copyrighting Shakespeare: Jacob Tonson, Eighteenth Century English Copyright, And The Birth Of Shakespeare Scholarship', *Journal of Intellectual Property Law* 19.1 (2011), 21–63, p. 31. Marino argues that even in the absence of what we now understand as copyright in intellectual property, the King's Men modified Shakespeare's plays for theatrical production idiosyncratically as a way of asserting their transformative authority and ownership of the plays they performed.
10. Gaba, *op. cit*, p. 44.
11. *Ibid.*, p. 62, p. 44, p. 43.
12. *Ibid.*, p. 44, p. 63. On Walker's penny parts, see also Robert B. Hamm Jr., 'Walker v. Tonson in the Court of Public Opinion', *Huntington Library Quarterly* 75.1 (2012), 95–112.
13. Don-John Dugas, *Marketing the Bard: Shakespeare in Performance and Print, 1660–1740*, Columbia, University of Missouri Press, 2006, 232.
14. I write here as a lay-person and a private individual and do not speak for my institution, the French Shakespeare Society, or any organization. Those with personal, financial, and institutional interests in copyright should consult a qualified expert in intellectual property law. I take my definitions from Cornell University Law School's invaluable Legal Information Institute; the definition of 'derivative work' appears at https://www.law.cornell.edu/uscode/text/17/101, accessed May 17 2016.
15. Pierre N. Leval, *Harvard Law Review* 103 (1990), 1104–1136.
16. *Ibid.*, p. 1111.
17. *Ibid.*, p. 1116.
18. Lawrence Lessig, *Free Culture: How Big Media Uses Technology and the Law to Lock Down Culture and Control Creativity*, New York, Penguin, 2004, http://www.free-culture.cc/freeculture.pdf, accessed May 21 2016; United States Court of Appeals for the Second Circuit, 'Authors Guild *v.* Google, Inc.', Argued Dec. 3 2014, Decided Oct. 16, 2015, http://www.ca2.uscourts.gov/decisions/isysquery/b3f81bc4-3798-476e-81c0-23db25f3b301/1/doc/13-4829_opn.pdf, accessed May 21, 2016.
19. Kevin Smith, 'A Wide-Angle Lens on Fair Use', *Scholarly Communications@Duke*, Nov. 17, 2013, http://blogs.library.duke.edu/scholcomm/2013/11/17/a-wide-angle-lens-on-fair-use/, accessed May 21, 2016; 'Google Books, Fair Use, and the Public Good', *Scholarly Communications@Duke*, October 18, 2015, http://blogs.library.duke.edu/scholcomm/2015/10/18/google-books-fair-use-and-the-public-good/, accessed May 21, 2016.

20. Barbara S. Murphy, 'The Wind Done Gone: Parody or Piracy? A Comment on Suntrust Bank *v.* Houghton Mifflin Company', *Georgia State University Law Review* 19.2 (2002), Article 7, p. 594, p. 598, http://readingroom.law.gsu.edu/gsulr/vol19/iss2/7, accessed May 18 2016; see also Richard Schur, '*The Wind Done Gone* Controversy: American Studies, Copyright Law, and the Imaginary Domain', *American Studies* 44.1–2 (2003), 5–33.
21. Patrick Cariou, *Yes, Rasta*, New York, Powerhouse Books, 2000.
22. Robert Nelson and Richard Schiff, *Critical Terms for Art History*, 2nd edition, Chicago, University of Chicago Press, 2010, p. 165; Kathleen K. Desmond, *Ideas about Art*, Oxford and West Sussex, Wiley-Blackwell, p. 151; Tom Williams, 'Appropriation Art', *Grove Art Online, Oxford Art Online*, Oxford University Press, 2010, accessed August 25, 2016, http://www.oxfordartonline.com/subscriber/article/grove/art/T2086713?q=appropriation+art&search=quick&pos=1&_start=1#firsthit.
23. Filmmaker and artist Greg Allen has written extensively about the case in 'Richard Prince's Canal Zone Paintings: Now With 83% Less Infringiness!', 'greg.org: the making of', http://greg.org/archive/2013/04/25/richard_princes_canal_zone_paintings_now_with_83_less_infringiness.html, accessed August 25, 2016, and archived Prince's 'Canal Zone' images at http://greg.org/archive/canal_zone_collage_rprince.jpg, accessed August 25, 2016.
24. Jonathan Francis, 'On Appropriation: Cariou *v.* Prince and Measuring Contextual Transformation in Fair Use', *Berkeley Technology Law Journal* 29 (2014), Article 10, available at http://scholarship.law.berkeley.edu/btlj/vol29/iss4/10, accessed May 21, 2016.
25. Jon Caramanica, 'What's Wrong With the "Blurred Lines" Copyright Ruling', *New York Times*, 11 March 2015, http://www.nytimes.com/2015/03/12/arts/music/whats-wrong-with-the-blurred-lines-copyright-ruling.html?_r=0, accessed 17 May 2016; Alex Sayf Cummings, 'The "Blurred Lines" of music and copyright: Part one', *OUP Blog*, 28 April 2015, http://blog.oup.com/2015/04/blurred-lines-copyright-part-one/#sthash.Gi1PA9Xq.dpuf, accessed May 17 2016.
26. Matthew D. Morrison, 'Gaye vs. Thicke: How blurred are the lines of copyright infringement?', *OUP Blog*, 26 March 2015, http://blog.oup.com/2015/03/blurred-lines-copyright-infringement/#sthash.CG3bws7g.dpuf, accessed May 17 2016; Guardian Music and Associated Press, 'Pharrell Williams wins back $2m in Blurred Lines case', *The Guardian*, July 15 2015, http://www.theguardian.com/music/2015/jul/15/pharrell-williams-wins-back-2m-in-blurred-lines-case, accessed May 17, 2016.
27. Cohn, *op. cit.*
28. Graham Holderness, *Tales from Shakespeare: Creative Collisions*, Cambridge, Cambridge University Press, 2014, p. 4.
29. Gary R. Bortolotti and Linda Hutcheon, 'On the Origin of Adaptations: Rethinking Fidelity Discourse and "Success"—Biologically', *New Literary History* 38.3 (2007), 443–458.
30. Henry Jenkins, *Convergence Culture: Where Old and New Media Collide*, New York, New York University Press, 2008; Henry Jenkins, Sam Ford, and Joshua Green, *Spreadable Media: Creating Value and Meaning in a Networked Culture*, New York, New York University Press, 2015.
31. Cory Doctorow, *Information Doesn't Want to Be Free*, New York, McSweeney's, 2014.

32. Brett D. Hirsch and Janelle Jenstad, 'Beyond the Text: Digital Editions and Performance', *Shakespeare Bulletin* 34.1 (2016), 106–27, p. 107.
33. Cory Doctorow, 'We'll Probably Never Free Mickey, But That's Beside the Point', *Electronic Frontier Foundation*, Jan. 19, 2016, https://www.eff.org/deeplinks/2016/01/well-probably-never-free-mickey-thats-beside-point, accessed May 21, 2016.
34. Creative Commons, https://creativecommons.org/, accessed May 21, 2016.
35. Copyleft.org, https://copyleft.org/, accessed May 21, 2016.
36. Jenkins, Ford, and Green, *op. cit.*, p. 67.
37. *Ibid.*, p. 68.
38. Harold Innis, *The Bias of Communication*, 1951, Toronto, University of Toronto Press, 1999, discussed in Jenkins, Ford, and Green, *op.cit.*, p.37.
39. Joe Queenan, *One for the Books*, New York and London, Penguin, 2012, p. 239.
40. Chris Anderson, *The Long Tail: Why the Future of Business is Selling Less of More*, New York, Hyperion, 2006.
41. PlayShakespeare.com, 2005–2016, https://www.playshakespeare.com/, accessed May 21, 2016.
42. The Candle Wasters, 'Whisper', *Lovely Little Losers*, Episode 45, https://www.youtube.com/watch?v=IUxpttxjyzs, accessed January 15, 2016.
43. On Shakespeare's sources for *Midsummer Night's Dream,* see Geoffrey Bullough, *Narrative and Dramatic Sources of Shakespeare*, Volume 6, New York, Columbia University Press, 1957, pp. 367–424. Whether or not Shakespeare used Moffett remains the subject of debate: see Katherine Duncan-Jones, 'Pyramus and Thisbe: Shakespeare's Debt to Moffett Cancelled', *Review of English Studies* 32 (1981): 296–301; Roger Prior, '"Runnawayes eyes": A Genuine Crux', *Shakespeare Quarterly* 40 (1989): 191–95.
44. William Shakespeare, *A Midsummer Night's Dream*, 3.1.172, ed. Barbara Mowat, Paul Werstine, Michael Poston and Rebecca Niles, http://www.folgerdigitaltexts.org/html/MND.html, accessed May 21, 2016.
45. Holderness, *Creative Collisions, op. cit.*, p. 8.
46. Shakespeare, *A Midsummer Night's Dream, op. cit.*, 3.1.174; 4.1.12, 15, 16, 41.
47. Katrina Brudzynski , Calvin Sjaarda, 'Antibacterial Compounds of Canadian Honeys Target Bacterial Cell Wall Inducing Phenotype Changes, Growth Inhibition and Cell Lysis That Resemble Action of β-Lactam Antibiotics', *PLOS One*, September 5, 2014, http://dx.doi.org/10.1371/journal.pone.0106967, quoted in Andrea Ford, 'Is Honey the New Antibiotic?' *Scope*, Stanford Medicine, January 18, 2015, http://scopeblog.stanford.edu/2015/01/28/is-honey-the-new-antibiotic/, both accessed November 14, 2016.

Afterthought
'Best for Winter'

Graham Holderness

Let me see: every 'leven wether tods; every tod yields pound and odd shilling; fifteen hundred shorn. What comes the wool to? My father's voice, grumbling and spitting, everything to him was money, how much would it come to, whether wool or leather for the market price, his ewes and rams were gold and silver, he made them breed as fast. What more could he do, for his little flock of hungry sheep, mouths bleating for food, all shorn fleece and wincing withers in the winter's cold? So lean that blasts of January would blow us through and through. Hand-fast and hold was the watchword, hard to come by as it was, money, nothing to spare and all devoured in a twinkling, flesh and fell. Sheep or men, eat or be eaten, he kept us penned warm together and we lived, most of us, while the wolves prowled outside in the darkness. Every spring, woolly buttocks quiver, new lambs drop, wringing wet and wriggling, from the ewe's heaving loins, no sooner on the ground than up and kicking, twisting back to the mother for a taste of udder in the hungry sucking mouth. *Enter a Shepherd.* In trouble with the law of course, my father, over the wool

Notes for this section begin on page 166.

gathering, likewise the usury, his trade being otherwise, and none should meddle with another man's trade, discrediting his mystery. But John first fed his family by any fair means, and let the law go hang. Anything could be turned to money, when the need arose: even the rubble of an old tumbled house. Pd to Mr. Shakespeare for one load of stone xd. They caught me too, holding ten quarters or forty bushels of malt or corn, I forget which, when women were dying in the hedgerows of hunger, and their babes mewled on the dry dead dug, but my babes never starved. A lawless family, then, we were, my own wild days no surprise to my father though a disappointment I have since redressed. I would there were no age between sixteen and three-and-twenty, or that youth would sleep out the rest; for there is nothing in the between but getting wenches with child, wronging the ancientry, stealing, fighting. Anne Hathaway, buxom and big-bellied at the altar in Worcester, her kinfolk standing close around me, she could testify to that, getting wenches with child. For she was the wench from Shottery o'er the dale, and with child, and there was none other nigh by whom the child in her womb might have been begotten. So I compassed a motion of the Prodigal Son, and married a tinker's wife within a mile. Young men will do't, if they come to't.

> When daffodils begin to peer,
> With heigh! the doxy over the dale,
> Why, then comes in the sweet o' the year;
> For the red blood reigns in the winter's pale.

There verily was some stair-work, some trunk-work, some behind-door-work. There was good smooth ploughing on that fair meadow ere the crop eared, but a goodly harvest it was to be sure, for she was fair and fertile as one of Laban's ewes. Mercy on 's, a barne, a very pretty barne! A boy or a child, I wonder? When she was delivered a child she proved, Susanna, a pretty one. Some 'scape it was, but I took her up for pity. For wronging the ancientry and stealing, old Sir Thomas Lucy can speak of that, for it was his deer I stalked, in the shadows of his park, and it was his men who seized me, as I bore the deer home over my shoulder to Shottery. The pale moon shines by night. They had me up before him, that very morning, and if lousy justice had taken its course I should not have 'scaped whipping. But the fellows who were to carry me to the goal were friends of my father's and owed him a good turn. They were good stout fellows who held that God put all the earth's beasts at man's service and cared nothing for the likes of Sir Thomas, who empaled his fields and kept food from the people's mouths, so they managed to lose me ere they reached the town, and I was away over the fields and bound for London before Sir Thomas brought me again to mind. And when I wander here and there, I then do most go right. And for fighting I had my share of that sport too, or would have, but that William Wayte being a coward who had wronged me and durst not stand like a man swore before the Judge of Queen's Bench that he stood in danger of death, or bodily hurt from William Shakespere.[1] Money was at the root of that trouble too, but I would have given money to beat the perjured rogue about the head with one of his own cudgels. Yet I staid my hand and kept the peace: beating and hanging are terrors to me: for the life to come, I sleep out the thought of it. Money can make all safe; money is a warm fire, and bread on the table; money is quiet children and a contented wife. Money is a fence against the wolf, a safeguard against the grasping hand of the law. I penned my dreams and spoke them on stage, and money fell around me in a shower like rain. Gold! all gold! It was told me I should be rich by the fairies. This is fairy gold, boy, and 'twill prove so. Keep it close: home, home, the next way. Away from London, take the road to Stratford. We are lucky, boy, good boy, the next way home. So home I went, not as a poacher escaped from justice, or a prentice run away from his master, but a gentleman, known about the court, and a man of means with gold to lay out on what I chose. I chose New Place, Clopton's house, and nothing in my life ever pleased me so much as to walk through its rooms, and warm myself before its many fireplaces, and take my ease in its gardens and orchards. Sir Thomas Lucy would not send his men to attach me here, nor William Wayte pursue me from far-off London with his ruffians. New Place: my place. Paid for in cash, £60 of ready money. House and home. Let my sheep go. I staid not long in Stratford, true, for it was off back to London, to make more money, pen more dreams. Now they come to me, my Stratford neighbours, feeling from afar the warmth of my wealth. Here is Sturley, I hear, who calls me his countryman, and asks if I am willing to disburse some money upon some odd yardland or other at Shottrei or neare about. Haply I will, too, for it may suit me to secure land thereabout, but if I do, for me it will be, and not for them. Here is Quiney, comes cringing to me for £30, calls me his loving friend and countryman, tells me I shall friend him much in helping him out of all the debts he owes in London. A mind free from debt is a quiet mind. So it is, but he begs to be indebted to me! What of my mind's quiet? Not even in his own hand either, this letter, but a scrivener's copy. If they bargain with me, or recover money therefore, let them bring their money home as they may. I am no fool to be fleeced and shorn by their avaricious shears. They called me dog, when I was young and wild and running mad with lust and want, and now they would have monies. Hath a dog money? Is it possible a cur can lend £30? I am sick of them, and must to my work. *Revenir a mes moutons*, the French say: let us return to our sheep. The French. Bastard Normans. Norman bastards. Mountjoy's wife is screaming at him now, down below, another dalliance with some baggage come to light. Listen to them, ungh, ungh, ungh, eow, eow, eow, nobody can understand them, least of all themselves. Let me shut the door, though the evening is hot, and the room close. Shut it tight. Let me dream. Ne'er was dream so like a waking. Perdita: the lost one. The seacoast of Bohemia: a child abandoned on a desolate shore, the father thinking it his friend's bastard, his wife an adulterous whore. Places remote enough are in Bohemia, to cast out an unwanted child. There weep and leave it crying; and, for the babe is counted lost forever, Perdita, I prithee, call't. Come, poor babe. I did in time collect myself and thought this was so and no slumber. Dreams are toys. I have heard, but not believed, the spirits o' the dead may walk again: if such thing be, may not my little Hamnet play there with lost Perdita, on that desert shore, stolen from the dead? Weep I cannot, but my heart bleeds. Blossom, speed thee well! Go into the mountains, and seek that which is gone astray. My land is before you, to dwell where you please. 107 acres of land and 20 acres of pasture in Old Stratford bought for £320 from William and John Combe. From Ralph Hubaud a half-interest in a lease of Tythes of Corne grayne blade and heye. What is a player? a coney-catching rogue, a mountebank, a poor fool. I have given everything for show, and nothing is left. I have sold all my trumpery; not a ribbon, glass, pomander, brooch, table book, ballad, knife, tape, glove, shoe tie, bracelet, horn ring, to keep my pack from fasting. They throng who should buy first, as if my trinkets had been hallowed and brought a benediction to the buyer. My verses, siren songs, so drew the herd to me that all their other senses stuck in ears: my sir's song, and admiring the nothing of it. So in this time of lethargy I picked and cut most of their festival purses. They flattered me like a dog and showered me with gifts, but I was nothing to them, at the last, but a poor player, that struts and frets his hour upon the stage, and then is heard no more. Till I became a landlord, a householder, a lessee of tithes, an aunciant freeholder in the fields of Old Stratford and Welcombe. Such a man is someone, a man of property, a gentleman of consequence. Combe and Mainwaring mean to enclose those fields, but I will lose nothing by it. I will be compensated for all such loss detriment and hindrance, by reason of any enclosure or decay of tillage, there meant and intended, by the same William Replingham, Attorney at Law. They are to fence round the smallholdings and common fields, the better to pasture the sheep. There is much profit thereby, and enrichment of the town. Yet Greene and his corporation oppose the enclosure and call upon me to take their part. Greene comes to see me, hearing I am in town, asking how I did. I told him they assured me they meant to enclose no further than to Gospel Bush and so up straight (leaving out part of the dingles to the field) to the gate in Clopton hedge and take in Salisbury's piece. And that they mean in April to survey the land and then to give satisfaction, and not before. And that I think, with Mr. Hall, there will be nothing done at all. Was I lied to, or lying? For truthfully I told him what I heard, though truthfully I knew it was all lies, and the work would begin in January. I will protect my tithes and secure against any loss reasonable satisfaction in yearly rent or a sum of money. Greene pleads for the poor and their memorial rights to graze their beasts on the common land. What do I care? I was poor enough once, and my father laboured to feed us, as I laboured to feed my own. I am a true labourer. I earn that I eat, get that I wear, owe no man hate, envy no man's happiness, glad of other men's good, content with my harm, and the greatest of my pride is to see my ewes graze and my lambs suck. Let the sheep graze and make some men rich, for they will need labourers in turn who will work for their food. Florizel and Perdita are to meet at the sheep shearing. Mountjoy's wife is scolding in the back kitchen. A stink blows up from the river: plague breath. A pestilent gall to me. O Proserpina, for the flowers now, that frighted thou let'st fall from Dis's waggon! I must go. Leave this place. Their nightly brawling wearies me. I lied on oath for Mountjoy, hoping it would bring me some peace and quiet. Said I could not remember the amount of the dowry promised to Bellott. I remembered it well enough, but I cared little for the young man, and landlords' palms need greasing. Much good it did me, imperilling my immortal soul for £50. And still it goes on, the shouting and banging of doors and clattering of pots and pans. Owy, owy, owy; nong, nong, nong. I must fly. To Stratford? My garden will be bright and fresh with the spring. Daffodils that come before the swallow dares, and take the winds of March with beauty. No: not there. If Silver Street is Purgatory, Stratford is very hell, with that scolding devil of a wife. Yet here I cannot entertain a friend or bring home a wench for a long night's solace. I must take a house in London. What of Henry Walker's gatehouse at Blackfriars? Black brows, they say, become some women best. If I buy it, Anne will have a third share for life in that part of my estate. I must keep it from her. Walker told me the house could be bought by trustees, and thereby become a joint tenancy. If I were to predecease the other trustees, Chancery would not recognize her privilege. That would serve: for I must not have her mingling in my London life, whether I am alive or dead. Knowing who I know, learning of who I lie with, turning o'er my things in a jealous rage ... No, I'll none of it. I'll take the Blackfriars house, be less in Stratford, make my home here. And when the burden of age presses down upon me, and I am too sick to stay here by myself, then I'll trudge slowly home to Stratford, to die in my own bed. This thought cheers me. At least they are quiet again downstairs now. Mountjoy is back in the workshop, I can hear him angrily hammering.[2] She will be sewing, jabbing her needle spitefully through the silk, wishing it were her husband's eyes. Venice gold in needlework. What a twisted skein is life: what a tangled web we weave. Gold and silver thread from Venice; silk from Damascus; pearls of the orient. Clattering pots in the kitchen; smell of frying onions. A man's anger; a woman's hate. My words too, precious jewels strung on cheap strings with counterfeit stones, to fool the senses, catch the breath, delight the eye. All is hybridity, promiscuity, miscegenation. For I have heard it said, there is an art which in its piedness shares with great creating nature. We marry a gentler scion to the wildest stock and make conceive a bark of baser kind by bud of nobler race. This is an art which does mend nature, change it rather, but the art itself is nature. The play goes well. A melancholy piece, with a jealous king, a virtuous wife suspected, a son dead from grief, a daughter left to die on a distant shore, a man torn to pieces by a bear. So let me bring them all together at the end and let reconciliation and forgiveness spring between them. A lost daughter returned; a wife back from the dead; a statue that moves and speaks. Nothing like life. Like an old tale still, which will have matter to rehearse, though credit be asleep, and not an ear open. It will do well though, the taste of the times being what it is, and make me some more money. A fleece against the coming cold. A sad tale's best for winter.

Graham Holderness is the author or editor of some 60 books. His work can be divided into three strands: literary criticism, theory and scholarship, especially in Shakespeare studies; the pioneering of an innovative new method of 'creative criticism'; and creative writing in fiction, poetry and drama. Key critical works include *The Shakespeare Myth* (Manchester UP, 1988), *The Politics of Theatre and Drama* (Routledge, 1992), *Shakespeare: The Histories* (Bloomsbury, 2000), and *The Faith of William Shakespeare* (Lion Books, 2016). Works of creative criticism, which are half criticism and half fiction, include *Nine Lives of William Shakespeare* (Bloomsbury-Arden Shakespeare, 2011); *Tales from Shakespeare: Creative Collisions* (Cambridge University Press, 2014) and *Re-writing Jesus: Christ in 20th Century Fiction and Film* (Bloomsbury, November 2014). He has also published two novels: *The Prince of Denmark* (University of Hertfordshire Press, 2001), and the historical fantasy novel *Black and Deep Desires: William Shakespeare Vampire Hunter* (Top Hat Books, 2015).

Notes

1. William Wayte took out an injunction restraining Shakespeare and others from offering him physical violence. This strange detail of the life has never been satisfactorily explained.
2. Shakespeare lodged in Silver Street between 1598 and 1604, while *The Winter's Tale* was probably written 1610–11.

Index

A
Account (Rowe), 130
Ackroyd, Peter, 135
Act for the Relief of the Poor (1597), 79
adaptation/appropriation, 12, 142–45, 148, 155n1
Agamben, Giorgio, 40
Albanese, Denise, 143
Allen, Greg, 158n23
An Alternative Biography, The Shakespeare Circle, 135–36
Amazon.com, 152
Appadurai, Arjun, 24
Appleby, Joyce Oldham, 43
Aristotle, 78, 125–26
    reciprocity and exchange related to, 29–30, 38–39, 42–43, 45, 46n2
The Art of Shakespeare's Sonnets (Vendler), 90
As You Like It (Shakespeare), 104
Austin, J. L., 23
Authors' Guild *v.* Google, Inc. (2005–13), 145–46
autonomous representation, of 'derivatives,' 18–19, 27
Ayache, Elie, 24–25

B
'balanced reciprocity,' 31
banking, 10–11, 88–89
banknote, 1–4, 6
Bank of England, 1–3, 88
'Bardbiz,' 7
Bardcard, 4–5
Bate Jonathan, 135, 141n38
Baudrillard, Jean, 16
Beal, Simon, 98–99, 103
Bearman, Robert, 12, 136–37
Benton, Michael, 129, 138n6
Bergson, Henri, 68n39
Bevington, David, 38
biography, 12, 125–28. *See also* Shakespeare biographies
Bishop, Matthew, 19
Blackfriars Playhouse, 112, 118–19
Booth, Stephen, 90
Borges, Jorge-Luis, 24–25
Bortolotti, Gary, 148
Branagh, Kenneth, 97
Braudel, Fernand, 41, 49–50, 88–89, 126
Bristol, Michael, 98
Brome, Richard, 111
brothels, 61–64, 69
Bruster, Douglas, 5, 66n14, 68n37, 121
Buckingham Palace, 4
Buffet, Warren, 16
business, 6–7
Butler, Judith, 23–24
Byron, May Clarissa Gillington (Maurice Clare), 140n26

C

Cambridge Guide to the Worlds of Shakespeare (Tratner), 90
capitalism, 5, 61–64, 143–44
Cariou, Patrick, 147
Carlyle, Thomas, 7
Catholicism, 79–80
Chambers, E. K., 130, 134
Cheney, Dick, 28n3
'cheque guarantee cards,' 4–5
Christian mercantilism, 70–71, 75
Church of England, 99
Clare, Maurice, 140n26
Clifford, James, 127, 133
Cohen, Ruby, 148
Cohen, Walter, 66n19
Cohn, Ruby, 148
Collingwood, Roger, 126
Collinson, Patrick, 46
The Comedy of Errors (Shakespeare), 9–10, 63–64, 68n44. *See also* historicity
    liquidity in, 57–59, 61, 68nn37–42
    Mediterranean world in, 51, 55–57, 58
commodification, 31–32, 41–44
commodities, 36–37, 47n20
commodity exchange, 31, 35, 36–37, 39–40
common land, 6, 164
community, 40
Contribution to the Critique of Political Economy (Marx), 29
copyright laws, U.S., 150
    'fair use' doctrine of, 146–47
    in hybrid economy, 142–49
    social media and, 142–43
    'transformative' in, 12, 146–48
Copyright Term Extension Act of 1998 (Sonny Bono Act), 150
Coriolanus (Shakespeare), 18
Cummings, Alex Sayf, 147–48
Cymbeline (Shakespeare), 118, 119

D

A Day with Shakespeare (Clare), 140n26
Dekker, Thomas, 113, 118
derivatives, 4, 9, 15, 28n3, 145
    autonomous representation of, 18–19, 27
    current value of, 16
    'deregulation' of, 16–17
    'exchange-value' of, 17
    idolatry and, 25–26
    iterability related to, 24
    performativity of, 25
    representation of, 20–22
    signifiers of, 22–23
    underlying of, 25
    usury and, 21–22
    volatility of, 16
derivative works, 145, 149, 152
Derrida, Jacques, 22–24, 44, 73
Descartes, René, 154
'digital currency,' 4
digital technologies, 149–51
DiPietro, Cary, 65n5
'disintegrationist,' 130–33, 140n25
distance and difference, 66n14
Doctorow, Cory, 149, 151
Donaldson v. Becket (1774), 145
'door-keepers,' 113
Drakakis, John, 9
drama, 68n39
Dugas, Don-John, 144–45
Duncan-Jones, Katherine, 135

E

Eagleton, Terry, 56
Ecclestone, Harry, 1–2
École des Annales, 126–27
Edel, Leon, 138n6
Edmondson, Paul, 131, 132, 135–36
Edward III (king), 88–89
Eliot, T. S., 15–16, 19–21, 28n10
Elizabeth (queen), 80
Ellis, David, 140n26
Ellmann, Richard, 129–30

emotions, money related to, 55, 67n32
Ephesus, 51–52, 66n16, 66n18
equality, 31–32, 35–36
Erikson, Erik, 131
European Commission, 67n26
European democracy, 104
European economies, 87
exchange, 61, 68n38, 69nn48–49
exchange-value, 15. *See also* reciprocity and exchange

F
false equivalence, 18
feathers, 118–19
Ferguson, Niall, 16
financial crisis, global, 50–51
financial recession, 97–98
financial symbols, 15
financing performance
  books in, 116–18
  clowns in, 115
  coaches in, 112–13
  'door-keepers' in, 113
  feathers in, 118–19
  food and drink in, 114–16
  'hawkers' in, 114–19
  players in, 109, 111–12
  playwrights in, 109–10
  prostitutes in, 119–20
  seating in, 113
  Shakespeare in, 110–11
  thieves in, 120
  tobacco in, 118
  transportation in, 111–13
  watermen in, 111–12
First World War, 19–20
Fitzgeffrey, Henry, 119
food, 60, 114–16
Ford, Sam, 150, 151
Forman, Valerie, 68n45, 69n52
Foucault, Michel, 143
free culture, 145–46

G
Gaba, Jeffrey, 144
Garrick, David, 2–3
Gaye, Marvin, 147–48
Gayton, Edmund, 114–15
gender, 23, 153–54
geopolitics, 8, 49–50
global economies, 8, 87
global financial crisis, 50–51
global geography, 66n19
Globe Theatre (London), 97, 112, 115, 118
gold standard, 15, 16, 19–21
Gone With the Wind (Mitchell), 146–47
Good Friday Agreement (1997), 108n20
Google Books, 145–46
Goux, Jean-Joseph, 17
Grady, Hugh, 56n7, 65n5, 104
Granville-Barker, Harley, 51–52
Grav, Peter F., 8, 56, 58, 66n18, 124n46
Great Shakespeare Jubilee, 2–3
Greek economy, 102
Green, John, 119
Greenblatt, Stephen, 53–54, 135, 141n38

H
Halliwell-Phillipps, J. O., 134–35
Hamlet (film), 20, 51
Hamlet (Shakespeare), 154
'hawkers,' 114–19
Hawkes, David, 41, 43
Hawkes, Terence, 7, 48, 65n7, 99
Heaney, Seamus, 65n6
Heinemann, Margot, 100–101
Heminges, John, 115
Henry VIII (Shakespeare), 115–16
Henslowe, Philip, 120
Heywood, Thomas, 109
Hirsch, Brett, 150
historicity, 48, 65n5
  mobility in, 50–54, 66n14, 67nn25–26
  place related to, 49–52, 65n6, 65n8, 66n16, 66nn18–19

history, biography related to, 125–28
Holderness, Graham, 131, 132, 141n38, 148, 154
'homology,' 17, 28n4
Honan, Park, 129, 130, 138n6
household management, 29–30
housekeepers (investors in company theatres), 110–11, 113, 115–16
Hutcheon, Linda, 148
hybrid economy
    appropriation in, 142–44
    capitalist cultural production in, 143–44
    copyright laws in, 142–50
    definitions in, 142
    Kickstarter crowd-funding in, 153–54
    'long tail' in, 152–54
    online open-access scholarly publishing in, 149–50
    payment in, 151–52
    publicly funded research in, 149
    Shakespeare related to, 151–55
    transform in, 143
'hybridity,' 13
Hytner production. *See Timon of Athens*

I
idolatry, 'derivatives' and, 25–26
images, power of, 8–9
inflation, 1, 19–20
information technology, 140n28
Innis, Harold, 151
institutional space, 2
intellectual property, 144, 157n9, 157n14
investors in company theatres (housekeepers), 110–11, 113, 115–16
iterability, 24, 151

J
Jackson, Ken, 103
Jenkins, Henry, 149, 150, 151
Jenstadt, Janelle, 150
jokes, 109, 120
Jonson, Ben, 65n4, 92
Jowett, John, 98, 103
Joyce, James, 140n26

K
Karatani, Kojin, 30–32
Keenan, Siobhan, 6
Kent, William, 1–2
Keynes, John Maynard, 5
Kickstarter crowd-funding, 153–54
King, Martin Luther, 65n5
King John (Shakespeare), 17
Knight, G. Wilson, 103
Knights, L, C., 45
Kurdi, Alan, 53, 67n25

L
Landreth, David, 68n39, 69n48
Lee, Benjamin, 28n3
legend, 131
Leighton, Alexander, 119
Leinwand, Theodore B., 67m32
Leishman, J. B., 91
Lessig, Lawrence, 145–46, 150, 152
Leval, Pierre, 145
Leviticus 24: 20, 73–74
LiPuma, Edward, 28n3
liquidity, 54–55
    in *Comedy of Errors*, 57–59, 61, 68nn37–42
The Lodger Shakespeare (Nicholl), 132, 133
London, 140n28
    Globe Theatre in, 97, 112, 115, 118
London Olympics (2012), 97
'long tail,' 152–54
Lord Chamberlain's Men, 89, 110–11
love poems. *See The Sonnets*
Love's Labour's Lost (Shakespeare), 153

M

Macbeth (Shakespeare), 20
Madélénat, Daniel, 126–27
Malone, Edmond, 130
Marino, James, 157n9
marriage, 55, 74, 76, 85n10
    reciprocity and exchange in, 33–36, 38
Marvell, Andrew, 91
Marx, Karl, 7, 10, 17, 27, 30–31, 98
    on 'power of money,' 87–88
Massinger, Philip, 61
McMenamin, Ciaráran, 108n20
Mediterranean world, 49–52, 55–57, 58, 66n16
The Merchant of Venice (*The Merchant*) (Shakespeare), 17–18, 21–22, 120–21
    anachronism in, 82
    bidding in, 74–75
    charity in, 79–83
    Christian mercantilism in, 70–71, 75
    Christian virtues in, 70–71
    Christian wealth in, 80–81
    conditions in, 72–73
    death in, 78, 79
    double-standard in, 77
    exchange economy and, 76–77
    greed in, 81
    homoerotic bonds in, 74, 76, 85n10
    identification in, 78
    ignorance in, 78
    institutional pawnbroker in, 82–83
    interest in, 72, 74
    judicial equity and common law in, 72, 85n5
    Leviticus in, 73–74, 81
    Marian pity in, 80–82
    marketable mercy in, 73–76
    Mounts of Piety in, 82–83
    new market economy in, 73, 74, 80
    piety in, 80
    pity in, 71–72, 75–80
    poverty in, 79–80
    Protestantism and, 71, 81, 82, 83
    refugee in, 75
    seasoned justice in, 73, 75
    shrewdness in, 81–82
    Sonnets' pity related to, 76–77, 82, 85n13
    victimization in, 78
    violence in, 72–73
    worthlessness in, 79
mercy, 10, 85n6. *See also The Merchant of Venice*
'microhistorical' biography, 140n27
Middleton, Thomas, 117. *See also Timon of Athens*
A Midsummer Night's Dream (Shakespeare), 117, 143, 153–55
migration, 52. *See also* refugees
Mitchell, Margaret, 146–47
mobility
    definition of, 54
    in historicity, 50–54, 66n14, 67nn25–26
    liquidity related to, 54–55
    refugees related to, 52–54, 67nn25–26
Modern Shakespeare Offshoots (Cohn), 148
Moffett, Thomas, 154, 159n43
Momigliano, Arnaldo, 125–26, 128
monetary subtext, 8
money, 12, 55, 67n32, 87–88. *See also specific topics*
    in *Pericles*, 60–63, 64, 68n45, 69nn48–52
    in Shakespeare biographies, 133–37
Morrison, Matthew D., 148
Much Ado About Nothing (Shakespeare), 153
Muldrew, Craig, 69n49
Muses Looking Glasse, 118–19

N

National Theatre, 98–99
'negative reciprocity,' 31
New Economic Criticism, 7–8, 84n1
New Place, 131, 136, 140n28, 162
Nicholl, Charles, 132, 133, 140n27
Nine Lives (Holderness), 132
No Fear Shakespeare, 152
Northern Ireland, 108n20
Notes from Blackfriars (Fitzgeffrey), 119

O

Occupy movement, 11, 99
online open-access scholarly publishing, 149–50
'open-source' creative repository, 142–43
Outlines of the Life of Shakespeare (Halliwell-Phillipps), 134
'Oxford Shakespeare Topics,' 90

P

parody, 146–47
Peltonen, Matti, 140n27
Pentapolis, 66n16
performative statements, 23
Pericles, 41
Pericles (Shakespeare), 9–10, 117
  money in, 60–63, 64, 68n45, 69nn48–52
  topography in, 59–60, 63–64
Perry, Curtis, 68nn41–42
pity, 10
  in *The Merchant*, 71–72, 75–82, 85n13
place
  currency of, 52, 67n25
  historicity related to, 49–52, 65n6, 65n8, 66n16, 66nn18–19
  immigrants related to, 52–53, 67n25
  New Place, 131, 136, 140n28, 162
Platter, Thomas, 114
players, 109, 111–12, 163–64
playwrights, 109–10
poaching, 161–62
The Politics (Aristotle), 29–30, 46n2
Pope, Horace Alexander, 134
Portugal, 49, 65n8
Poulantzas, Nicos, 45–46
Pound, Ezra, 21–22, 92
power, 8–9, 87–88
presentist approach, 11
Price, Diana, 133
Prince v. Cariou (2013), 147
private banking, 88–89
prostitutes, 119–20
Protestantism, 71, 79, 81, 82, 83
Prynne, William, 121
publicly funded research, 149

Q

Queenan, Joe, 151

R

Randall, Alice, 146–47
reciprocity and exchange, 9
  Aristotle related to, 29–30, 38–39, 42–43, 45, 46n2
  balance in, 37–39
  commodification in, 31–32, 41–44
  commodities in, 36–37, 47n20
  commodity exchange in, 31, 35, 36–37, 39–40
  competition in, 45
  'dependence' in, 39
  equality in, 31–32, 35–36
  exchange process in, 31
  friendship in, 41–45
  hospitality in, 41–45
  in household management, 29–30
  imbalance of, 33–34, 37–40, 43–46
  intertextuality and, 32–33
  paradox of, 33–34
  resistance in, 34–35

value in, 36–40
volatility in, 34, 42, 44–45
refugees, 52–54, 60, 67nn25–26, 75
Richards, Nathaniel, 119
ritual magic, 25–27
Romeo and Juliet (Shakespeare), 6, 9, 32–36
Rowe, Nicholas, 130, 133
Ryan, Kiernan, 104
Ryner, Bradley, 68n39, 69n51

S

Sagnes, Jean, 128
Sanders, Julie, 142–43
satire, 51, 57, 68n37, 68n39, 98, 99, 146–47
Scheemakers, Peter, 2–3
Scheil, Katherine, 131–32
Schoenbaum, Samuel, 130, 134–35
Seafaring prowess, 56n8
sexuality, 74, 76, 85n10, 119–20, 153–54
  brothels, 61–64, 69
Shakespeare, William, 89, 110–11.
  See also specific topics
  homes of, 131, 136, 140n28, 162, 165, 166n2
  'self-reflections' related to, 160–66
Shakespeare: A Life (Honan), 129
Shakespeare biographies
  'disintegrationist' related to, 130–33, 140n25
  money in, 133–37
  probabilities in, 136
  'self' in, 134–35, 137
  theoretical debate on, 128–29, 139nn12–13
  traditionalism of, 137
The Shakespeare Circle (Edmondson and Wells), 132
Shakespeare 'Globe to Globe' Festival (2012), 97
Shakespeare in the Present (Hawkes), 48

Shakespeare's Money (Bearman), 12, 136–37
Shapiro, James, 129, 132, 140n26, 152
'sharers' (investors in acting companies), 11, 109, 110, 111, 113, 115–16
sheep, 160–61
Shell, Marc, 28n4
Shellard, Dominic, 6
Shylock, 17–18
Skylax of Caryanda, 125–26
Smith, Kevin, 146
society, 88
The Sonnets (Shakespeare), 6, 10–11, 22, 88, 134
  commercial language in, 90–92
  competition and, 93
  'dear' in, 91
  'dyer's hand' in, 89
  financial images in, 91–92
  greed in, 92
  'husbandry' in, 94
  indebtedness in, 93
  'love merchandized' in, 94
  'lust' in, 94
  The Merchant related to, 76–77, 82, 85n13
  metaphors in, 90
  'procreation' in, 92–93
  surplus value in, 93
speculative financial derivatives, 9
statue, 1–3
Statute of Anne (1710), 144–45
Stavrakakis, Yannis, 102, 108n14
stream-of-consciousness, 13, 160–66
subjectivity, 88
Sullivan, Ceri, 68n39
Supreme Court, U.S., 145–46
symbols, 3, 15, 17

T

Tarlton, Richard, 115
Tarsus, 66n16
Tatham, John, 114–15

Taylor, John, 112
The Tempest (Shakespeare), 97, 118, 119
Thicke, Robin, 147
Thucydides, 41
Timon of Athens (Shakespeare and Middleton), 11, 17, 87–88, 107n8, 121
  accent in, 99–100, 108n20
  class-conscious and, 99, 105
  counterpart in, 103–4
  extremism in, 102–3, 105
  Greek economy related to, 102, 108n14
  limitation of, 106–7
  misanthropy in, 100, 101–3
  pastoral criticism in, 101–2
  'presentism' of, 98–99, 101, 102–7
  production challenges of, 98, 99, 105–6
Titus Andronicus (Shakespeare), 117
Tonson, Jacob, 144–45
toponymy, 55–56, 59
trafficking, human, 62
'transformative,' 12, 146–48
Tratner, Michael, 90
Troilus and Cressida (Shakespeare), 36–40, 47n20, 121
Trojan horse, 60
Trump, Donald, 60

Turner, Frederick, 85n6
Tyre, 66n16

U
Unorthodox Biography (Price), 133
usury, 21–22, 30, 82–83, 100–101

V
Vendler, Helen, 90
venereal disease, 62
virginity, 62–63, 64

W
Walker, Robert, 144
Ward, John, 132
Wayte, William, 162, 166n1
Wells, Stanley, 131, 132, 135–36, 141n38
Westminster Abbey, 1–2
Wilkins, George, 117
Williams, Pharrell, 147
The Winter's Tale (Shakespeare), 12–13, 116, 119, 166n2
Woodbridge, Linda, 18
'writing,' 23–24

Y
Yes, Rasta (Cariou), 147

Z
Žižek, Slavoj, 11, 103

www.ingramcontent.com/pod-product-compliance
Lightning Source LLC
Chambersburg PA
CBHW072156100526
44589CB00015B/2255